THE
THIRTY-SIX

TO DR. STEPHEN SMITH

WITH BEST WISHES.

22.10.2009.

To my great-grandchildren,
Kai William Yehoshua,
Sienna Reilly Halit,
Noa Emmanuelle Shoshanna,
Amielle Hava Victoria,
and all yet unborn.

In memory of
my father, my hero,
my gorgeous mother,
the 169 members of my family, including 76 children,
who perished in the Holocaust.

Their lives ended abruptly, not even a grave or a tombstone to
mark their passage through life. To my family and to all who
knew them and loved them, their spirit lives on.

I dedicate this book as a tribute to the six million Jews who
perished in the Holocaust as well as to those who helped me to
survive, risking their own life – Jews and non-Jews,
those Righteous amongst the Nations.

THE
THIRTY-SIX

SIEGMUND SIEGREICH

VINTAGE BOOKS
Australia

A Vintage book
Published by Random House Australia Pty Ltd
Level 3, 100 Pacific Highway, North Sydney NSW 2060
www.randomhouse.com.au

First published by Vintage in 2009

Addresses for companies within the Random House Group can be found at
www.randomhouse.com.au/offices

National Library of Australia
Cataloguing-in-Publication Entry

Siegreich, Siegmund.
The thirty-six / Siegmund Siegreich.
ISBN 978 1 74166 843 8 (pbk.)

Siegreich, Siegmund.
Holocaust, Jewish (1939–1945) – Poland – Biography.
Holocaust survivors – Australia – Biography.
Jews – Poland – Biography.

940.5318092

Cover illustration by Getty Images
Cover design by Christabella Designs
Typeset in Times New Roman 13/16.5 pt
Printed and bound by Griffin Press, South Australia

Random House Australia uses papers that are natural, renewable and recyclable products and made from wood grown in sustainable forests. The logging and manufacturing processes are expected to conform to the environmental regulations of the country of origin.

10 9 8 7 6 5 4 3 2 1

CONTENTS

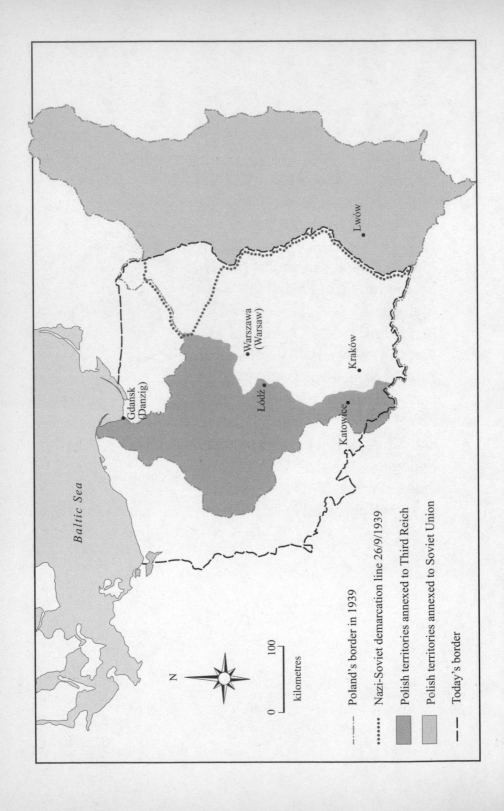

Baltic Sea

Gdańsk
(Danzig)

Łódź

Warszawa
(Warsaw)

Kraków

Katowice

Lwów

N

0

100

kilometres

Poland's border in 1939

Nazi-Soviet demarcation line 26/9/1939

Polish territories annexed to Third Reich

Polish territories annexed to Soviet Union

Today's border

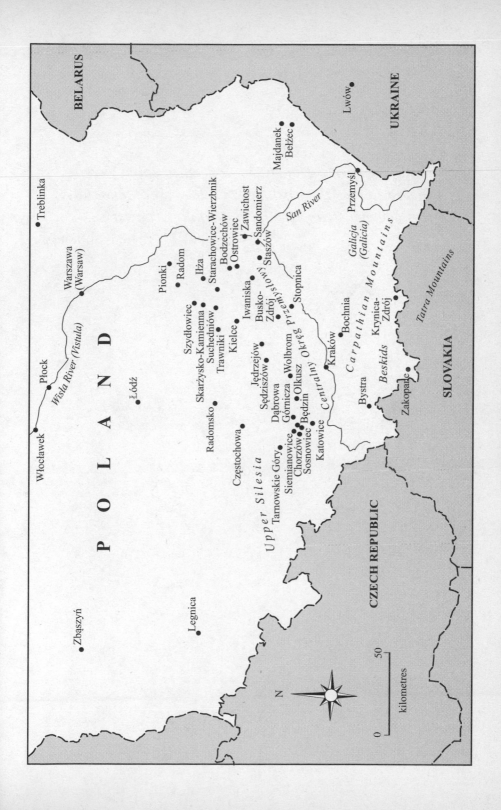

BELARUS

UKRAINE

Lwów

Majdanek
Bełżec

Treblinka

San River

Warszawa
(Warsaw)

Przemyśl

Zawichost
Sandomierz
Staszów
Ostrowiec
Bodzechów
Starachowice-Wierzbnik
Iłża
Radom
Pionki

Galicja
(Galicia)

Stopnica
Busko-
Zdrój
Iwaniska

Carpathian Mountains

Tatra Mountains

Szydłowiec
Skarżysko-Kamienna
Suchedniów
Trawniki
Kielce

Wolbrom
Olkusz
Bochnia

Kraków

Krynica-
Zdrój

Płock

Jędrzejów
Sędziszów
Dąbrowa
Górnicza
Będzin

Wisła River (Vistula)

P   O   L   A   N   D

Łódź

Radomsko

Bystra

Beskids

Zakopane

Włocławek

Częstochowa

Upper Silesia

Tarnowskie Góry
Siemianowice
Chorzów
Sosnowiec
Katowice

Centralny Okręg Przemysłowy

SLOVAKIA

CZECH REPUBLIC

Zbąszyń

Legnica

50

kilometres

N

0

For the sake of the thirty-six concealed saints,
God preserves the world, even if the rest of humanity
Has degenerated to the level of total barbarism.

The Kabbalah

PROLOGUE

'HOLY MOTHER OF GOD!' exclaimed Aniela. 'It must be God's punishment. This boy is going to be my undoing.'

This was our Polish housekeeper ranting as she cleaned my shoes on the balcony outside our kitchen. Seated on a low stool, her skirt covered by a large apron, Aniela leaned over to protect herself from the sticky brown mud that caked my brand-new shoes. She shook her head from side to side in utter disbelief. Hoping to gain some sympathy from my mother she whined, '*Where* did he find this mud? It's not rained for days, and there's no mud on any of Katowice's streets. He's ten years old and should know better than to play in puddles. *Where* does he manage to find this mud?'

My mother tried to hide her amusement. Looking at the shoes, she imagined how much fun her darling angel had stomping in the squishy gooey mud.

'Don't worry, Aniela,' she replied, her face full of sympathy. 'He's only doing what any other boy his age would do. He'll grow out of it soon and will pay more attention to his appearance. You'll see, before you know it he'll be asking you to style his hair.'

I recalled this scene some nine years later while standing in ankle-deep mud during a rollcall. I was in Poland's Skarżysko-Kamienna slave labour camp, and the weekly 'selection' of the

1

so-called *entlassene Juden* – the weak and the sick who could no longer work – was under way.

Mud. It was one of the most depressing aspects of imprisonment. Mud was *always* present; it never froze and never dried out, even on rainless and hot days. But on a true list of suffering I'm not sure where it belongs. Should the first item be hunger or the beatings, hard labour or the lice, scabies and terror of the 'selections'? Or perhaps it should be the bitter winters or the stifling summer heat? But then where on the list would I place dysentery, typhus, tuberculosis? The loneliness and hopelessness? And what about the loss of loved ones?

Everyday privations also belong somewhere on the list: the endless queues for the latrine and the absence of paper, any piece of paper or leaf to wipe yourself; that piece of rag that served as a towel; the absence of shoes, clogs, shirts, trousers and blankets; and using a discarded paper cement bag as clothing.

Those of us who were incarcerated in these camps and survived endured a great deal. So much happened; so many things happened to those who survived that a list – no matter how long – would not do at all. Instead I will simply tell my story.

PART I

JULY 1939 – OCTOBER 1940

CHAPTER 1

IN THE SUMMER OF 1939 I had just turned fifteen. I spent July at a Hanoar Hatzioni scout jamboree in the Beskid Mountains in south-western Poland and then, with the start of the new school term still more than five weeks away, I travelled on to the Zakopane resort in the High Tatra to join my schoolfriends for another camp.

On my way there, I stopped briefly at Krynica-Zdrój, a renowned resort and spa. My mother was waiting for me there with fresh clothes and sweets. She was spending her summer holiday there while my father was busy overseas – a business trip to England and a New York visit for the International Exhibition of 1939.

My older sister Halinka was also away, trekking and climbing the East Carpathian mountains. This group was led by her boyfriend, Don Grünspan, the handsome eldest son of a wealthy industrialist. Halinka and Don were planning to announce their engagement very soon.

I spent a few hours with my mother in Krynica-Zdrój and arrived in Zakopane in the late afternoon. Zakopane is one of the most beautiful resorts in Europe, located some 1000 metres above sea level and surrounded by mountains as high as 2655 metres. It is as magnificent in summer as it is in winter where we, as a family, would regularly ski and ice-skate to our heart's desire.

Mr Silber managed the camp. He was the headmaster of the Mława boarding school where I was a student. He had a mass of bushy blond hair and an upturned pointy nose; round metal-rimmed glasses framed his bright brown eyes. Mr Silber was a stickler for discipline at boarding school, but here he was jovial and jolly.

My best friend Jurek Tenenbaum had already arrived, as had Henryk Rosental, Janek Fiszer, Mietek Sonenberg and others. Mietek was a talented artist, particularly skilled in drawing caricatures and cartoons. These boys, like me, were also boarders at Mława. Other members of our party, such as Lilka Flaksbaum, Lillian Lichtenstein and Jack Gilinski, were from different schools.

I was one of the tallest boys in my class, having already reached my adult height of 174 centimetres. I had a lean sporty physique with broad shoulders. My hair was short and wavy and its once golden colour was now getting darker. (My mother lovingly called my hair colour liquid gold.) My mother said that I looked like my father although my eyes were brown, like hers, and my father's were grey-blue. I did, however, have my father's nose.

Those four weeks were such fun. We swam, played games, listened to records and learned the latest dance craze – the 'swing'. We laughed and sang and had a great time. We were so innocent, so free, so full of optimism. The entire world was at our feet – literally. Mr Silber was a passionate mountain climber and took us to conquer Tatra's summits. We began with a ride in a cable car to the top of Kasprowy Wierch, and then progressively climbed Zawrat, Giewont, Świnica and Rysy, sometimes using ropes, chains and iron hooks. It was scary and it was hard work but it was worth it to see the breathtaking views from the peaks.

Us boys had recently 'discovered' the opposite sex and there was no shortage of pretty girls to admire. We discussed the girls' breasts and joked about those who were slow developers. Zenek, the camp jester, made us constantly laugh, especially when suggesting using a pair of tweezers to fondle the breasts of one flat-chested girl. But we also noticed that the sparkle in the girls' eyes was somewhat different too. I immediately set my sights on pretty Lillian Lichtenstein, who had large blue-green eyes and long blond braids that framed her oval face.

While strolling in the forest picking wild strawberries, Lillian and I lingered well behind the others and I placed my arm around her waist. We talked about our schools, favourite books, movies and parties. I was giddy with happiness. We had invented this great game while picking the fruit. The berries normally grow in pairs on a single stem; we picked a stem and both of us tried to remove the berries, our lips touching slightly. As our lips met, we pretended that nothing had happened.

A few days later my parents arrived for a weekend visit. My father had cut short his New York trip on hearing rumours of impending war in Europe. I introduced them to Lillian and eagerly asked my father for permission to take her for a drive. My father instructed Stefan, our chauffeur, to take us in the car. When we turned the first corner Stefan stopped to let me drive; we had done this many times before. This time he climbed into the back seat so that Lillian could sit next to me. Stefan left the engine running and all I had to do was adjust the rear-vision mirror. I pressed the clutch all the way to the floor and eased the gearstick into first. Pushing the accelerator with my other foot, I slowly released the clutch, feeling the car move as gently as if I was an experienced driver. I could feel Lillian's eyes on me but looked straight ahead in a grown-up manner. This was the highlight of my holiday: showing off my driving and becoming a hero in Lillian's eyes.

We had another two unforgettable weeks in Zakopane

before it came to an end. And it ended with a big bang on 23 August 1939. The newsflash on radio and in all the papers, as well as on billboards, was the announcement: GENERAL MOBILISATION.

At first we did not fully grasp what this meant; we were busy thinking about the new school year, which was to begin on Friday 1 September. But on that August day the camp came to an abrupt end. The girls panicked and the boys teased them with false bravado. We packed and were ferried to Zakopane train station where we said our farewells, expecting to meet again in just over a week at Mława boarding school. Lillian and I promised to write to each other after exchanging photographs that we had inscribed on the back. I would never see most of my friends again.

CHAPTER 2

MY FATHER WAS SAMUEL DAVID SIEGREICH, the eldest son of Isaac
and Raizel. He had five sisters – Rozka, Hela, Eva, Gita and
Cesia – and three brothers – Julius, Abraham and Felix. My
mother, Eva, was also a Siegreich, the daughter of David and
Rachel. She had four sisters – Regina, Gusta, Zahava and Hela
– who were all married with families of their own. My parents
shared the same paternal grandfather and were first cousins.

The name Siegreich is German for 'victorious'. Our family was
large and very close-knit, and for many generations had lived in
the Upper Silesia and Zagłębie area of south-west Poland. This
region was Poland's main industrial centre and was a landscape
of coal, steel, chimneystacks and mining towers. The Siegreichs
played an important role in Polish commerce and industry,
especially after the country regained independence after the end
of World War I.

Our family's main source of income was in the chemical
industry, sawmills, building materials, supplying mines and
the steel industries. The ELTES Company, named for my great
uncle, Leo Tobias Siegreich, owned dolomite and chamotte
quarries and kilns, as well as factories producing quicklime and
slaked lime, industrial porcelain and ceramics. It employed more
than 20,000 people. The IMS Company, named for Isaac Meir
Siegreich, my paternal grandfather, manufactured furniture, and

employed about 150 people in its carpentry plant, sawmills and timber yards.

The family had two branches. The Polish-speaking branch lived in the towns of Będzin, Sosnowiec, Dąbrowa Górnicza and Ząbkowice, while the German-speaking branch lived in the towns of Katowice, Siemianowice, Wielkie Hajduki, Chorzów and Tarnowskie Góry. My family belonged to the German-speaking branch and lived in Katowice, the capital of Upper Silesia. Katowice is situated by the small river Rawa, and despite having some decent parks and buildings – including Poland's first skyscraper (a fourteen-storey building), the first department store and the country's only undercover ice-skating rink – it was much polluted. The city was often gloomy and depressing; the sun was rarely visible.

Katowice's population in 1939 was 250,000. The Jewish community, of which my family was part, numbered just over 9000. The majority of the town's inhabitants were native Silesians or Poles, and the rest were *Volksdeutsch*. (The term *Volksdeutsch* was used to describe ethnic Germans living outside Germany's borders. Many of the Volksdeutsch in Silesia held Polish citizenship.)

Katowice's Jewish congregation was predominantly German-speaking and its religious and social networks were well organised and financially sound. The town had an impressive Moorish-style synagogue with a huge dome that accommodated over 2000 worshippers. Another, Orthodox, synagogue catered for the Polish Jews who had settled in the area when a large part of German Upper Silesia was incorporated into Poland's territory at the end of World War I. There was a visible difference in the culture, lifestyle and architecture of Upper Silesia and other Polish towns and villages; Katowice Jews were more affluent than those in other parts of Poland and we enjoyed a comfortable, even privileged, lifestyle.

I grew up in a modern, cultured home. My parents embraced life and enjoyed all it had to offer. They never missed a lecture, a concert, a show, a play, a party, a movie or any other event that gave them pleasure. They loved dancing and regularly attended five o'clock tea dances on Saturdays. In summer, they visited health spas and other holiday resorts, while my sister and I usually went to youth camps. In winter, they holidayed at ski resorts. My father was a keen skier who would tackle the most difficult runs in Zakopane. Sporting activities were an important part of his life – but his greatest passion was travelling with my mother to exotic destinations. They were always either on holiday, returning from holiday or planning a holiday. After their return, the numerous colourful labels of famous international hotels on their luggage always fascinated me. Some suitcases were completely covered with these labels, as was Mother's hatbox.

My father, who was in his early forties when the war broke out, had been blessed with an enchanted life. Besides his family's wealth, he had amassed his own small fortune in the timber and construction industry. He was highly respected in the Jewish community for his involvement in philanthropic activities. He was gentle but strict, yet possessed an aura of casual confidence. He had aristocratic good looks, with dazzling blue-grey eyes and blond hair which he brushed back. As was fashionable at the time, he wore a small clipped moustache and was always impeccably dressed in suits tailored from fine English cloth. He was well read and interested in international affairs, and possessed an almost wicked sense of humour which endeared him to young and old. He was the best father in the world – my mentor and my hero, the greatest influence in my life.

My mother was a striking-looking woman and, with her dark hair and lipstick, always appeared smart and sophisticated. But she was an exceptional woman too: sensitive, intelligent and blessed with a wonderful sense of humour. Her life was a whirlwind of activities. She had a large circle of friends whom she met almost daily at a fashionable cafe house in the city. Our chauffeur, Stefan, would drive her back home in time for lunch. Sometimes she would stop at Borinski delicatessen to purchase some treats or visit her dressmaker, lingerie seamstress or milliner. She was an active member of the Women's International Zionist Organization, supporting scores of charitable and social causes. She also possessed extraordinary psychic abilities, and often had premonitions of future events, though this was something we never spoke about outside the family.

My sister, Halinka, was a slim and attractive teenager who had many friends. She was a member of the Bar Kochba sports club and one of the leaders of the Hanoar Hatzioni Zionist youth movement, an organisation to which I also belonged.

When Halinka and I were in our early teens we finished school at one o'clock and at 1.30 sharp the family used to sit down together for lunch. My parents were very strict about having our meals together. This was when current affairs were discussed and we children were encouraged to participate and share our experiences. Both my parents discussed many topics in front of us, as my sister was practically a grown-up, or so she thought. We were a close and active family.

We lived on the second floor of a five-storey corner building at 16 Zabrska Street. Our apartment, one of ten in the building, was spacious and elegant with central heating and glossy parquetry floors. We had both a formal drawing room and a separate dining room. The drawing room furniture was intricately carved rosewood upholstered in sky-blue silk brocade. The floor was covered with handmade Persian rugs. Valuable oil paintings acquired over the years adorned the walls and heavy velvet drapes framed the lace-curtained windows. A dazzling Austrian crystal chandelier dominated this room, though it competed with a glossy black upright piano. My mother was an avid collector of fine porcelain figurines, favouring Meissen, Rosenthal and Hutschenreuther, which were proudly displayed in a special cabinet. The most prominent and best-illuminated position in the room, however, was reserved for the silk paintings of birds, flowers and butterflies hand-painted by my grandfather.

This was my mother's favourite room and she loved to entertain her friends and family there. Our home was always filled with people. Sometimes my mother would host piano soirees, showing off her talent or inviting other pianists to perform, but the most frequent entertainer in our house was Halinka, who in my opinion was quite an accomplished pianist. Sometimes she and I would have to recite poetry in front of our parents' guests or sing and dance to a popular folk song such as 'Die Tiroler Tänzl', which meant dressing in Tyrolean costumes and performing a duet. Fortunately I was never asked to play my violin: I was still learning and the sound I produced even frightened the neighbourhood cats.

The dining room was large and bright. The walls were covered with pale aqua moiré silk and matching curtains and drapes. On the floor, as in the drawing room, lay an oblong Keshan Persian rug. Two large aquarelles by the famous local painter Maurycy Applebaum hung on one wall. In each corner was a large, beautifully hand-painted porcelain jardinière containing exotic indoor palms. The furniture was carved from Caucasus walnut trees and consisted of a grand table with twenty-two matching upholstered chairs and two carvers – enough to seat twenty-four people. An antique silver candelabrum, which was lit on Friday nights for the Jewish sabbath and other festive dinners, took pride of place in the centre of the table. All the formal and family dinners took place in this room. On special occasions my mother would hire extra staff to help Aniela, our live-in housekeeper, Franciska, our nanny, and our cook, Jadwiga.

The furniture in my parents' bedroom, carved from palisander, was modern art deco. Two large beds stood side by side, covered with a hand-embroidered bedspread; two alabaster lights stood on matching bedside tables. A long wardrobe with seven doors flanked one wall; on the other were a three-door linen cabinet and a dresser with a huge round mirror. On top of the dresser were crystal *flacons* of perfume, cosmetics, ornamental trinkets and a silver mirror, comb and brush set. Fresh flowers were always on display; my mother's favourites were mimosa for their delicate feel and hyacinths for their fragrant scent. When our parents were out for the evening or away on a trip, Halinka and I spent many wonderful nights in their beds pretending to be in a train's sleeping compartment travelling to exotic European cities, re-enacting the stories they had told us about their travels.

My father's study was private and I had to knock before being invited to enter it. The furniture was heavy oak, varnished in dark brown. There was an imposing desk, a high-backed leather chair, and a vast cabinet filled with leather-bound volumes in German and Polish, with a special section on Judaica. There was also a leather couch and two armchairs, which surrounded a low square table with a large ashtray and lighter. Although my father never smoked, one could always smell the scent of cigars in his study, because he received guests there so frequently. A heavy cabinet contained crystal decanters filled with various local and imported spirits.

I remember my father invited me to his study after my bar mitzvah service, when I had just turned thirteen. As always, he was immaculately dressed, in a hand-tailored grey woollen suit, a white shirt with pale blue stripes running through the Swiss voile fabric and an elegantly knotted silk tie. He asked me to sit in the heavy leather armchair across from him.

'I was very proud today, hearing you read from the Torah,' he began. 'Your speech at the end of the service was excellent. Well done! From this day on you will be responsible for your deeds, and while attending prayers and services you will be acknowledged as an adult and counted as part of the prayer group. Further, you are allowed to access any of my books except those on the upper shelf.'

I wondered why those books were taboo. Later, when my parents were away, I went into his study and found that they included medical and scientific books about sexuality, as well as Boccaccio's *The Decameron* and an illustrated *Kama Sutra*. I was utterly fascinated and bewildered by it all.

Our family room was comfortable and functional, with a gramophone cabinet housing many records and an eight-lamp Telefunken radio, a sophisticated model in its day. At one end of the hallway was a guestroom, elegantly furnished and occupied only occasionally. Then there was the room where my sister and I slept. Our furniture was painted a high-gloss white lacquer. Two wide single beds hugged opposite walls. We had two identical desks, two identical cabinets and one bookshelf, which we both shared. Halinka was four years older than me and as children we had ongoing problems regarding this sharing business, so exact measurements were taken to define our territories. We teased each other mercilessly, though I'm sure only as much as a younger brother and older sister would in any family.

As for the rest of the apartment, we had a modern tiled bathroom with running hot and cold water, a bathtub, handbasin, toilet and bidet. And we had a very large kitchen, which was Aniela's domain. To her I was a real nuisance: always wanting to look into the cupboards and drawers, touch the utensils and pinch biscuits left lying to cool. The best sweets, though, were kept under lock and key in the credenza in the dining room. Imported chocolate, marzipan, truffles, fruit jellies and pralines filled with cherries or plums were kept for guests and special occasions. Sometimes my sister and I would find the key and help ourselves to treats.

Passover Seder was a special event. It is a Jewish tradition that no Jew should be deprived of attending a Seder, so each year my father would invite anywhere between six and twelve Jewish soldiers serving at the local garrison to join us at the Seder table. The invited soldiers were privates serving in the Polish army. (In Poland, Jews could rarely advance in the military and very few reached the rank of officer.) They came from faraway villages in eastern Poland, with no connection to anyone in Katowice.

One Passover Seder, when I was eight or nine years old, remains etched in my memory. It happened that the leader of this group of eight soldiers was a corporal. They rang the front doorbell. Our nanny Franciska greeted them and asked them to come in. They hesitated and seemed overwhelmed by the bright lights of the apartment. Franciska opened the door wider, stood back and beckoned them in. 'Come in, please. Come in.'

The soldiers turned around and were about to leave when the corporal spoke up. 'Please excuse us, but it seems we've come to the wrong address. We're looking for Mr Siegreich's residence. We've been invited for Seder dinner.'

My father soon appeared and took charge. 'Welcome, gentlemen. Please come in. Happy Passover and welcome to our Seder.'

Now the soldiers seemed even more bewildered since my father was blond with a fair complexion. 'Are you Jewish?' asked one man outright.

'Of course I'm Jewish,' he reassured his guests, 'and the food in our home is strictly kosher.' But it was only when he confirmed this in Yiddish that they were convinced they were in a Jewish home. (Though we spoke German at home, my father also spoke Polish, English and Yiddish, and had studied Latin. My mother spoke Polish, French and Yiddish.)

It took the men about ten minutes to wipe their boots and

remove their belts and bayonets. They hesitated, however, in taking off their caps. Unlike my parents, who were liberal progressives, these men were orthodox Jews. My father understood immediately and sent me to get skullcaps for them.

Shown to the table, they could not stop looking around in utter disbelief and were dazed by the splendour of the room, leaving them speechless and a bit uncomfortable. Finally, my father started asking everyone who they were and where they came from. Answering in a clipped military manner, they each stood to attention, as they had been trained in the army. I got the giggles, and Halinka poked me in the ribs with her elbow. My mother gave me a beseeching look. Slowly though, the guests started to relax and the corporal tried to explain. 'We've never, ever seen an apartment like yours before, or knew that such apartments exist. Nor have we ever seen a Jewish man with fair skin dressed like a nobleman. If we were to describe this to our family and friends they wouldn't believe us.'

For me, the most amusing part of the evening was watching the soldiers try to make sense of the numerous pieces of cutlery on either side of their plates. I found their table manners very funny. I was a cheeky boy and turned to one of the soldiers as he was eating his chicken soup and matzo balls. 'You're enjoying that, aren't you?'

'Yes, very much,' he replied politely. 'This is the best chicken soup with matzo balls I've ever eaten.'

'Yes, yes. We can hear that you think so too!' I started to laugh, thinking how smart I was making fun of his slurping noises.

The soldiers were very embarrassed and clearly felt uneasy again. My mother tried delicately to restore some decorum, gently explaining the order of the cutlery. She whispered that she would deal with me later.

After drinking the customary four glasses of wine everyone's mood improved. The corporal showed me his bayonet and allowed me to play with it and I remember being impressed by the heroic romanticism of the military. As the soldiers were leaving, my mother gave them each a parcel of kosher Passover cakes and packets of matzo to take back to the barracks.

*

In 1937 I was boarding at Mława and Halinka was at the Ognisko finishing school in Kraków. With their children away, my parents were looking forward to their second honeymoon. That year, however, the German government began to revoke the citizenship rights of Jews and proceeded to expel them from Germany. In response to an appeal by the Jewish welfare society, my father dispatched our chauffeur Stefan to the border town of Zbąszyń to collect refugees and bring them to Katowice. Stefan spent almost four weeks shuttling back and forth, bringing these poor people to safety. They were mostly families who had been taken from their beds in the middle of the night with nothing more than a dressing-gown or overcoat. Some even remained barefoot.

My parents opened our apartment to a young family with two small children – they lived in our bedroom and guestroom. They were not the only family to shelter with us; some people stayed in our apartment for only a few days, while others stayed for several months. Everyone under our roof was treated like family. My mother busied herself with the collection of funds, badly needed clothing items and other commodities. She helped organise temporary and long-term accommodation, employment and anything else that was needed. At least once a week she wrote to me with all the news, and I could only feel compassion for these poor people, evicted from their homes. In time, some of the refugees found their way to America, England and other overseas countries. Others were to share the fate of all the rest of the Jews in Poland.

At the end of February 1938, shortly before Germany annexed Austria, my mother's sister, Aunt Regina, her husband Karl and my three grown-up cousins arrived in Katowice from Vienna with only their hand luggage. My uncle, Karl Reichmann, was the sole coal importer for the whole of Austria and represented a number of Silesian and Zagłębian coalmines. Their daughter Lotte, whom we all called Lunia, was a beautiful young woman, a member of the famous Hakoah swimming club in Vienna. Her brother Harry was a chartered accountant and the youngest brother Severin, known as Sevek, was a graphic designer. Karl had left his employees in charge of his business, confident that the League of Nations would prevent Germany from annexing Austria and that he and his family could soon return to Vienna.

They stayed with my grandparents and we all helped in every possible way. Lunia was eager to meet an eligible bachelor and my father introduced her to a business associate, Henryk Mesing, from Rozwadów, a town in eastern Galicja. They married soon after, and within a few months Lunia was pregnant.

The following year, 1939, was a busy one for my family. At the end of the autumn we planned to move to Kraków, Poland's former capital, about 100 kilometres south-east of Katowice. My father had commissioned a construction company to build an apartment block of forty-eight units there, as well as a new two-storey family home. At last Halinka and I would have our own rooms; I would have all the space a fifteen-year-old needed, and my sister all the privacy she had craved for so long. We were all very much looking forward to the move and Father commuted regularly to oversee the builders' progress.

As well as arranging a house-warming party, my parents were to celebrate their twentieth wedding anniversary, which would also coincide with the official announcement of Halinka's engagement to Don Grünspan. We had great hopes for the future.

CHAPTER 3

AFTER MY ABRUPT DEPARTURE FROM ZAKOPANE, I arrived back in Katowice at about 1 am. Stefan retrieved my luggage while my father waited for me in the car.

'Sigi,' he said, greeting me warmly. 'Tomorrow, early in the morning, you will travel to Olkusz with Mummy and Halinka.'

'Why do I need to go to Olkusz? I've just come back after nearly eight weeks away.'

'War is now imminent and in Katowice we're geographically and strategically very vulnerable. We're too close to the German border.'

'But it will be so much fun, Father. I've not been in a war yet,' I said. 'I can't imagine that a frontline would be established in our town. If I go to Olkusz, I might miss the war.'

'When hostilities start, Sigi, anything could happen and people could get hurt. You need to take care of your mother and Halinka. I must stay behind to attend to business but I'll commute as often as I can.'

My father made it clear that any further protests were futile.

The next morning, 24 August 1939, I noticed suitcases lining the hallway and strangers in various rooms. I tried to explain to my parents that I needed to get back to boarding school. 'Don't worry about your school for now, we'll discuss it later' was their only response.

'I don't think you'll be going to Mława right now,' Halinka agreed. 'Your holiday will be extended for at least another four weeks.' She had just graduated from her finishing school in Kraków, but that morning she seemed pensive. At the breakfast table that morning there was none of the usual laughter or conversation, only silence and tension.

Katowice was only eight kilometres from the German border, which placed it in immediate danger should Germany invade Poland. German nationals predominantly populated the town, and despite having many German friends and business associates, as Jews we were vulnerable. Olkusz, some sixty kilometres east of Katowice, was the birthplace of my maternal grandmother Rachel. The plan was to stay there for a few days until the situation had resolved itself. Many people refused to believe that there would be a war at all. They assumed that the Germans would back down before the military might of England and France. Personally, as a naive fifteen-year-old, I was hoping for some 'action'. It all sounded so exciting.

Our chauffeur carried three suitcases from the hallway and placed them in the boot of our black automobile. We could not know as we drove away that we had just become homeless refugees. The lifestyle we enjoyed as a privileged family was about to come to a sudden end and all that was safe and familiar would be left behind.

Stefan drove towards the highway where columns of military vehicles, tanks and artillery were heading west towards the Polish–German border. We were travelling in the opposite direction. Once we arrived in Olkusz my mother bought a round loaf of bread and pound of salt to bless our new home. This old custom was to ensure that we would always have a well-stocked pantry.

My father had arranged a furnished apartment for us. It had two rooms, a kitchen, bathroom and an indoor toilet, which was uncommon in this town. There were some wardrobes, one double bed and two singles, a couch, a table and four chairs. There were framed prints on the wall, and the windows, which looked out onto the street, had simple curtains.

After we unpacked, my mother and Stefan went back out to do some shopping. They bought loads of groceries and Mother took charge of preparing our meals. The chauffeur then returned to my father in Katowice. As there was nothing for us to do, my sister and I went out to explore the town. The weather was exceptionally pleasant. The unusually high temperatures that summer had caused the chestnut trees to bloom for the second time that year. It was a typical *babie lato* (Indian summer) and some people saw this as a bad omen, as they remembered that the weather in the autumn of 1914 was almost identical.

We passed through the market. The stalls were stacked high with mounds of green, red and yellow apples, aromatic pears and luscious plums. Colourful vegetables, strings of dried mushrooms and plaited garlands of garlic were all on display to tempt passers-by. Strolling on, we saw a playground, where noisy, happy children were running around, skipping, swinging on swings and playing in the sandpit. Like children everywhere, their joy and laughter filled the air.

The next day David and Rachel Siegreich, my maternal grandparents, arrived in Olkusz from Katowice and, like us, moved into a rented apartment. But their chauffeur, after unloading their luggage and pretending to check that nothing had been left behind, simply drove off in my grandparents' car. We never saw him again. My grandfather David was, among other things, a member of the Silesian *Sejm* (parliament) and an honorary treasurer of the Jewish congregation. He was in his sixties and possessed an aura that was equal parts power, polish and nobility, but even he was at a complete loss for words at such behaviour and just rolled his eyes in exasperation. My grandmother Rachel was not even told the news and so she remained confident that her beloved David was looking after everything and that all was well.

In his latest speech, Hitler had demanded free access through Polish territory to East Prussia and the annexation of Gdańsk (Danzig) to the German Reich. In response to this the radio played Polish military marches, patriotic songs and transmitted propaganda speeches. Two popular slogans of the time were 'We are strong, united and ready' and 'We won't give away one button of our uniform'.

Soldiers dug trenches in public parks and gardens for use as bomb shelters. We saw older scouts fill sacks with sand and place them around the entrance of public buildings. On the Olkusz streets placards went up calling for volunteers and giving details about air-raid drills. This was how I imagined life had been at special times in history; it was as if I were on a sightseeing journey – a witness to events but not necessarily a participant. I considered myself lucky – that extraordinary things were about to happen. At school we had learned about Poland's war of independence as a grand act of glory, full of heroism, sacrifice, patriotism, camaraderie, military parades, bugles, drums and stirring war songs. Such romantic rhetoric was strongly appealing to a fifteen-year-old boy.

My mother spent time with her parents and worried about them. They were elderly and suddenly living in very different conditions, without hired help and without transport. Halinka was unhappy because we had left so suddenly she had been unable to contact Don Grünspan. Don lived in Łódź and was studying postgraduate chemistry at the Jagiellonian University in Kraków. Things were in such chaos she could not get word to him. My family's intensive search for him over the following weeks was unsuccessful.

My father commuted from Katowice almost daily. He had to look after his business, secure our assets and organise funds.

Each time he arrived he brought more belongings. I begged him to bring my pushbike and my stamp and coin collection but was told that there were more important things to consider.

A few days later there was a knock on our door. My mother opened it to find a young woman holding a baby in her arms. 'I'm your neighbour and have come to welcome you,' she said.

My mother invited her in. Sabina was an attractive Jewish woman in her mid twenties. She was bright and friendly, the wife of the local doctor who had been drafted into the army the previous week. She had been married for almost two years and her daughter was nine months old.

Mother saw that Sabina was having some difficulties and offered her support. Sabina was unhappy. Her husband, after finishing medical school, had been forced to accept a position in this small town. My mother suggested that in a few years they would be able to move to a larger city but that in the meantime Sabina needed to be positive and concentrate on her baby.

Later that afternoon my aunt Hela, my mother's youngest sister, arrived from Katowice together with her husband Jerzy Manela and their poodle Bobby. Jerzy's parents lived in Olkusz.

The next day was Friday 1 September 1939. The sirens started howling in the early morning. The German army had crossed the border and the Luftwaffe began strafing Poland's strategic targets. Civilians on roads and in towns and cities were also subject to deliberate attack. We heard aeroplanes but were unable to see them; and, from a distance, we heard explosions.

My father arrived with Czeslaw Borensztejn, his brother-in-law, who was also his business partner. Both men were extremely agitated. Stefan had driven them; now he parked the car in the barn, locked the gate, handed the keys to my father and left to catch the train home to his family in Katowice. My father and Czeslaw were out of breath, wet with perspiration, and almost collapsed on the couch. Czeslaw, who was in his early thirties and slightly overweight, seemed about to pass out. They asked for a cold drink and my father took a deep breath.

'We left Katowice very early this morning,' he began. 'When we got onto the highway there was heavy traffic in both directions. All types of military vehicles were travelling west towards the German border. Going in the opposite direction were heavy government trucks – probably moving documents, archives, artefacts and God knows what else to safer locations. For the first half-hour, we moved at a snail's pace, bumper to bumper. Two hours later as we were nearing Olkusz, out of nowhere, German bombers attacked the highway. The shrieking sound was deafening and the earth trembled. A car just four in front of us was hit, and everyone in it was killed.

'The car behind crashed into it and also burst into flames. We were lucky to stop just metres away. We tried to pull people out of the burning car. There was panic, chaos and confusion. People were screaming, jumping out of their cars and running into the fields. Then a new wave of planes appeared and sprayed the road with machine-gun fire. Many people were killed or injured and scores of trucks went up in flames. Shaken, we continued our journey using the side roads. And here we are.'

My poor mother was so distressed that my sister gave her a sedative. When the all-clear siren sounded, the whole family gathered in our apartment to discuss what to do next. Everybody had a different idea but finally it was decided that the family should move east to central Poland. After all, the Polish army was strong and had many allies. Surely we could sit out the war safely in the centre of Poland?

The air-raid siren began again. This time we could hear and see the bombers flying overhead, and the response of the anti-aircraft artillery. One German plane was shot down. We decided to move on as quickly as possible, though my mother insisted we leave our car for her parents – we would travel by train.

The next morning we packed for the second time in ten days, though we would now have to leave many of our belongings behind. My father reassured my mother that eventually we would replace everything. He pointed to his leather briefcase and explained that we had to keep an eye on it at all times as it contained numerous important papers: titles, share certificates, bonds, promissory notes, securities, insurance policies and local and foreign banking details.

My father and Uncle Czeslaw went to make inquiries about trains heading east. The stationmaster told them that there were no trains operating any more. The entry to the eastward tunnel had been bombed and was destroyed, leaving the line jammed by a queue of previous trains hundreds of kilometres long. He suggested that they call again in about two hours, as the situation could change. When Czeslaw returned he was informed that the return track would soon be opened to allow an official evacuation train through, but the stationmaster said he could not be certain that it would take any passengers. He added, 'Be here early in the morning and try your luck. I may be able to do something.' This indicated his willingness to accept a bribe and money promptly changed hands.

Early next morning, 3 September, there was an announce-ment on the radio that England and France had declared war on Germany, followed by Australia, Canada, South Africa and New Zealand.

'The war will now be over within weeks,' said Father.

Nevertheless, we headed off to the station to board the train. After an hour it pulled slowly into the station. It was very long, consisting of a dozen Pullman carriages occupied by high government officials and their families, about forty sealed goods carriages and some ten empty flat-bed freight carriages. We were not the only ones waiting for the train, and more and more people were arriving continually. A mass of frantic, desperate people pushed hard to get onto the platform, but were held back by police, who were trying in vain to control the crowd.

I ran ahead along the train tracks to reach an empty flat-bed carriage and jumped onto one, reserving it for us. The train overran the station by a few hundred metres; there was no platform or ramp and my mother could not climb up, as it was far too high. We improvised and constructed makeshift stairs using our suitcases. Finally, with the help of my father, Czeslaw and a bystander, my mother managed to climb up onto the open carriage.

After checking that all our baggage had been loaded, and particularly Father's leather briefcase, we arranged the luggage in such a way that we could sit on it and face each other. It was surreal to see the five of us sitting on suitcases in an open carriage – especially Mother and Father, who were both so elegantly dressed.

All of a sudden Sabina appeared with her baby in one arm and carrying a small case. Though we had only recently met her, she had visited my mother three or four times over the past week, and now she insisted on joining us, claiming she would feel much safer with us rather than remaining alone in Olkusz. My family was firmly against her decision: not knowing our destination or the outcome of the journey she would be much safer with her baby in her own home, waiting the return of her husband. But Sabina's mind was made up and she would not be left behind. She handed her baby and case up to us and the men relented and helped her.

My father gave Halinka and me some money in case we were separated, as well as instructions where we should meet, and then, at around midday, the train began to move. It was a typical golden Polish autumn day with plenty of sunshine and not a cloud in the sky. As time passed we became more relaxed and tranquil. Everyone was lost in his or her own thoughts and the rhythmic movement of the train made us lethargic.

After a slight bend we were parallel to the highway and saw a long caravan of horse carts with supplies heading west, followed by thousands of weary Polish soldiers. They must have been marching for many hours, as they appeared to be sleepwalking; their officers were on horseback. Thousands of civilians tramped along in the opposite direction, carrying their belongings or small children. Some pulled handcarts, others pushed baby prams; cars low on petrol were pulled along by horses. Children struggling to keep pace were crying.

German saboteurs had spread rumours that the invading soldiers were raping women and killing men. As a result people were abandoning their homes. This created the chaos and traffic jams the saboteurs hoped for, which was intended to slow down the progress of the Polish army. This line of people went on for many kilometres, but after the next bend we lost sight of the road. We travelled through a forest then approached a tunnel that was several kilometres long.

There we were, sitting in an open carriage in total darkness, engulfed by smoke, struggling to breathe. The rhythmic noise of the carriage wheels against the joints of the iron tracks was amplified in the confined space. If German planes bombed the tunnel we would be buried alive. We sat there, jolted from side to side, terrified, coughing and gasping for air. This stretch took at least twenty long minutes, though it seemed endless. At last we glimpsed the light at the end of the tunnel becoming bigger and brighter and felt fresh air rushing towards us.

As we emerged into the light, rubbing soot and dust from our eyes, our ears ringing, the sun was still shining. We were travelling between fields ready for harvesting, but there were no farmers or workers in sight; the fields had been abandoned. We were happy that the worst was over. But suddenly, out of nowhere, a squadron of German bombers attacked us. Bombs exploded everywhere.

The train came to an abrupt halt, and people stumbled and tripped over each other. We were thrown off our cases and onto the floor of the carriage. People started screaming as they jumped from the train. Someone cried out, 'Under the wagons!', others yelled, 'Run into the field!' Salvos of machine guns were fired at those who ran for shelter. There were no military personnel on our train.

My father jumped out first and held out his arms to my mother. He then motioned for Halinka and me to follow when I noticed his briefcase among the luggage. I snatched it in one hand and with the other grabbed my sister. We started to run while Czeslaw helped Sabina and her baby off the train. We escaped into the field, hiding in potato furrows. With her baby in her arms, Sabina decided to go back to grab her little case. We saw her go and screamed at her to come back. She did not make it. A barrage of bullets killed her and her baby daughter instantly. We were so shocked, so horrified. We found ourselves in the middle of a battle. We were surrounded by the dead and wounded. Many of the train's carriages were ablaze.

'Sabina and the baby are dead,' Halinka cried hysterically. 'Sabina died. Oh God. The baby. Where are you, God? What have you done?' Mother fainted and we slapped her face to revive her. We lay clamped together in the trench with our heads down, waiting for it all to end. There were hundreds of people screaming and crying, running around, searching among the dead, among the injured, for mothers, children, sisters and brothers. The noise of the exploding bombs was indescribable; it tore at our eardrums causing piercing pain and temporary deafness. The ground shook with every blast and the air was filled with dust, smoke and dirt.

Finally the air raid was over and people slowly began to rise from the ground and look around them. The pandemonium had lasted about twenty minutes but it seemed like hours. My family was totally traumatised. Only two weeks earlier we had been living a normal and peaceful life but now the four of us were in the middle of a war. Many people had died and it was a real miracle that we had been spared.

Some nearby villagers arrived and tried to help the injured and bury the dead; others started looting. Hurriedly, we returned to our carriage for our belongings. We had to move our luggage to a safe place. Everything was still there, including Sabina's suitcase. It was then that we realised Czeslaw was missing – we had been separated from him in the fields during the attack, and he had not returned to the train. We called out and looked for him among the dead and wounded but he was nowhere to be found. We searched for more than an hour, but no-one had seen him. Finally, Father went to the village for help while we stayed with the luggage, hoping that Czeslaw might still appear.

At dusk my father returned with two hefty men pulling a cart. The suitcases were moved to a farmhouse in the village; the farmer promised to look after the luggage overnight and was paid handsomely for this favour. This long day was Sunday 3 September 1939.

CHAPTER 4

THE TRAIN WAS BOMBARDED somewhere between Sędziszów and Jędrzejów, near some isolated farms. At the farmhouse, and still shaking, we asked for some water to rinse the bitter taste from our dusty mouths. We were covered in grime and dirt, our hair askew. We looked like coalminers.

Our immediate concern was to find a place to spend the night. We decided to make our way to Jędrzejów, six kilometres away. We set out on foot and, luckily, as it was a full moon and a clear sky, we could walk quite safely. Years earlier my father had had a business in Jędrzejów and a few acquaintances still lived there, but nobody answered when we knocked on their doors. They had all left town, trying to escape the advancing German army. Desperate now, we knocked on every door we passed. At one very shabby house we saw a tiny light penetrating from a crack in the door. We knocked and a short woman wrapped in a knitted woollen scarf stood before us and asked, 'Are you looking for the opportunity?'

'I don't know what you mean,' my father answered. 'We're looking for a place to spend the night. We were travelling on the train that was bombed by the Germans a few kilometres from here. Please, will you take us in?'

To our relief the woman stepped back and waved us into her small home. 'We've only one room where my husband and I sleep, but you can sleep in the barn on fresh hay. It's all I can offer. I know it's not much but you're welcome to it.'

We dropped down onto the hay exhausted. A few hours later a choir of roosters roused us. My mother, who was distressed and still traumatised, noticed that she had lost a golden brooch of great sentimental value. It was a family heirloom and had belonged to her grandmother. Strangely, she reacted as if nothing had happened. We searched for it, hoping to cheer her up, but did not find it. In turn, my mother tried to cheer us up, reflecting that we were lucky to have only lost a brooch and not our lives.

Our landlord turned out to be a horse cab owner and called his cab 'Opportunity'. He listened to our story and offered to take us back to the farmhouse to collect our belongings. I went along with my father and on the way we passed hundreds of refugees trying to escape the invading German army. We rode against the traffic and were abused by the crowd on the road. It took us two hours to get to the farmer's house.

Once our belongings were loaded, including Sabina's little bag, we were invited inside for a glass of homemade buttermilk. My father paid the farmer and asked if he had heard any further news about the air raid.

'Early this morning two firefighters arrived to assess the scene and then called for volunteers to bury the dead,' he told us. 'Thirty people went and dug a huge pit in the field nearest the forest. They buried more than 120 people there, but before doing so they emptied the pockets of the dead and stole their belongings. We looked for the local priest but he had obviously fled. Hopefully the poor souls will find their way to heaven without a final blessing.' He made the sign of the cross. 'Some of the wounded were transferred to surrounding houses but the majority are still lying there in agony.'

'Poor Sabina and her baby,' Father said to me once we left. 'Her husband won't have any idea what has happened to his wife and child. I'll find a way to notify him as soon as we get back home.'

We returned to Jędrzejów exhausted and depressed. On the outskirts of the town was a sawmill that belonged to one of the Horowicz brothers. Mr Aaron Horowicz, a friend of my father's, welcomed us warmly and said that we could stay as long as we wished. We asked if anyone had seen Czeslaw, but no-one had. We were extremely worried about him.

It was on this day that the German army entered Katowice. They set the magnificent synagogue alight and used dynamite to destroy it utterly, to the amusement of a cheering mob of ethnic Germans and Poles. Without any real warning, this was the end of Jewish life in Katowice; the city was to be *Judenrein* – cleansed of Jews.

The next day, 5 September 1939, the German army marched into Jędrzejów and proceeded to execute a random number of Jews and Poles to intimidate and humiliate the population. They then set the local synagogue alight. It would become a ritual repeated in almost every town and village they occupied. In many cases they burned the synagogues when worshippers were still inside.

We stayed at this sawmill for a few days and then decided to travel via Będzin – 100 kilometres away and the home town of my paternal grandparents – back to Katowice. We hired a horse cart and while loading our belongings my father noticed Sabina's suitcase. 'What should we do with this, Eva?'

'I suppose there's no use taking it with us now, but could we keep something to remember them by?'

'Let's see,' Father said and opened the lid. Sabina had been able to bring so little with her in her tiny case: a small bar of baby soap, baby powder, two glass feeding bottles, nappies and a few items of clothing. My mother pulled out a cream-coloured woollen shawl, lovingly embroidered by Sabina's mother for her first grandchild. She buried her face in the soft pile of the shawl and cried. 'I shall treasure this forever. May their dear souls rest in peace.'

CHAPTER 5

WE TRAVELLED TO BĘDZIN SLOWLY, sometimes sitting on the cart, sometimes walking next to it. We were all in shock, particularly my parents. On the second night we stayed with family in Ząbkowice, where I met up with my favourite cousin, Lusia Frenkel. We finally arrived at our destination on the third day.

In Będzin we moved into Czeslaw's apartment in Piłsudskiego Street, even though he was not there and still nowhere to be found. We asked many people, but no-one had seen him. Czcslaw's wife, Cesia, my father's sister, had left a few days earlier with her two young daughters to stay with her parents-in-law in Lublin. There was no communication – no transport, telephone or post. The whole country was on the move and in disarray. Everyone was trying to flee the invading army.

I left the apartment to buy some food. Many businesses were closed due to shortage of supplies, some because their owners had fled. I walked along to Małachowskiego Street, then turned right and walked up to the shops. A covered German army truck was parked there and uniformed soldiers surrounded a group of civilians – some Poles but mainly Jews. I was not aware of any danger nor did I suspect a trap; being a curious teenager I wanted to know what was going on.

As I moved closer to the group, a soldier grabbed my sleeve and ordered me to climb onto the truck with the other civilians.

This was my first encounter with a German. I was baffled, but presumed that they were grabbing us off the street to do some work. I had no reason to be nervous – I had heard of this happening numerous times before, though it hadn't happened to me personally.

As the truck moved off, I grabbed the rails to steady myself. There were picks and shovels lying on the floor in the back. We drove for about half an hour, the men in the back joking a little together, and when we arrived at a forest we were ordered to grab a tool, climb down and start digging. The soldiers marked the area we were to dig, pointing with their submachine guns, and supervised while smoking cigarettes. At no time did they intimidate or harass us. I had no idea at all why we were digging.

As we began to sweat we removed our jackets; some of the Poles even removed their shirts. One of the soldiers told us that the sooner we finished the sooner we could go back home. As there were not enough tools for the twenty-odd men in the group, we were told to take turns, which gave us the opportunity to rest a while. My hands were sore and blisters were forming where my skin rubbed against the wooden handle.

When the soldiers were satisfied with the depth of the pit we were told to finish digging and line up at the edge, facing the hole while they stood behind us. Without any warning the soldiers began to shoot. Unable to see them, I thought the soldiers were shooting in mid air. Just as I turned to look at the bearded Jew next to me, his body jerked, hit by a bullet, and I heard him whisper, 'Trust me'. Within a split second, he had grabbed my arm and pushed me ahead of himself into the ditch. He fell on top of me and died. One by one the other men fell into the ditch too, some already dead, others fatally wounded.

We lay there, a mass of bleeding corpses, the dead and dying in a mass grave somewhere deep in the forest. Innocent men who had left their homes on a simple errand, planning to return home to their loved ones, were now consigned to a nameless grave. The soldiers stopped firing, came closer to the edge and emptied their magazines directly into the pit, aiming at the still-moving bodies. The bearded man shielded me from the onslaught. His heavy lifeless body pinned me down, leaving me unable to move, while his warm blood gushed freely, covering my back and sliding along my neck onto my chest. I felt the flow of blood ease to a trickle and finally subside. I heard the truck engine rev up and move out but the sound of the soldiers' laughter lingered, so I lay still and made no noise.

I do not know how long I lay there before I heard the truck return with Polish peasants from a nearby village. One of the soldiers ordered them to fill the ditch. Their reward for this work was permission to empty the pockets of the dead, help themselves to the jackets discarded earlier and keep the tools.

I heard the sound of the truck driving off again, but I could not tell if any soldiers remained, so I kept quiet. For a while nothing happened as the peasants tried to make sense of what was before them. They could not understand what in God's name was going on. They noticed that not only Jews were in the pit, but also some of their 'own'. The mumbling went on for a long time until one of them called out, 'Boys, come on, let's get the job done. Let's get on with it.' But they did not climb down into the pit to rob the dead. They just began to shovel dirt back into the pit.

I was petrified then that I would be buried alive and I struggled to free myself from the pinning weight of my saviour, the kind Jewish man. Finally, I managed to claw my way out of the pit. One of the villagers spotted me and cried out, 'Look, this one is still alive!'

Some of them ran over to help me. 'Have you been shot? Are you wounded?' one man asked.

'I don't really know,' I said. 'I'm not sure. I have no pain and I seem to be in one piece.'

'Hey, he's one of us. He's just a kid. He must be from the city by the way he talks. He sounds educated.' He had assumed I was Polish, like him.

The man led me aside and insisted that I urinate. He thought it was important to relieve oneself after a terrible experience such as mine. He led me to a nearby tree stump. 'Sit here for a while and just take it easy.' Suddenly I began to tremble uncontrollably. He brought over some of the jackets from the pile to cover me, thinking I was cold and not in shock. 'When we finish here, I'll take you to my place,' he said, and tried to calm me down.

When we got up to go, I looked for my own jacket. I was covered in blood and dirt and when I found it, I held it out carefully to stop getting any blood on it. At the man's hut they helped me clean up and gave me an old but clean oversized shirt. After a hot glass of milk his wife showed me the barn and gave me a thick blanket, heavy with the odour of horse manure. I was glad to spend the night, not daring to violate the curfew.

In the morning, the hospitable peasant introduced me to his neighbour and asked if he would take me back to Będzin. Two hours later I was standing at the threshold of Czeslaw's apartment. My mother, who was out of her mind with worry, had not slept. She greeted me with a huge hug and sighed with relief.

'Where were you? You *cannot* just go off like this without telling anyone. What happened? Did you get stuck somewhere after curfew?'

'That's exactly what happened,' I said and told them the whole story. My parents and Halinka were torn between believing my story and suspecting that I had fabricated it to avoid being punished.

I held out my hands and showed them my blistered palms,

and my mother, having inspected my peasant's shirt, noticed traces of blood behind my ears, in my hair and on the back of my neck.

'Oh dear God,' she cried out. 'It's all true! Our baby was to be executed in a forest. What are we to do? You poor boy, you must have been terrified. How can this be happening to us?' She started to weep and shake with fear. She turned to my father. 'David, you must forbid Sigi to go out on his own. I cannot endure it! It is too dangerous.'

My father held my mother and told me not to tell anybody what had happened. 'Someone might inform on you. We can't trust anyone. The Germans could return if they found out that you survived the execution. They are sticklers for perfection and do not like to fail in any mission. They would want to silence an eyewitness.'

My sister helped me run a bath and instructed me to shampoo my hair and wash thoroughly behind my ears and neck. When I'd finished, I changed into clean clothes and returned to the lounge room. 'Sigi, tell us some more about the man who saved your life,' my mother asked. 'Who was he? What exactly did he say?'

'I don't know who he was. I didn't notice him in the truck, or see him digging the pit with us. I only turned to look at him when the Germans started shooting. I only looked at him for a second. His face was so peaceful even though he had just been shot. He had the most incredible eyes – deep, dark and luminous – and a sense of peace emanated from them.'

'I now understand,' my mother whispered. 'It was divine intervention.' She nodded her head. 'The man was a Lamed Vav.'

According to the kabbalah, in each generation there are thirty-six righteous people who sustain the world and preserve humanity. The term 'Lamed Vav' is two Hebrew letters that represent the number 36. These people are frequently unknown and obscure but they bear all the sorrows and sins of the world. They also appear and help ordinary people in times of extreme need. Their deeds are often unrecognised and unexplained. If I wasn't convinced that this was how I came to be saved, my mother certainly was.

That same day notices were posted on every billboard in town: *Twenty-five residents of Małachowskiego Street were executed for shooting from their windows at incoming German troops.* No names were listed.

We wanted to return to Katowice, but the Germans had annexed Upper Silesia to the Reich. They had immediately deported the remaining Jewish population to the Russian demarcation line and, shooting above their heads, chased them over to the other side. We were cut off from our home town and not allowed to return. We tried to settle into Czeslaw's apartment for the time being, but after only a couple of nights we were jolted from our sleep by violent knocking and kicking at the door.

'*Aufmachen! Schnell! Aufmachen! Geheime Staatspolizei, aufmachen!*'

The *Geheime Staatspolizei* were the Gestapo. My father put on his gown and opened the door. Four Germans in plain clothes barged in, screaming, 'Are you Czeslaw Borensztejn?'

'No, I am not,' my father answered.

'Who are you? Show us your papers! What are you doing here?'

My father explained that this was his sister's apartment, and that we had come to visit but found no-one at home. The Germans screamed louder and louder and demanded to know where Czeslaw was. My father could not answer, so one of them raised his arm and slapped him twice – hard.

My mother's face twisted and her scream froze in her throat. We all felt the sting of the slap, but my father did not betray a flicker of emotion lest he antagonised the German further. The brute then demanded to know where we lived.

'In Katowice,' my father answered.

'You're a liar!' the German retorted. 'You do not live in Kattowitz. There are no Jews any more. *Kattowitz ist Judenrein.*'

The men then vandalised the apartment, tearing down curtains, cutting into mattresses and breaking everything in their path. They 'confiscated' all of our money and some of my mother's jewellery – even my sister's modest gold chain and charm were ripped from her neck. Intimidated and threatened, we watched these thugs help themselves to our possessions. We had no right to object; instead, we had to be profoundly grateful that they did not kill us on the spot.

Once they had left we still stood there, stunned and silent. Father's face started to swell, revealing red welts left by the gloved hand. I was keenly aware of his embarrassment at being humiliated in front of his family. I avoided his gaze so as not to see the pain in his eyes and add to his shame.

'Thank God they did not come for Sigi,' my father sighed, breaking the spell. 'For a moment I thought that we were going to lose him.'

CHAPTER 6

ON 24 AUGUST 1939, the Germans and the Soviet Union had signed a 'treaty of non-aggression', renouncing warfare between the two powers. It is known as the Molotov–Ribbentrop Pact, named for the German and Russian foreign ministers serving at the time, but it is also called the Nazi–Soviet Pact or Hitler–Stalin Pact.

The treaty contained a secret protocol for the division of much of northern and eastern Europe into German and Russian 'spheres of influence' – in effect, a plan for the expansion of the German Reich and the Soviet Union through the invasion and occupation of Finland, Estonia, Latvia, Lithuania, Romania and, of course, Poland.

Poland shared borders with both Germany and the Soviet Union and so would be partitioned between its bigger neighbours, with the eastern territories going to the Russians and the western territories to the Germans. The existence of this secret protocol was only revealed after Germany's defeat at the end of the war.

The Germans had acted on the protocol almost immediately, attacking Poland from the west on 1 September. The Red Army then invaded Poland from the east on 17 September, forcing Poland to fight on two fronts. The Polish government never surrendered, but by 1 October, the country had been entirely overrun.

The Soviet army occupied all the territory east of the Narev, Wisła and San rivers. The Germans annexed some territories directly into the German Reich, making them part of Germany. The remaining German-occupied territories were grouped into a 'Generalgouvernement' administered by the Germans.

The Polish people now changed their old slogan for a new, sarcastic version: 'We are strong, united, and ready to surrender Poland to Hitler.' My family and I were in Będzin, fourteen kilometres from Katowice, and so found ourselves living in the Generalgouvernement.

Conditions deteriorated rapidly. The Germans had seized the country's food supply and very little of it remained for the civilian population. Food prices were exorbitant and buying privately from farmers or producers was forbidden. The occupying forces saw it as black-marketeering, and it was dangerous for both buyer and seller. In serious cases it was punishable by death.

Although Father's briefcase and most of Mother's jewellery had been safely hidden from our German visitors, we had no money. Mother and Halinka decided to return to Katowice to salvage what they could from our apartment and to withdraw funds from our bank accounts. They had nothing to fear as they did not look Jewish and could easily pass as Poles. They also went to talk with Ernst Waida, a German business associate, to ask him to run our business, as trustee, until our return. After receiving instructions and guidance from my father they left together to catch the train back to our home town. It was not far – just three stops away.

At the far end of our old street, Mother and Halinka saw men in overalls, supervised by uniformed Nazi Party men, taking furniture, paintings, rugs and other items from our apartment and loading it all onto a furniture truck parked outside. They dared not move any closer in case they were recognised by neighbours.

They left very distressed and went to find Mr Waida, who had helped broker numerous business transactions for Father over many years. He generously agreed to look after our business. My mother gave him the documents Father had prepared and signed giving him full power of attorney over the business, then asked him to access some funds for us, as our bank accounts had been frozen. He gave my mother a single twenty-mark note (around US$5 today), saying that was all he had on him. He promised to look after our business as if it were his own, but made no effort to arrange any more money for us.

My mother was at a loss what to do next, but they left his flat. Halinka was furious at Waida's attitude and lack of respect. They returned to Będzin late that afternoon, humiliated and exhausted.

My father now attempted to contact the manager of the construction company that was building our new home and the apartment block in Kraków, but the company had ceased to exist. Worried that the building site might have been ransacked, he went to Kraków to investigate. He was met with a shattering sight. The entire site had been looted and vandalised – even the bathtubs and vanities had been ripped out.

The world he knew was disintegrating right before his eyes and he was helpless to do anything about it. In desperation, he called on some old friends and to his surprise found that the Jewish community in Kraków still lived some kind of semi-normal life: people there still lived in their own homes and the Jewish high school was still open to students.

He returned to Będzin and described everything he had seen and heard. My mother insisted that we move there at once. 'The war will be over in a few months,' she said, 'and it's most important that Sigi continue his education.' Halinka supported Mother and the two immediately started packing. We arrived in Kraków by train in mid September.

One of my parents' friends, who had moved to the territory occupied by the Russians, allowed us to stay in his vacant apartment located in an exclusive part of the city, at 2 Łazarza Boczna Street. My mother was noticeably less agitated in these more comfortable surroundings, but her happiness was short-lived. Three days later the Germans evicted us. Early one morning, four men in the black uniform of the SS loudly stormed the apartment and gave us half an hour to vacate. They did, however, let us take our few belongings.

Once again we were homeless. My father hailed a horse cab and went to his friend's relative, Mr Ptasznik, to ask for help. The Ptasznik family had a large apartment at 27 Radziwiłowska Street and offered us one of their rooms. We were lucky.

When Father returned, we prepared to move. While Halinka was struggling to get a suitcase loaded on the cab, a group of young people walking past stopped to lend a hand. At once there was excited cheering. The young people were close friends of Halinka and her boyfriend, Don Grünspan. As it turned out, Don himself was in Kraków and searching for Halinka. One of the young men went to find him and they soon returned together.

Halinka and Don embraced each other warmly, elated that they had finally found each other. Don told us that a group of them was preparing to cross the border that night into Soviet territory. Halinka was excited by this news and, urged on by Don, decided to join them immediately. My mother was taken aback while, for a moment, my father was speechless.

'What's the hurry?' he finally said. 'Let's talk about this. We need time to prepare ourselves, and so does Halinka. Maybe we will join you, as we have just been evicted.'

'Sorry, there's no time to wait,' Don insisted. 'We must leave now. *Immediately.*'

'Such decisions should not be made in haste,' my father argued.

'We have to catch a train to Przemyśl in forty-five minutes. A guide is waiting to smuggle us over the border this evening.'

Don was adamant that there could be no delay. But there was no way we could join them at such short notice. There were my grandparents to think of, the family business, our new home under construction in Kraków . . . And crossing the river secretly by night would be very dangerous. But Halinka begged my father to let her go. Don promised to send another guide to take us over the border and that we would reunite in the Russian-occupied territory.

My father reluctantly conceded. Perhaps it was best for Halinka to go now and be safe and we would follow as soon as everything was in order. It might even be easier for the three of us to cross the border later. He took the young man aside, gave him some money and said, 'Don, I'm giving you my most precious possession, my beloved daughter. I beg you, take good care of her.'

Halinka transferred her belongings into a backpack and was ready. My mother's anguish exploded into a hysterical cry. She embraced Halinka with such force that my father and Don were unable to separate them. It seemed as if they both knew that this hug would have to last a very long time. Don tucked his arm under Halinka's elbow and, leading her away, whispered, 'Keep walking, don't look back, keep walking forward.' Floods of tears were shed and then, before we knew it, Halinka was gone.

We moved into the Ptasznik family apartment a few hours later. We unpacked in silence, each of us preoccupied. My thoughts were of the exciting adventure in being smuggled across the border under the cover of night. My mother was inconsolable that Halinka had left for an uncertain destination in such dangerous times. Her only consolation was that Halinka and Don were heading towards Lwów, where her sister Hela and brother-in-law Jerzy Manela now were, having managed to escape there from Olkusz. (Lwów was a provincial capital in south-eastern Poland, and was part of the territory annexed by the Soviet Union.) My father reassured my mother that Don had promised to look after their little girl with his life. 'In any case, this war will soon be over. We shall return home, somehow finish building our new house and celebrate the children's engagement. Life will return to normal.'

Within five days the Germans closed down the city's schools and transformed them into military barracks for the German army. They proclaimed Kraków the capital city of the Generalgouvernement and Hans Frank the General Governor. A curfew from dusk until dawn was introduced throughout the entire occupied territory. But at last the postal service was properly reinstated and we were able to notify our family of our whereabouts.

Within days we received a postcard from my grandmother Rachel informing us that they were safe in Olkusz and my aunt Regina and cousin Lunia had arrived – with Lunia's new baby, born on 1 September, the night of the German invasion. While on the run trying to escape the invading army, Regina and Lunia were caught up in Kielce by low-flying planes that bombarded the city. When Lunia's contractions began, they searched the city for a safe haven and found a cellar, used as an air-raid shelter. The basement was packed with the building's inhabitants huddled together in almost total darkness with only the sound of crying children, frightened by the bombs exploding above and shaking the ground. When Lunia's contractions intensified, some people found an old table, cleared its dusty surface and covered it with a thin blanket. Lunia gave birth to a baby girl surrounded by total strangers without a doctor or midwife to assist her. Regina, who had recently lost her husband, delivered the baby alone. Lunia's husband Henryk Mesing had deserted his pregnant wife and fled to eastern Poland to save himself.

My education had been interrupted a second time by the closure of schools so my father enrolled me in a private school of commerce that was owned and managed by an acquaintance, Mr Nycz. There were about twenty-five students in the class, the majority being Poles. We learned a little bit of everything: typing, shorthand and basic accountancy. I was quite happy there as the students were very nice and I made a few new friends.

Three weeks later, however, four black-clad SS officers, skull badges on their caps, entered the classroom. They apologised for the interruption and introduced themselves to our female teacher.

'Are there any Jews in this class?' one of the soldiers demanded.

'I don't know,' she answered, sweeping her eyes across her class.

Another soldier stepped forward. 'In accordance with the order proclaimed by the General Governor Hans Frank, no Jews are allowed to attend any educational institutions on any level. Jews stand up!'

I stood up, along with five or six other students. 'Take your belongings and leave the class immediately,' the SS-man ordered, pointing an accusatory finger. The rest of the class watched, embarrassed. The teacher lowered her head in shame and confusion.

As we left the room each of the Germans kicked us from behind yelling, 'Get the hell out of here! On the double, you filthy Jews!'

I was used to strict school discipline, but this was something quite alien to me. Nobody had ever spoken to me that way before. I was extremely offended. Even during my near execution in Będzin I wasn't kicked or verbally abused. This was my first direct experience of German oppression. I was fifteen years old and had been brought up to behave with propriety, courtesy and respect and I was stunned and angry that I was unable to defend myself, protest, or even to ask why. That day marked the end of my formal education.

CHAPTER 7

A *JUDENRAT* or Jewish Council of the Elders had been established by the Germans in every city and town to represent the local Jewish population. These councils were responsible for all Jewish affairs including food supply, accommodation, welfare and so on. Most importantly, they organised workers for several German institutions and public works. The Judenrat was the go-between for the German authorities and the Jewish community. The Council of the Elders paid for the forced labour with money levied from the wealthier members of the community.

A law was soon proclaimed that all Jews over the age of twelve had to wear a white armband with a blue Star of David on their right arm, and that all Jews between twelve and sixty-five years of age who were not employed elsewhere would work for the Germans. But this arrangement did not stop Jews being seized from the streets for immediate tasks such as cleaning up snow or shovelling coal or coke into cellars of public buildings. Some satirical lyrics were even sung to the tune of a popular song at the time. Translated from the Polish, they went like this:

'Come on, Jew! Come on, Jew! On the double,'
Behind me roared a vulgar voice.
'If you don't want any trouble,
Make it now, your proper choice.

You see the coal pile at the cellar door?
Immediately start to shovel.'
'With pleasure, sir – it's my profession.
Not only coal, but also mud and snow,
Were always my obsession.'

Things had become so difficult that we were forced to sell or exchange our personal belongings for food. As soon as the night curfew was over, I was up every morning, queuing up at the local bakery. I would remove my armband because Jews were usually thrown out of the queue. Flour was so scarce that the bakers would limit the number of loaves they would sell to each customer. Sometimes I managed to buy more than one loaf, which I would sell, making a small profit.

Once, while crossing the street I came across a Dr Wander's bakery displaying the famous and exclusive Dr Wander's Health Bread. This was my mother's favourite. Surprised, because bread was so rare, I went into the shop to ask if I could buy a loaf. To my amazement they sold me three! I was able to buy this bread for another two weeks until the Germans shut down the shops.

One evening during a frugal dinner my father proposed that I start an apprenticeship. In the basement of the house where we were living was a shoemaker, and my father had visited him that day to hide some gold ingots in the soles of a pair of my shoes. The visit had started him thinking, he said – I should become a cobbler.

His rationale was that tradespeople were very much in demand in wartime. A barber was the best profession as you did not need many tools and could keep them in one hand. But it would take me too long to qualify for that so a cobbler was the next best thing. He assured me that should I turn out to be only a mediocre cobbler no-one would complain too much, but if I was an inferior hairdresser I could accidentally clip someone's ear or give them a style they did not like. There was a shortage of shoes to buy and people needed to mend their old ones so work was guaranteed. I liked the idea of being able to earn money and help my family. My mother, however, was affronted. 'This must be a joke. This absurd war will end soon. We'll re-enrol him as a boarder into Mława College as soon as possible.' Finally, though, she accepted my father's plan.

The shoemaker lived together with his wife and young child in one small room. They also had a little kitchen, and he had his workshop set up there. When we first went to see him, he was crouching on a very low stool nailing soles with wooden pegs. Without lifting his head he asked what he could do for us. My father explained and offered to pay him for teaching me his trade.

As Father spoke, I looked through the open door into the windowless room to see a shabby iron bed covered by a threadbare blanket, a dirty pillow and no bed linen. A few pieces of clothing hung from a hook on the wall. A crucifix was mounted on the opposite wall and a small light globe hung from the middle of the ceiling. In the kitchen was a small iron stove and next to it a wooden cradle with a crying baby in it. In front of the tiny and only window was the shoemaker's work area. I could see people's legs rushing by as the window was at ground level. On the floor around the worktable, among scraps of leather, lay a dozen pairs of shoes. The shoemaker agreed to my father's terms and I began my apprenticeship at once.

My father left and I was given a cloth to tie around my waist, a stool to sit on next to the shoemaker and instructions to watch him as he worked. But first I asked him a few questions, starting with one that I had always wondered about while accompanying Aniela on her visits to the shoemaker. Why did he crouch over on such a small stool rather than sitting on a regular chair at an ordinary workbench? He looked at me with a baffled expression and said that he was doing as his father had done before him.

I considered this and imagined that if I were to succeed and become a world-renowned shoe designer and manufacturer one day, I would oversee rows and rows of employees with black aprons tied around their waists, sitting on tiny little wooden stools hunched over little benches, their mouths full of nails, buried ankle-deep in scraps of leather. It was such a funny image that I nearly laughed out loud.

The shoemaker then asked me about my life and family and became so interested that he put down his tools and stopped working. That is how we spent the rest of the day. The next day was much the same: me, explaining the current political situation and why we were at war, and him listening.

On the third day he asked to see my father. When Father came down, the shoemaker took some money out of his pocket and handed it to him. 'Sir, I'm returning the money you gave me because I'm unable to teach your son. He will never be a shoemaker. Not only could I not teach him, but I'm neglecting my own work. We were spending the whole day talking. When I engage an apprentice I have to ask him to do basic tasks, like sweeping the floor, chopping wood, delivering repaired shoes and even taking care of the baby when my wife is away. I cannot ask your son to do this kind of work.'

To my mother's delight, my career as a famous shoemaker ended before it even began.

Forced labour was now obligatory for all Jews and the Judenrat had to organise this. The Germans did not pay for the forced labour, but the Judenrat had developed a scheme that allowed people to hire 'substitute workers'. The wealthier members of the Jewish community could pay the Judenrat a certain amount, exempting them from forced-labour duty, and this money was used to pay the wages of the poor who worked in their place. I registered with the Judenrat and was selected to join a working brigade of sixty young people. Coincidentally I was reunited with two schoolfriends, Jurek Proper and Ernst Tahler, who had also moved to Kraków. We worked as cleaners at a huge complex of German police barracks. They had been working there for a while and were familiar with the conditions and the routine. We worked every day for ten hours starting at 7 am and earned around one quarter of the wages of a non-Jewish worker. This was the only income available for our family.

Ernst Tahler's brother Wili worked at an adjoining brigade. I knew him well, as he had once been Halinka's boyfriend, long before she met Don. He was killed one day when a heavily loaded truck overturned. Poor Wili had been on the top of the truck holding the load. His death shocked us greatly. With time we grew used to it, that people were killed for no reason, but this was still at the beginning of the war.

In addition to the daily struggles, my parents worried about Halinka, Czeslaw and their own parents. The Ptasznik family was supportive: sometimes they invited us for dinner and sometimes my mother would lunch with them.

Mrs Ptasznik was an attractive, kind woman who was expecting her first child. While we were staying with them, her husband organised a room for her in a private clinic, at great expense and effort. This was around the time that the occupying authorities changed over the old Polish currency for the new zloty. The maximum amount of money a person was officially allowed to exchange was 400 zloty – a small sum, equivalent to about one and a half month's wages. Money, however, could be exchanged on the black market for an exorbitantly inflated price. Mr Ptasznik was forced to look for such a contact to change his money so he could pay the clinic's fees; he was happy that his wife would deliver in a private facility and utterly unaware that he was exposing himself to possible blackmail.

That same evening, just as we had finished dinner, fierce

knocking at the front door interrupted our conversation. Although there was a doorbell, the Germans never used it; they always knocked with a rifle butt or kicked with their boots. And they never spoke normally when approaching Jews – they always yelled.

Four Germans entered the apartment. Two of them were dressed in plain clothes, with characteristic leather coats, and two were uniformed SS-men. Without asking any questions, they started to search the apartment. They pulled out everything from the cupboards, dressers and drawers. They stripped the beds and moved the furniture. They separated the men from the women and ordered us to undress, then inspected each piece of clothing. One of the men pulled a wad of cash from Mr Ptasznik's jacket, which he had exchanged that morning. They confiscated the money as well as my father's address and notebook.

'You filthy Jew!' one of them yelled. 'Are you aware that it's an offence to have more than four hundred zloty in your possession?'

'Yes I know,' Mr Ptasznik said. 'But my wife is expected to give birth very soon and I needed the money for the hospital.'

They ignored his explanation and punched both my father and Mr Ptasznik in the face. 'You bloody Jews!' they yelled. 'You're coming with us and will learn what it means to disobey orders and regulations.'

They took both men away, leaving behind them a terrible mess. We were so intimidated, so terrorised and terrified, that we could barely breathe. We did not know what to do, we were completely helpless, broken-hearted, the two women and I. We had no-one to turn to for help or advice and nowhere to go for protection and justice. We tried to clean up, stumbling around, each in our own misery. We were not sure if we would ever see the men again. My mother was crying with the faint whimper of a frightened child, while Mrs Ptasznik was crying aloud, remonstrating with God for putting her through this pain. I was trying not to cry but tears kept spilling out of my eyes, pouring down my face, and my nose was running. That night we could not sleep. In the morning I went to work as usual but couldn't stop wondering and worrying about my father and Mr Ptasznik's fate. I returned home to find my mother and Mrs Ptasznik just as I had left them: grief-stricken and in a state of complete despair. They had red puffy eyes and darkened faces from continuous crying.

This went on for the next three days until my father and Ptasznik returned. They had been in the Montelupich prison, where they were beaten and tortured. They were also forced to clean all the toilets in the building with toothbrushes. It was incomprehensible to me that my father, who was such a refined gentleman, who commanded respect from business colleagues and was a pillar of society, should be reduced to this.

Mrs Ptasznik gave birth to her son in mid November. Fortunately, everything went well and they were very happy with their new baby. As we had expected, Mr Ptasznik politely explained to us that they would now need our room for the baby. Once again it was time to look for another place to stay.

Mrs Giza Leichter was a close friend of my mother's. They used to holiday together at spa resorts. Mr Leichter was CEO of the Helia chocolate factory in Podgórze, a suburb of Kraków on the other side of the Wisła River. Until now my parents had been too embarrassed to contact the Leichters – even just to let them know that we were in Kraków. My mother now swallowed her pride and set out for the Leichters' apartment.

Giza was very surprised but happy to see my mother in Kraków. They were hugging and kissing, crying and smiling, all at the same time. They spent about half an hour talking and reminiscing. Then my mother told her of our experiences since we left Katowice three months earlier. Giza was aghast. Here she was, still living her old lifestyle, untouched by war or persecution. Mother then asked if she could help us find an apartment or room, or any kind of shelter. Giza replied that she did not know of any, but would gladly take us in if we didn't mind sharing a very small room. It must have been a maid's room once: it was two metres long and one and a half metres wide with a single bed and a small bedside table. Mother explained that there were three of us. Giza reassured her that she had a fold-out bed for me to sleep on, if I didn't mind sleeping in the kitchen. They already had one boy sleeping there who came from Bochnia and was the same age as me.

By the end of November we had moved in with the Leichters at 22 Smoleńsk Street. This was our sixth move since we left Katowice. We were very grateful, as winter had started with a vengeance. Food became even scarcer and movements were restricted. Round-ups, persecutions, arrests and body searches became a daily occurrence. My father continued to look for work and we continued living from day to day.

It was in December 1939 that my mother, who possessed extraordinary psychic abilities, had her first premonition of the Holocaust, visions of unimaginable horror. 'All the Jewish people in town had to line up in the main square and were shot,' she told us. 'Women, children, babies, all shot dead!' Of course no-one took it seriously. The whole family tried to convince her that it had only been a bad dream. The idea that entire Jewish communities could be killed seemed ridiculous and extreme.

On 3 March 1940, we received our first postcard with marvellous news: Halinka had arrived safely in Lwów and, remarkably, Czeslaw had turned up there as well. We had given him up, thinking he must have been killed in the bombardment of the train and buried somewhere in a mass grave, so it was an enormous relief to us to hear that he was safe. Aunt Hela and

Uncle Jerzy were also in Lwów and Halinka stayed with them a while. Our life now focused on mail from Halinka and surviving one day at a time.

We had to communicate via postcards, as all mail was censored and letters sealed in envelopes were no longer permitted. The post was unreliable at best, so my sister often sent us duplicate postcards, hoping that if one went missing the other would get through. She also sent news to Don's parents and to my mother's sister Regina, who lived in territory that had been incorporated into the German Reich. The Grünspans and Regina often received news before we did, because mail was more reliable and faster in the Reich than in the Generalgouvernement, and they passed it on straight away. That is how we came to learn of my sister's marriage to Don at second-hand, a week before we heard it from Halinka herself. She had written two postcards, both dated 21 April 1940. They arrived the following month, and my parents replied at once.

My father wrote:

Dearest children and all of you close to my heart,
  Today, Saturday 25 May 1940, we received two postcards from you dated 21 April where you officially and directly informed us of your marriage. We heard of your wedding last week from Don's parents Mr & Mrs Grünspan from Łódź, and from Mummy's sister Regina Reichmann. You cannot imagine how we felt. Our tears wet the postcard, partly from joy and partly from anger that we could not be present at our dearest and only daughter's wedding, somewhere far away in a foreign country in exile without parents. We imagined the wedding of our dearest Halinka to be different. However, thank God for this, and we wish you and all who took part in the event a hearty mazel tov. We send you parental

blessings, lots of happiness and all the very best. It is most important that you are together and happy, because your happiness is also our happiness.

We and Mr & Mrs Leichter (we do not have anyone else) toasted everybody mazel tov and l'chaim on news of your wedding. The routine here is all the same. We would like to move to Olkusz or to Będzin to be with the other members of our family. We receive mail from them quite often. We also received a parcel of food from Czeslaw's mother. We wish you all the best, good health and maintain good hope.

Kisses and hugs,
your father

My mother wrote her own note on the same postcard:

My dearest children,
I am so moved by all of this that I am unable to concentrate to write at length. From the bottom of my heart, I am sending you sincere motherly wishes of happiness. Wishes for better times for all of us.

Kissing you,
your mother and best friend

This latest news made my parents much less anxious and depressed. At least once a week, my parents received a postcard from Halinka. They sent her one every week in return – the maximum the German authorities allowed – and also continued to correspond with Don's parents in Łódź. Later, as conditions in the ghetto there worsened, my parents would send them a loaf of bread every fortnight. (A food parcel could not exceed one kilogram in weight and was only allowed to contain a single loaf of bread.)

Unfortunately bad news was soon to follow. In early April 1940 Denmark surrendered to the Germans, followed by Luxembourg. Holland surrendered to the Germans in May 1940, and Belgium was next. Norway capitulated on 10 June. On 22 June France signed its capitulation to the Germans near Compiègne village, in the same railway carriage the Germans had signed theirs to France after World War I.

My father approached former business associates, Germans whose companies had established new branches in the occupied territory, and asked them for work. The Grabowski Brothers, customers of Father's before the war, offered him a position selecting, sorting and allocating cut logs for use in the mining, transport and communications industries. This meant he had to move to Starachowice-Wierzbnik, a small village 190 kilometres northeast of Kraków. My father was overjoyed that at last he was able to provide for his family and at the same time do what he loved most. He had trained in forestry, and before the war had supplied timber to heavy industry in Upper Silesia. There were very few people skilled in this profession.

At the same time, the authorities decreed that all Jews who were not permanent residents of Kraków prior to the war must leave by the end of August 1940. Failure to comply would result in compulsory deportation to an unknown destination. We thanked the Leichters for their hospitality and left Kraków on 14 August 1940.

My father obtained the necessary travel documents and went directly to Starachowice-Wierzbnik. My mother and I only had permission to travel to Częstochowa and from there we had to apply for an additional permit to join my father.

CHAPTER 8

CZĘSTOCHOWA'S JEWS had endured a terrible tragedy at the beginning of the war. On Sunday 3 September 1939, the German army had moved into the town and the Jews were falsely accused of shooting at the entering soldiers – just as they had been when the Germans entered Będzin. Almost everywhere the Germans used this excuse to intimidate the local population. It was a common occurrence. The next day the Germans killed 300 unarmed Jewish civilians, including women and children, and wounded many more. This event was known as 'bloody Monday'.

At the beginning of the war, my father's sister Rozia Aronowicz moved with her husband Abraham and two children from Radomsko to Częstochowa. She was one of my favourite aunts. They had a wholesale textile business selling all kinds of fabrics, clothes and manchester. Rozia's son, twenty-one-year-old Bolek, was an industrial and architectural draughtsman and her fourteen-year-old daughter, Paula, was still at school. In Częstochowa, they had a very small flat so they could not take us in. They were themselves refugees.

My mother's cousin Tekla Faktor was in a much better position to offer us help. She lived in a very modern apartment at 6 Kilińskiego Street with her husband and two children, Mark and Hanka. They received us with open arms. The Faktors were still in their own home and not much had changed in their lives. Tekla had lost her job as a college teacher, but her husband still worked at his sawmill, now under German administration. The Faktors were very good to us; they treated us with dignity and respect.

We stayed in Częstochowa for about four weeks. I met a few kids my own age and we spent some time together, reminiscing about the Zionist youth movement, dreaming of a Jewish homeland, and trying to forget the war. Marian Kongrecki, the son of the landlord, even taught me how to play bridge. For a short time I felt like I was on vacation.

Early one morning German gendarmes surrounded the neighbourhood and announced through a loudspeaker that everyone had to vacate their apartments within the hour. We were allowed to take personal belongings but only as much as we could carry. People roused suddenly from their sleep were confused and began to panic: children cried and sobbing women ran about helplessly in the street. Then an energetic man stepped forward and spoke to us. 'People, calm down. Go back into your apartments and start packing. We have less than an hour and there is nothing else we *can* do.' They listened and did as they were told.

We had been through this experience a few months earlier in Kraków. As we lined up in the courtyard, Mother approached the commanding officer and explained that we were in transit on our way to Starachowice-Wierzbnik, where her husband had just commenced an important job for a German company; we were waiting for a travel permit to join him. The officer was impressed by Mother's perfect German and allowed us to keep our belongings. He also told Mother to come to his office that afternoon where he would issue her the appropriate permits. The next day we were on our way to Starachowice-Wierzbnik.

The 120-kilometre journey was not easy. At every stop a new squad of gendarmes or German police boarded the train, checking the identity of the passengers, searching their luggage and confiscating all foodstuffs.

We were the only Jews in our carriage, easily identifiable by our armbands, and received 'special treatment'. It would start with an exclamation: 'Ah, what have we got here? Jews! Let's see how clever they are.' The whole compartment would burst out laughing. Then, after they had checked our travelling permit and identity cards, would come the questions.

'Where are you travelling to?'

'We're going to Starachowice-Wierzbnik,' my mother would answer in Polish. It was safer in this circumstance not to admit that she spoke German.

'What for?'

'To join my husband.'

'Don't bother. He's found himself another Jewess, prettier than you.' My mother would ignore this.

'And what is your husband doing?'

'He works for a German company.'

'You are a *liar*. Jews do not work, they cheat, swindle and count money.' Then: 'What have you got in your suitcase? Let's see. Open it.'

One German would then take out a few things – towels, sweaters and blouses – and drop them on the floor. Looking deeper into the suitcase he would pull out some of Mother's underwear, holding it up for all to see, and the other passengers laughed their appreciation. My mother began to tremble and burst into tears. I wanted to attack the German, but I froze, watching the scene in horror.

At last the train would reach another stop but the gendarmes would leave only for another lot to replace them. We experienced half-a-dozen similar incidents before reaching our destination in the early morning of 18 October 1940. At Starachowice-Wierzbnik station Father was waiting for us.

PART II

OCTOBER 1940 – SEPTEMBER 1942

CHAPTER 9

Starachowice-Wierzbnik is in central Poland. In the 1930s this region, known as the Centralny Okręg Przemysłowy (COP), was developed as a major industrial centre and foundries, steel mills and munitions factories were established. The area, rich in iron ore, ranged from Pionki through Radom, Suchedniów and Starachowice-Wierzbnik to Skarżysko-Kamienna and Stalowa Wola. Many people were attracted to the region because housing was supplied to employees and the working conditions were better than elsewhere in the country. As all factories belonged to the government, the workers were government employees – they were, in effect, a kind of public servant. In 1940, after the Germans had invaded, Starachowice-Wierzbnik's industry was taken over by Hermann Göring Werke, a company with the German state as its majority shareholder and senior Nazi leader Hermann Göring as its director. Stahlwerke Braunschweig was a subsidiary company of Hermann Göring Werke and employed many people in Starachowice-Wierzbnik as miners and in its steel mills.

My father had rented a ground-floor room at the back of a house at 16 Iłżecka Street, occupied by a family with three small children. The toilet was in the backyard. Father managed to 'furnish' our room with some second-hand furniture: a bed, a small table and two wooden chairs. He bought a lamp and a can of kerosene, and borrowed a fold-out bed and a tiny wardrobe.

To cook we used a Primus kerosene burner, offered to us by a neighbour.

The first thing Mother did when we arrived was to sit at the table and write Halinka a postcard. Then she organised a cleaning bee. First we had to buy two buckets, one for clean water and the other for the waste. We carried water from a well located in the town square about 150 metres away. We scrubbed the walls, the floor, the furniture, the only window and the door. After we finished cleaning, we unpacked and put our clothes away. Somehow, the room now appeared larger.

My mother shook out a tablecloth and used a large glass as a vase for flowers. Father went out to buy food and, of course, bread and salt for our house-warming ritual. As we sat down to our first meal we felt very happy – we three were finally reunited – despite the primitive conditions. With only two chairs one of us had to sit on the bed; this became my permanent seat. Father talked about his job and his coworkers. He said that he was happy to stay where he was until the end of the war. That night we put the chairs on top of the table to make room for my fold-out bed.

It was still dark outside when Father got up and ready for work. He prepared his lunch of bread, cucumber, a few radishes and a bottle of substitute tea. (Tea and coffee were not grown in Europe, and supplies had run out soon after the war began.) He had to walk almost five kilometres to work.

My first night on that bed was terrible: it took minutes of stretching and flexing before I could straighten up. My mother slept on and I started to prepare breakfast. I needed some water.

At the well a group of young people were waiting in line. 'Is there always a queue here?' I asked the boy in front of me.

'No, just in the mornings,' he answered. 'What's your name? I haven't seen you here before.'

'I just arrived,' I said.

'Have you been re-settled here as a refugee?'

I told him no, explaining that my father had a new job here. I asked him if he was a local.

'No,' he replied. 'When the Germans incorporated Łódź and surrounding areas into the German Reich two months ago, they deported many Jewish families to the Generalgouvernement. About twenty families were sent here. We were one of them. Other families from Włocławek and Płock have also been sent here. It's a nice place and the people are decent and helpful. We were the first refugees in this town.'

We chatted for a while longer and he pointed to his house nearby. 'Why don't you come over tonight around six o'clock? I finish my shift at five. I work at the steel mill in the Hermann Göring complex.'

I thanked him and told him I would see him that evening. Mother was just waking up when I got back and we sat down to eat our breakfast in silence. She hadn't slept well and was cranky and moody: we had not received any mail from Halinka since leaving Kraków and she was getting very worried.

Father returned from work tired but happy. He praised my mother for preparing a wonderful dinner and told us funny work stories. He then suggested that I get a job working with him. 'I'll teach you gradually while you work as a labourer, still earning a reasonable wage,' he said.

Mother was concerned that it would be too exhausting for me but I assured her that I was strong enough. I wanted to work. I then excused myself from the table and, to the amazement of my parents, declared that I had an important engagement. They were astonished.

Five minutes later I knocked on the door of the house that the boy had pointed out to me. A small porch led to a well-lit room and at first I was blinded by the light's brightness. There was still a blackout and the windows were covered. As my eyes adjusted

I was surprised to see about a dozen girls and boys my age. I finally shook hands with the boy I'd chatted to that morning. He told me his name was Mundek, and then went around the room introducing me to everyone else; I was very pleased to be welcomed and included in the group. I spent an hour there chatting to them all, and a few of the girls asked if I needed help with anything.

'Actually, I need to organise a few things in the morning and don't know where to start,' I said. 'I have to register my family with the police and the council and register myself at the labour exchange.'

'Easy!' exclaimed two girls simultaneously. They were sisters, Hanka and Rozka Laks. 'Our father's the manager of the labour exchange, and we can also help you register with the police and the council.'

I was delighted. They gave me the address of the labour exchange and we arranged to meet there the following morning.

Rozka was a few months younger than me, but just as tall. She was very pretty with shiny, long, dark-brown hair, braided on top of her head like an angel's halo. Her large brown eyes added to her attractiveness. Hanka was a couple of years older and very tall with short hair, very dark eyes and a permanent smile on her face. Both girls were gorgeous.

Hanka introduced me to her father the next morning and I had to stop myself from laughing out loud on first seeing him. Mr Laks looked like someone straight out of the nineteenth century: he wore his hair parted in the centre, had a funny waxed and curved moustache and a pince-nez perched on his long and pointy nose. But he was very helpful. Besides my family, Mr Laks was probably the only person in Starachowice-Wierzbnik who spoke fluent German and I learned he had been an officer in the Austrian army during World War I.

The sisters then took me on a tour of the town, past the town hall, the church and the remains of the synagogue, which had been destroyed by the Germans at the outset of the war. They did this to prove that they had come, to leave their mark. While we were walking a German police patrol marched towards us. Hanka immediately warned me to step down off the pavement – it was forbidden for Jews to share the pavement with the Germans – and remove my hat. 'Sometimes, if you don't take off your hat you get whacked for disobeying orders,' she explained. 'Other times, if you do acknowledge them by taking your hat off, you get whacked for thinking that you're worthy of acknowledging them!'

We stood still with our heads bent, our eyes cast down, holding our breath, waiting for them to pass.

'Look at these filthy Jews shitting themselves with fear,' one of the policemen sneered. The rest laughed. I did not translate for the girls. As soon as the patrol turned the corner, we took a deep breath, put our hats on and stepped back onto the pavement.

We walked to the river, where we found a bench under the shade of an old weeping willow. We sat and admired the trees along the riverbank, the birds in the sky, the wild ducks on the river diving for food and reappearing. The fresh fragrant air and the beauty and calm about us made us forget about the war. The girls began singing a song about love and happiness, sacrifice and loyalty, life and hope. I sat there transfixed – even after they had finished.

Rozka broke the silence and declared that it was time for lunch, insisting that I join them. Mrs Laks, a tall woman with sad eyes, was expecting me. After I had praised her cooking, she asked me a few questions, then told me she believed that it had been a big mistake for her family to settle in this little town of 20,000 people, of which 3500 were Jews.

Jews had been banned from holding public employment throughout all of Poland since 1918, and as local industry in this region had been nationalised, Jews could not obtain work in the government-owned mines or factories. Before the war most made a living from trade and small retail shops, supplying the relatively better off local population, though many relied on charity. Mr Laks, a qualified accountant, had tried to make a living by helping the poorly educated folk by writing petitions, filling in forms, copying documents and writing letters on their behalf. It had been tough, and the family had been able to afford to educate only one of their daughters – the eldest, Hanka. The war had in fact improved their financial situation, as Mr Laks, one of the town's few German speakers, had been made the manager of the local labour exchange.

From that day I was a frequent guest of the Lakses. Their courtyard had a well that was easier to operate than the one at the main square and more convenient, since their house was just across the road from ours.

The first Friday after our arrival my mother wanted to light Sabbath candles. I bought her a packet of twelve candles and a box of matches. Each Friday night my mother always lit two candles – but to save money she now cut them in half. She laid out a fresh tablecloth, prepared the candles and suddenly realised that she did not have any candlesticks. My father took a large potato, cut it in half and put the pieces flat side down on a little tray. He then cut a hole in each half and inserted the candles. 'How ingenious!' Mother cried. 'After all the beautiful silver candelabras and candlesticks, it's now the humble potato that helps our Sabbath blessings.'

Around this time I began my new job as a timber labourer. On my first day Father woke me at 5.30 am. We had a quick breakfast of hot porridge, packed our lunches and left for work. We walked alongside a railroad, jumping from sleeper to sleeper.

I was full of energy and the crisp morning chill invigorated me. I asked how much money I would make.

'First you have to prove yourself and then we'll see,' Father replied. 'The team is paid according to its productivity, all sharing equally.' Because of his expertise, my father had been appointed manager of the whole operation.

We arrived at 6.45 am and started work at 7 am. Dawn had broken and the rising sun soon illuminated our workplace – in the middle of dense forest was a large clearing where a lumberyard had been created. A temporary rail sidetrack had been laid for easy connection to the main rail network. Some twenty non-Jewish workers were already there, preparing their tools and sharpening their saws. There were two teams: one was hand sawing timber logs; the other loaded them onto a goods carriage. In the middle of the yard was a small shed with a stove that served as the site office – the workers stored their lunches and bottles of tea there to keep them warm. (They brought their substitute tea to work with them in old vodka bottles.)

After the trees were chopped down, branches trimmed and bark stripped, the logs were transported to the yard for cutting. These huge logs were twelve to fifteen metres long and laid out in rows to be sorted and categorised by my father. Most of the timber was for the mining industry but some was used for railway sleepers and some tall strong logs for telegraph poles. My father had to mark each log using a special knife: firstly to determine the best use for the log, then to indicate the best cutting spot. Usually the cuts were on the knots to allow for greater strength, but as this was pinewood or spruce, both very knotty woods, it was much more difficult to cut. Chainsaws were yet to be invented. The logs were generally 25 centimetres in diameter and 2.5 metres long.

I was assigned to the loading squad, whose job it was to stand the logs upright onto the carriage. As the logs were freshly cut, they were still wet and very heavy. Struggling to get them onto my shoulder, I tried to pick the thinner ones. Other workers managed to carry two logs at a time. Climbing the steep ramp to the carriage was the most difficult part, but I was happy working in the fresh air, breathing the aromatic, resinous scent of pine.

At noon we had a half-hour break for lunch. I ate quickly so I could find a spot on the soft moss to lie down and rest. 'You were such a big hero in your Hanoar Hatzioni scout group. What's happened to you?' my father teased. 'It shouldn't be a problem for you to throw a few sticks onto a carriage.' Somehow I made it to the end of the day and returned home exhausted. My mother placed a vinegar compress on my bruised and throbbing shoulders and I went straight to bed. But the job got easier.

On our march to work I began to spot pieces of coal lying alongside and between the tracks, which must have fallen off the engine. I suggested that we take them home for heating. I found an old sack and transformed it into a backpack to carry the coal in and my father organised an old cast-iron stove that we installed in the room. We removed part of the glass from our only window, replacing it with a piece of sheet metal, and then hooked up the stovepipe, which became our flue. We now had enough coal and firewood for heating and cooking. Things were looking up.

I worked with my father until the end of November, then Mr Laks found a position for me at the firebrick factory, Rogalin. The day I started there was the day I began to smoke, encouraged by my coworkers. The job was not very stimulating, but it was undercover and in a well-heated building, thanks to the constantly fired kilns. We were manufacturing firebricks, fire mouldings and fireclay. When I first started two of us had to load lumps of heavy fireclay into cradle-tip carriages on a narrow-gauge rail at the nearby quarry. Then we pushed the carriages about 100 metres to a chute, where we tipped and emptied the load. It was repetitive work. The day shift was from 7 am to 3.30 pm, and the night shift from 3.30 pm until midnight. We swapped shifts every six weeks.

Many young Jewish people found jobs working at the Hermann Göring complex. Some positions paid better than others but the better-paid jobs were more gruelling, especially at the grand furnace and the steel mills. About twenty kilometres from Starachowice-Wierzbnik was another industrial centre, Skarżysko-Kamienna. There, we were told, the conditions were much tougher, the work much harder and the working hours longer. There the workers were treated like slaves. It was forced labour, and they were paid less than the workers in Starachowice-Wierzbnik.

Alternating between the two shifts meant that I could still help out at home and see my friends. For the time being, I was content. Very often, I would meet Rozka at the well. We became very good friends and, eventually, we fell in love. I was as much in love as only a sixteen-year-old boy can be. I spent most of my free time with Rozka, sometimes strolling along the narrow streets with their dilapidated, white- or green-painted houses, past shabby shops displaying faded garments as the latest fashion, and grocery stores showcasing bottles of tea-flavoured liquid and imitation coffee made from roasted barley.

At least once a week a group of us used to visit the Parzęczewskis, a very nice couple from Łódź who had a daughter a little older than me. Mr Parzęczewski was a professor and the principal of one of Łódź's Jewish colleges. He gave us fascinating talks on Greek and Roman mythology, ancient Roman and Greek history, Persian, Assyrian and Babylonian history and European history. Some of his lectures were so enthralling that we sat there mesmerised – so starved were we for knowledge.

It was only when we received a much-awaited postcard from Halinka that our home life began to settle into a rhythm. Before it arrived my parents had been always anxious, always waiting, obsessed. My aunt Hela had told us that Halinka and Don were no longer in Lwów; they had been deported to an unknown destination by the Soviet authorities. We'd had no further news in the entire time we'd been living in Starachowice-Wierzbnik – more than a month.

I had been working night shift and was home when the postman came. My mother woke me, crying and laughing at the same time. 'Look! Look what I have. It's a postcard from my darling Halinka!' She was so elated that she jumped up and down and began to dance in our little room. 'Get dressed and let's go and show it to Daddy.'

Even though I was still half-asleep, I was nearly as excited as her. And so too was Father. My mother jumped on him, hugging and kissing him. In fact the whole squad of workers in the timber yard stopped to watch the two of them beaming at the card. I urged my mother to calm down as she was embarrassing me, but she read the postcard out loud, repeatedly. The news was that they were well, though she and Don had been forced to relocate to Siberia.

In 1939, there had been a massive influx of refugees into the eastern part of Poland occupied by the Soviet Union. For a while the number of refugees was much higher than the local population. In the early days, many people ended up travelling back across the border into the German-occupied territory in the same illegal way they had left, because they couldn't make a living or establish themselves as refugees in the Russian-occupied territory – but many others remained. The authorities had tried to convince them to settle permanently in the area and accept Soviet citizenship, but without much success. The Russians didn't want people living in the border territory whose political orientation was uncertain, so they decided to find out who was friend and who was foe.

The first step was to register all refugees. In 1940 the Russians announced that an agreement had been reached with the German government, and whoever wanted to return to their home and family in the German-occupied territories could do so – but first they would have to register, giving the authorities their names and addresses.

People lined up in endless queues for this opportunity; some even camped out not to miss their chance. After they registered they were instructed to wait for notification. A few weeks later, tens of thousands were rounded up and deported to villages and small towns in Siberia and other places in central and eastern parts of the USSR. They were seized at night, when they were unprepared, but the evacuation was conducted in a relatively humane manner. The Russians allowed the refugees to take their belongings, what they could carry, and even helped them with their luggage. The areas to which they were deported had harsh climates, the elderly people suffered, and many died, but there was no mass murder, no-one was singled out or killed. There is no doubt that this deceitful evacuation did save lives, but it was deception all the same.

As we returned home, Mother was the happiest I had seen her in a long time. That night all three of us wrote back to Halinka.

My dearest darling children,

Yesterday we received your postcard dated 14/11/40, which was the first letter from you in three months. You cannot imagine how ecstatic we were. We were very worried. We did not know what to think. We wrote to Hela and the Diamants and no-one replied. Mummy and Sigi ran 5 km to my workplace, filled with joy to tell me the good news. Mummy was singing and dancing with excitement. Thank God you are well, have enough food and some clothes. We will investigate the possibility of sending you something. We immediately notified Don's parents in Łódź, since they had not heard from you either. We normally correspond with them at least once a week. We are helping them as much as we can. So do not worry about them and us. Here all is well. Sigi and I have jobs and we have sufficient provisions. The only thing missing is you. It is such a pity that we cannot all be together, we would have been so happy. We live in hope that one day we shall all be reunited. Hearty regards and kisses, do not lose your high spirits, and keep well.

Your loving father

Dearest children,

I can't tell you how overjoyed I was to receive your postcard. I was very worried about you. I did not know what to do.

I could not sleep at night. I have been crying for days. Thank God, you are well and in good health. I believe that, please God, one day we will be joyfully reunited. I will write to Łódź.

Hugs and kisses,
Mother

My dear Mr & Mrs Grünspan,

I would like to write a few words to you. I advise that I am presently working in a firebrick factory, earning on piecework quite well.

Other than that, I am having a good time with my friends. I also learned to play harmonica. I wonder when I shall become an uncle!

Please reply soon.
Best regards and kisses,
Sigi

At dinner my mother sighed and said ruefully, 'I wish I had my Electrolux vacuum cleaner here. It would be so much easier than all this sweeping.'

My father began laughing. 'If you're going to make a wish, why not let it be for your housekeeper? That would make much more sense.'

'You wouldn't be able to use it anyhow,' I added.

'Why not?' my mother asked.

'Because we have no electricity!'

It was clear that my parents were happy, making me even happier, but it pained me too. It must have been so hard for them to bear all this without losing dignity and pride. They had led a full and exciting social life, regularly attending operas, concerts and other cultural events. They would invite guests to our house, and were invited out. Now they were content to have a friendly chat from time to time with our landlords, Mr and Mrs Tencer, who lived in the same building. Sometimes they stayed longer with the Tencers to play a game of bridge, without having to worry about the curfew.

The winter of 1940–41 was a typical Polish winter – very cold. At home it was not difficult to keep such a small room heated, but as I worked away in an overheated room at the firebrick factory I often thought of my father exposed to blizzards and frost in the forest. Our meals were very frugal, millet or maize gruel. Potatoes and bread were freely available, although expensive.

To have lived always in comfort and luxury and suddenly having to adjust to this new life was extremely difficult for my mother and father. They were deprived of almost everything – starving physically, spiritually and intellectually. Even reading material was very scarce. Now the only luxuries remaining were their memories. When mother was in a good mood, she would often sing songs from popular operettas and even arias. To cheer herself up, she would lay a tablecloth and some flowers on the table. My parents maintained their fine physical appearance, never neglecting and never letting themselves go. My heart was bleeding. They never complained, never. On the contrary, they helped people who were less fortunate – if not financially, at least morally, by counselling, encouraging and consoling others. I admired their courage and determination.

We received a few more cards from Halinka; the last one, which arrived on 13 May, had a postmark of 7 April 1941. We couldn't know it, but this would be last news we would hear of her until the war was over. The Germans attacked Russia on 22 June and all contact between the Russian-occupied and German-occupied territories ceased.

*

Reports began to circulate in May 1941 of how the Germans were extorting monies and riches from the Jewish population, affecting the entire community, not just in Starachowice, but everywhere else too. Rumours also started to spread that the Germans were killing Jews for no reason.

In the early spring, large numbers of German military vehicles and personnel carriers were on the highways and railroads moving troops and hardware east, day and night, towards the Russian border. This operation took about three months. One unit stopped in Starachowice-Wierzbnik for about four weeks. German soldiers were everywhere. Small retailers revived their businesses and the pubs and coffee shops really thrived.

One afternoon I went for a walk with Rozka and a soldier stopped me for directions. He was astonished that I spoke perfect German and, as we were going in the same direction, he joined us. After chatting for a bit he said that he wanted to meet us again the next day. I had never had a friendly conversation with a German in uniform before, and was surprised. He was in his early twenties, very handsome and well spoken. At first he asked me what I was doing in such a place and I explained that Jews were banned from living in Upper Silesia. 'I live in Silesia too!' he exclaimed. 'In Lower Silesia. My name is Joachim Hesse, and I live in Heinrichau, Wüstewaltersdorf.'

We met a number of times in those few weeks. Sometimes he brought cigarettes, chocolates or tinned meat. Joachim was very curious and wanted to know if there was a synagogue in town, if there were many Jews, which Jewish holidays we had recently celebrated and when the next one would be. He wanted to know about our lives before the war and how things had changed. At our last meeting he told me outright that he was leaving that night for an unknown destination, and did not know if he would return. He gave us some parting gifts and then asked something of me. 'Next time you enter a synagogue, could you please pray for me?' I was baffled but said I would, and began to wonder if he was of Jewish descent. I never heard of him again.

Around this time about half-a-dozen Jewish families from Płock, a town annexed to the German Reich, were deported to Starachowice-Wierzbnik. Among them were a young man, Salek Warman, and his elderly father. My mother saw them in front of the Judenrat looking so helpless that she invited them to eat with us. They had been herded up by German police in the middle of the night and were allowed to take only the clothes on their backs. They were escorted to the station and, under guard, endured a two-day journey to Starachowice-Wierzbnik without any food. Salek's mother and sister had been deported to a different town and he had no idea where they had ended up. The Judenrat had promised them mattresses but blankets were not available. My mother offered them a bedsheet, a towel and a cake of homemade soap. Soap was the most sought-after product and nearly impossible to obtain. The Germans confiscated all soap products and any dealings in this commodity were forbidden, though some entrepreneurs tried to produce it at home to sell, placing their own lives at risk.

Salek and his father were invited for lunch and dinner every day for months. Sitting in our tiny room, Mr Warman senior told us about his career as a successful diamond merchant. They both spoke of their lives in Płock and Mother made sure they felt at home at our table.

Around June 1941, the German authorities advised us, via big placards, that new identity cards would be issued to restrict our movements even further. Each member of the community was ordered to provide two portrait photographs (with the left ear visible) and report to the authorities. This *Kennkarte* contained a photograph and fingerprints. For Jews, a bold red J was stamped on the front cover to further identify them.

One morning not long after, I woke to the sound of my mother's crying. 'What's happened? What's wrong?' I asked anxiously.

'Nothing's happened,' she said between sobs. 'I just need to cry from time to time.'

Her crying intensified. I was frightened at seeing her so distressed and decided to fetch my father. I threw some clothes on and ran. Without wasting a second, we hurried home and found Mother still sobbing. My father held her in his arms, hugged her and stroked her head. He asked her why she was so upset but she could barely speak. 'The dream,' she mumbled. 'The dream.'

'What dream?' we asked.

'Remember? At the beginning of the war I had a dream that all the Jewish people in town had to line up in the main square and were shot. Women, children, babies, all shot dead! I had the same dream again, but this time it was somewhere else, in a small Jewish town. It was horrifying.'

'It was just a bad dream, a nightmare,' my father said gently. 'You shouldn't take all these rumours to heart.' He gave her some valerian drops to calm her. My poor mother was wretched, saying she felt like Cassandra, the prophet who was never believed.

My mother's dream coincided with the German invasion of the USSR in June 1941. We were hopeful that things would soon change for the better and that the Soviets would successfully retaliate and shorten the war. But on that same day in Starachowice-Wierzbnik, a little Jewish boy – his family's only son and the youngest of four children – was killed by a German gendarme in front of the offices of the Judenrat. Moishele Ben Koppel was only ten years old and therefore not obliged to wear the Star of David armband. He was on an errand for his mother when a Polish police officer arrested him for not wearing the band. Moishele tried to explain that he was only ten and begged the officer to ask his parents to confirm this. He swore on his life that he was telling the truth, but his pleas fell on deaf ears. He was dragged before the German policeman, who, without the slightest hesitation, pulled his pistol from its holster and shot the boy on the spot. Almost the entire Jewish population of Starachowice-Wierzbnik was present at his funeral. Everyone was distraught at this murder and feared what was yet to come.

A week later, Father's company informed him that they would soon relocate to Staszów. We had expected to stay in Starachowice-Wierzbnik until the end of the war; the prospect of finding new accommodation was bad enough, but having to leave my girlfriend behind left me heartbroken.

Rumours about the killing of Jews became more common and on the very day we left Starachowice-Wierzbnik, four Jewish men from the nearby town of Iłża were executed in the main square because they did not have travel permits. It was mid August 1941.

CHAPTER 10

STASZÓW is one of Poland's oldest settlements, dating back as far as 1245. The first Jewish settlers arrived in 1526, were expelled in 1610, and then readmitted in 1718. My parents and I reached the small town after sixteen hours on three trains. We had our armbands on and the German police and the train crew harassed, abused and humiliated us throughout the journey.

On arriving Father went to find his cousin Zahava. Before long he returned and we boarded a horse cab and soon pulled up in the main square in front of a large shoe store – one of the town's few two-storey buildings. On the ground floor was a shop with two large display windows; at its rear were the wholesale store and warehouse with an adjoining small office. Zahava's family lived upstairs.

Zahava and her husband welcomed us into their home and helped unload our belongings, which we placed in their storeroom. They invited us in for breakfast and to stay with them while we looked for our own place. Zahava was an attractive twenty-five-year-old with long dark-blond hair and a constant smile. Her husband, four years her senior, was tall and athletic. They had an adorable three-year-old son, Joel, who spoke only Yiddish. He was forever calling out for someone to open the door for him, as he could not yet reach the handle. He had a head full of curly blond hair and the most angelic face. At their house, one did not feel there was a war raging outside. Not much had changed for them here. They still lived in their own house and ran their business, but an Aryan manager would sometimes visit, sign a few documents and collect a handsome wage.

Staszów's population was less than 10,000 people; more than half of them were Jews. It was located in an isolated area with no industry and no natural resources except for limited forestry and a sugar beet plantation with a sugar mill. Here though, the Jewish community still traded and prospered, mainly through the black market. Once or twice a week, farmers and peasants from surrounding villages would bring their goods to the marketplace. There was an abundance of fruits, vegetables, poultry, fish and home-baked bread, as well as clothing and shoes. It was such a wonderful sight, and so rare in the rest of the country. From time to time four or five German gendarmes would suddenly appear, but the peasants must have had advance warning because their illegal goods were hidden in time – apparently the Polish police had something to do with this. A major source of income for the town came from the cottage industry of tanning and sawing leather uppers for shoes – leather had become much sought after.

Three days later, thanks to Zahava, we found accommodation on Kolejowa Street, in a house that belonged to a family named Bigos. Mr Bigos was a Polish police officer who, at the beginning of the war, had escaped to eastern Poland, later annexed by the Soviet Union. He had never returned, leaving behind a wife, her mother and two small daughters. Our room, which was even smaller than the one in Starachowice-Wierzbnik, had a kitchenette with a small wood stove.

This was our ninth home since we left Katowice. There was room for just one bed, a small table and a wardrobe. We unpacked some luggage but kept most of our belongings in cases under the bed. There was no room for chairs, so we sat on the bed. As before, I slept on a fold-out bed. Eventually, in the warmer months, I moved into the barn. In the backyard was a well with a bucket on a chain and opposite was a lavatory with a manure pit. In the back was a barn, a pigsty with a pig and two piglets, a cowshed with one milking cow, half-a-dozen chickens and a dog.

The simple daily task of washing and bathing became a huge undertaking. Water had to be brought from the well, which was then heated on the small stove and poured into a large bowl. Bending over the bowl, we would wash our face and upper body, move the bowl from a stool to the floor and then strip and step into the bowl to wash from the waist down. We had to carry the heavy bowl outside to toss out the dirty water and repeat this procedure until all three of us had washed.

Father reported to Mr Andretzky, a Polish-speaking German from Upper Silesia, who was the manager of Grabowski Brothers' Staszów branch. This time the timber yard was next to the train station, a two-minute walk from our house. I would also have to find a job, but in the meantime, I helped with some shopping, housework and registration formalities.

One of my first tasks was to go to the registration office in Staszów and register our new address. The clerk at the counter took my *Kennkarte* and was about to cross out my old address in Starachowice-Wierzbnik when he took off his glasses, looked me directly in the eyes, and for one moment – a split second when our eyes met – I felt a strange sensation of recognition. I had never seen this man before and yet I knew him. There was something very familiar about his eyes; they were luminous and comforting. He shook his head and said that he wouldn't change my address for now. 'It will have to stay as it is.' He issued me with the correct receipt yet left my ID card intact. It seemed odd, but at the time I thought no more about it.

In front of the Judenrat just a few days later I saw a very pretty girl wearing a pale blue coat with a matching hat tilted to one side. She had olive skin and beautiful sparkly eyes. 'I never expected to meet such a beautiful girl in a place like this,' I said boldly. She blushed. Her name was Hanka – just like Rozka's sister back in Starachowice-Wierzbnik – and she was the daughter of the president of the Judenrat, Mr Ephraim Singer. She invited me to her home the following evening to meet a group of other young people.

On my way home I walked through the market. There was butter, cottage cheeses, eggs, white flour, barley, dried butter beans and peas, sugar, fresh and dried mushrooms. There were loads of cheap potatoes. Mother was delighted.

The next evening I met the gilded youth of the town. Most were locals, though there were a few refugees from Łódź, Kraków and Warszawa (Warsaw). We were all much the same age, except for David Najman, who was a teacher at a primary school in Łódź. Prior to the war the teenagers in Staszów had been active in various Zionist youth movements, from the extreme left to the far right. Now they gathered in private homes to learn Modern Hebrew, Jewish history, and the history of Zionism. They studied the Jewish settlement movement in Palestine as well as the geography and topography of Palestine. They also spoke about self-defence and active resistance to the German occupation.

I became friendly with most of them. Some of my particular friends were Heniek and David Nisenbaum, Hanka Groshaus, Sara Nojman, Tusia Huzarski and her brother, and the sweet Hinda Jaskółka . Every time we met there would be new faces in the group. David Najman, who excelled in running our meetings, had a wealth of knowledge, which he generously shared.

CHAPTER 11

ABOUT TWO WEEKS after our arrival in Staszów, I began working with my father. My job was to collect superfluous logs and offcuts and arrange them in piles to be sold as firewood. I also had to chase away young urchins who tried to steal the timber. One of these boys, Wacek, was especially cheeky. He was a Pole, about half a head shorter than me, with wavy light brown hair that bounced when he walked, a fair complexion and a small turned-up nose. He wore a constant smirk on his face, exposing a chipped front tooth. His pants had been patched so many times that it was difficult to identify the original fabric. He would steal anything he could get his hands on, darting in and out between the goods trains' carriages. He seemed smarter than his companions, very light on his feet yet shrewd and cunning. I would try to chase him away, throwing small pieces of wood, but he would just tease me with a mischievous and defiant smile and hurl stones in my direction. Neither of us intended to hit or hurt the other.

I watched my father closely to learn as much as I could and earn more money and within three weeks he had recommended me to his manager. I became a log sorter for the mining industry – what a long way from my apprenticeship as a cobbler! With this promotion, I now walked four kilometres every morning to Golejów, where we established a delivery station for pine and spruce logs to be cut and shipped to Germany. My father showed me how to calculate the cubic volume of the logs and how to report them.

Six weeks later the job was done and the Golejów station ceased to operate. Soon after I received an assignment to establish a new, short-term station to receive logs in Iwaniska, a village about ten kilometres north. The company provided me with a pushbike and organised my accommodation. Mr Andretzky introduced me to the local authorities, requesting a yard adjoining the train station and a workforce of ten to fifteen men. As it turned out this was impossible: Iwaniska had a large sugar mill that worked only for six months of the year, and the season had just commenced. Every pair of hands was busy. Wacek and his gang were also very busy during the sugar season, stealing large numbers of sugar beets and selling them on the black market.

I returned to Staszów and continued working together with my father. One Sunday morning he asked me to help him fetch some firewood from the Bigos family's cellar. Once there he unwrapped a small bundle of white linen no larger than a fist. 'Sigi, here are the few remaining pieces of your mother's and my jewellery.' He held out his hand and showed me rings with glittering diamonds and dazzling coloured stones. I picked one and asked him about it.

'That is a blue sapphire which I gave your mother when you were born. But her favourite ring is this solitaire diamond I gave her on our tenth wedding anniversary.' He held out the ring and even though it was dim in the cellar, the stone was so brilliant that one could see all different colours in it.

There were two of Father's rings – a diamond and a signet ring – as well as two or three gold coins. My father removed one heavy and rather plain ring from the bundle and placed it on his ring finger. He re-wrapped the bundle. 'I think this is a safe place. We shall hide it here,' he said, pointing to a spot where a brick had come loose in the wall. He removed it, inserted the bundle into the cavity and pushed the brick back into the slot. 'These pieces are very valuable, Sigi. Memorise the spot and one day we'll recover them.'

*

I would meet my friends after work, sometimes at Słodka Dziurka, or 'Sweet Little Niche', a little coffee house we liked where we drank substitute tea, coffee or lemonade and ate homemade cookies. Sometimes the manager, a woman called Idesa, baked a cake or pie.

Although my father and I both worked, we could hardly make ends meet. My mother wanted to help and I suggested that she bake some cakes and offer them to the cafes in town. Before the war, guests in our home would praise her excellent cakes, which she had indeed baked herself. Even though she supervised the cook with all other food preparation, she enjoyed the cakes too much to let anyone else bake them.

My father was delighted with this idea and Mother agreed to bake a cheesecake. I asked her to prepare a shopping list and my father instructed me to record all expenses. After my father summarised all the outgoings and added the profit margin, he then determined the selling price. As soon as the cake had cooled, I rushed it to the Sweet Little Niche and placed it on the counter. 'This is the best cheesecake in the world,' I announced. 'Would you add it to your selection of tortes and pastries?'

Idesa hesitated for a moment then agreed. The cakes were an instant success and Idesa increased her orders. Unfortunately, though, we failed to make much of a profit: my mother used only the finest ingredients, which were pricey and difficult to obtain. Still, the emotional benefits to my mother in being useful were worth all of it.

My maternal grandmother, Rachel Siegreich, passed away

while we were living in Staszów. My father learnt of her death through a postcard sent by my Aunt Regina. He was concerned how the news would affect my mother, as their relationship had been more like best friends than mother and daughter. They had kept in contact as best as they could under these difficult circumstances and my grandmother's postcards were the most beautifully written cards, containing an enormous amount of information. In her neat, small calligraphy, she managed to fit so much onto such a little space. My father told my mother that due to a stroke, my '*babcia*' Rachel was unable to write any more. My mother never learnt the truth.

*

Around this time the German authorities demanded that every Judenrat in the Generalgouvernement establish units of *Ordnungsdienst* or 'regulation officials', later known as the *policjanten* or Jewish police. Their duty was to serve the Jewish population and assist with their communal needs. These included escorting Jewish workers to and from their workplaces, collecting taxes, helping to distribute food, guarding the ghetto gates, settling complaints, and supervising sanitary conditions. Eventually the Germans exploited the Jewish police to collect ransom payments, seize valuables and confiscate personal belongings.

There were fewer Germans in Staszów than elsewhere in the country but they did not forget us. Every so often an SS officer from the regional command appeared at the Judenrat demanding monies or items from the Jewish community. It started with smallish demands such as fifty pairs of boots for the SS. Then all silver objects were to be handed over as well as twenty kilograms of gold. The Judenrat posted these ever-increasing demands on billboards and waited while the Jewish policemen were sent house to house to collect the spoils – with very little success.

This in turn incited the Germans to visit the Judenrat and beat up the members, threatening them with imprisonment and even death. One member could not stand the pressure and committed suicide.

The day after this visit to the Judenrat, trucks carrying about 150 Germans in full uniform, under the command of the high-ranking SS officer Maluschke, arrived. The Germans jumped out of the trucks and immediately began a house-to-house search, screaming, knocking down doors with gun butts and spreading panic and terror. The Germans forcefully removed and confiscated vast quantities of jewellery and other valuables, as well as clothing, household items and even food. To cause further humiliation, they destroyed prayer books and ripped open *tefillin* (Jewish religious boxes) expecting to find hidden treasures inside. Earrings were ripped from women's ears, even little girls', tearing their lobes and causing serious injuries.

At one house they uncovered large quantities of leather hidden beneath the floorboards and inside a false wall at another. The two families were shot: the children were killed first to intensify the parents' (and our) grief and then their houses were demolished. During this pandemonium, at least sixteen people lost their lives. The discoveries of the leather led to more houses being storm-searched and demolished and, over several weeks, tonnes of leather were confiscated. Maluschke became infamous for his brutality, cruelty and ruthlessness.

*

One morning I asked Mr Andretzky if I could take three days off and use the company's pushbike to ride to Starachowice-Wierzbnik to visit my friends. Rozka and I had been sending each other postcards from time to time, and the Laks had invited me to come and stay with them. Mr Andretzky not only agreed to my absence, he gave me a certificate stating that my journey to Starachowice-Wierzbnik was work-related and advised me on how to behave if stopped by the Germans. 'Stay calm. Don't make any sudden movements and let them know which pocket your documents are in,' he said.

Early on a Saturday morning in August, I packed some clothes and a tyre repair kit, kissed my parents goodbye, removed my Star of David armband and began my ninety-kilometre bike ride. The weather was good and the road almost empty. An hour later I had a puncture in my rear tyre. I had to push my bike for a few kilometres before finding water, which I needed to locate the puncture then check the repaired site.

Six hours after I had first left home – and after a few near misses with German police patrols – I arrived safely in Starachowice-Wierzbnik. I passed the house of Guta Blas, one of my friends. She saw me and insisted that I come in. I ducked inside to say hello for five minutes but was soon on my way to see Rozka. Mrs Laks had prepared a festive dinner, which must have strained their already meagre budget. I had brought small gifts for each member of the family. We talked a lot at the dinner table that night and after a while I began to feel very tired. The guestroom had a small bathtub and I had my first hot bath in months. It was heaven. That night I slept like a baby.

After breakfast the next day, Rozka and I could not wait to be alone. We went for a long walk and reminisced and talked about love and our future together. I promised her that as soon as the war was over I would take her to Katowice; we would marry and build our life in Palestine. It was all so romantic and innocent. Everything seemed so real, so genuine, that nothing could destroy our dream. Our love was stronger than this war. We just needed to be a little bit more patient.

The next day after lunch three of my old friends, Mundek, Unger and Mincberg, arrived for a walk around the village. I thanked Mrs Laks for the meal we had just eaten and assured the family that I would be back within the hour. My friends and I walked towards the Rogalin factory and I looked through the gate hoping to find a familiar face. No-one was there. We walked to the Wilczeks' restaurant and turned back. We stopped in front of Unger's house, then at Mundek's house. The village looked very dull and depressing – despite the beautiful weather, the streets were almost deserted.

At the other end of the main square a patrol of three gendarmes headed in our direction. We stepped off the footpath and prepared to greet them, as ordered. We took off our hats and bowed. As they passed, one of the Germans suddenly turned. '*Halt! Stehen bleiben!*'

We froze, petrified.

'Your documents. On the double,' he barked.

We fumbled trying to find our papers. Then one of my friends handed his *Kennkarte* to the German.

'Not you,' yelled the German. Pointing his finger at me he barked: '*You!*'

I handed him my document. My friends grew deathly pale: now I was trapped. The German examined the ID card, looked at me, then back at the photo, turned it over and, shaking his head, handed it back to me. Then they continued on their way.

My friends sighed with relief. If the Germans in their town spotted a non-local Jew they shot him on the spot. This later became the rule everywhere, but it was common practice in Starachowice-Wierzbnik long before it became general law. Afraid of sabotage or partisan activities in this important industrial area, the authorities had forbidden Jews to move from village to village. The gendarmes had recognised my friends but could not identify me. But my friends did not know that my documents had originally been issued in Starachowice-Wierzbnik and had not been updated.

I thought back to the clerk at the registration office in Staszów and his strange behaviour when I had gone to register our new address. He had issued me with the correct receipt, yet left my ID card unchanged. This little piece of paper had saved my life.

I was lucky that the gendarmes had not questioned me, as I would have told them that I was a visitor and would have been killed. I was shaken to the core of my being. I decided to cut short my visit and left early the next morning.

Alone with my thoughts on the long ride home, all the wonderful dreams I'd had evaporated, leaving me gloomy and depressed. All I could think about was the misery, pain and hardship this war was causing. How many people had lost their children, parents, brothers and sisters? How many had lost their homes, their livelihood? What was the *point* of it? And why hadn't the world done something to stop this madness and mindless destruction? Did the rest of the world even know what was going on in the German-occupied countries? And why hadn't we left Poland when we still could, when we had the means to do so? Could we ever have foreseen all of this? And if we had, what would we have done differently? I wondered how it was possible to be so miserable.

CHAPTER 12

A COUPLE OF MONTHS LATER, Mr Andretzky informed me that in a fortnight's time, on 1 November, I would be sent to re-establish a station in Bodzechów, some 100 kilometres north of Staszów and twenty kilometres from Starachowice-Wierzbnik. I proudly announced my news at dinner that night but failed to get the response I wanted.

'This is not good news,' my mother said grimly. 'I'm not happy about this.'

'Will I earn as much as you?' I asked my father, ignoring my mother's comment.

'I don't think so, but you'll receive a substantial raise.'

'That's great!'

'David,' Mother interrupted, 'do you think Sigi should go so far away in these dangerous times? I'm scared.'

I left the room while my parents argued for a while, unwilling to participate in their conversation. When I returned, Father had persuaded my mother to let me go. 'It will be safe and Andretzky will issue the appropriate documents.'

The very next morning Mother began mending a few things for me and tried to finish crocheting a woollen sweater that she had started weeks before. She did not know how to knit; back in Katowice she preferred needlepoint, embroidery and lace making.

'Mummy, you don't have to rush. I'm not leaving to-morrow.'

'I know, but I've already unravelled Halinka's jumper and I'm going to crochet socks and gloves so you won't freeze.'

'I'm sure I'll be protected from the worst frost: I have a good cap with ear-protectors, a warm overcoat, ski boots and a woollen scarf.'

'Still, I'll feel better if I finish these items for you in time.'

'You're the best mum in the whole world, a real angel,' I said, knowing how she liked to pamper me.

I sent a postcard to Rozka saying that I would be stationed nearby and would try to visit for the Christmas holidays. During my previous visit to their family I had also promised Rozka's sister Hanka that, if at all possible, I would ride to Busko-Zdrój to meet her boyfriend Moniek Topioł.

That Saturday morning I jumped on my bike and two hours later arrived at the Topioł family's impressive villa.

Busko-Zdrój was a well-known health spa. Before the war the Topioł villa must have been run as a family hotel, but when the Germans arrived they had appropriated it and established gendarmerie headquarters there. They did, however, permit the Topiołs to stay in the upper floor of the house. Mr Topioł became chairman of the local Judenrat and, unusually, these gendarmes even employed Moniek as a driver. Hanka had not exaggerated; Moniek was a very handsome man with enormous charisma and a wicked sense of humour. After a pleasant lunch with his parents, he took me to a house in town where a group of young people performed a comedy on an improvised stage to an audience of about fifty. The show, which was funny but very amateurish, was performed in the attic and afterwards we hung around for a while talking. On our way back, I jokingly pointed out that maybe one day we would be brothers-in-law.

*

Every day we heard that Jews had been killed in nearby villages, and conditions in Staszów were also deteriorating. A gendarmerie command post had been established, manned by about ten gendarmes, who constantly harassed the Jewish population. On market days especially, after completing shopping errands, Jews were stopped, searched and their goods and money usually confiscated. The gendarmes did not harass the Poles.

By the end of October 1941, my father's cousins Felix and Samuel Siegreich had arrived in Staszów along with Samuel's wife Andzia and their two children, Stefanie and Ludwig. Felix and Samuel were Zahava's brothers and Zahava gave them shelter in her own house. Before the war, Felix and Samuel were the owners and company directors of the ELTES company. They had come from Lwów. We were very happy to see them but disappointed too – we had hoped that they had been safely deported to Siberia like Halinka and Don.

Felix and Samuel were unaware of the harsh conditions the Jews experienced in occupied Poland: it was tough and dangerous in Russia, but nobody was targeted for extermination. At the same time, my mother's sister Hela, her husband Jerzy and Bobby returned from Lwów to settle in Sędziszów, where Jerzy had relatives. My mother was very happy to have family closer to her – and now that Hela was back in German-occupied territory, they could communicate via the post, so my parents finally had first-hand information about Halinka and Don again.

During their stay in Lwów, Samuel and Felix had worked in a large brewery: Felix worked in the storeroom and dispatch area and Samuel in distribution, driving a huge brewery wagon pulled by giant Clydesdales, delivering barrels and bottles of beer to restaurants, hotels, inns and pubs. My cousins Stefanie and Ludwig had continued their education.

Ludwig, who was two years younger than me, was a strapping young man with a good sense of humour. I used to call him *comsomolets* (the name given to members of the USSR communist youth movement) because he used to tell me funny stories about Soviet people. Generally, he said, they were obsessed with watches and alarm clocks. Apparently after the invasion of eastern Poland the Soviet soldiers bought all the watches and alarm clocks they could lay their hands on. They strapped them on both arms by the dozens, from wrist to elbow, and wore alarm clocks on a string or a chain around their necks. The Soviet women acquired nightgowns and wore them as evening dresses. The soldiers drank eau de cologne, thinking that it was liqueur, and even managed to get drunk. And yet they claimed that Polish people were uncivilised and uncultured because there was not one delousing station in the whole occupied territory.

They were obsessed with comparing food prices, Ludwig said. For example, they had asked him about the price of sugar in Poland before the war. One zloty was the price of a kilo of sugar but they wanted to know the price on the black market, which was ten groszy. (There were 100 groszy to one zloty, so the black market goods were much, much cheaper.) 'How is it possible that on the black market it is cheaper than in a shop?' they wanted to know.

Because Russia had a centralised economy with fixed prices, goods in shops were cheap, but the shelves were often bare. Everyone in Russia bought on the black market, but prices were expensive. The pre-war system in Poland was the exact opposite, and it amazed them.

They were even more surprised to learn that before the war Poland had virtually no black market at all. 'Only stolen goods were illegally sold and bought,' they were told. My cousin told me this whole story in a perfect Russian accent accompanied by comic gestures. We laughed until we cried.

I had a lot of fun with Ludwig. I introduced him to my friends and he got a job at Ömler, a road-building company where many young Jewish men were forced to work. It was backbreaking work and poorly paid, but it was the best he could get. Ludwig did not complain.

CHAPTER 13

On Saturday 1 November 1941, Mr Andretzky came to take me to Bodzechów. My mother had packed my suitcase days in advance, but she now also handed me a neatly wrapped shoebox, full of sandwiches, apples, a freshly baked cake and other goodies. My father gave me a reckoner for calculating the cubic volume of the logs. He offered many useful tips and, in the short time we had left, advised me about my new assignment.

I hugged my parents goodbye and my mother kissed me, shedding a few tears. 'May God protect you, and a Lamed Vav keep you safe,' she whispered, running her hand through my curly hair.

It sounded like a blessing and for a moment I wondered if I might really meet a Lamed Vav.

Once we got to Bodzechów, we turned off onto a dirt road and drove deep into a forest. The road ran alongside a single sidetrack of a railroad. After about twenty minutes, we stopped in front of a forest lodge, just opposite a parked train engine. It was picturesque in its fairytale setting: very tall pine trees surrounded the log cottage. Beside it there was a small shed, full of firewood, and behind that, a vegetable garden enclosed by a white picket fence. The weather was unexpectedly mild for this time of the year. Usually 1 November, a Catholic day to honour the dead – All Saints' Day – was rainy, dark and cold.

I unloaded my bike and suitcase and we went to the house. Mr Andretzky introduced me to a man called Stanisław and his wife, Maria. Stanisław was in his thirties, his wife maybe a little younger. They had no children. He was an engine driver, servicing the local sidetracks. Their home was very neat and clean, and there was a distinctive smell of cooked cabbage and melted pork lard. The house had three rooms and a kitchen.

My room was at the back of the house. There was a bed with a side table, a wardrobe and a table with two chairs. A small rectangular window without blinds or curtains looked out onto the forest. In the corner were a washstand with a bowl and a pitcher with fresh water; beneath it was a bucket for waste. On the wall behind the bed was an oversized picture of the Holy Virgin, and on the two sidewalls were two kerosene lamps. A cast-iron stove stood in the corner opposite the washstand, protected from the wall by a sheet metal lining. The room was neat and tidy.

The company paid for my accommodation and I had to pay for my meals. Mr Andretzky gave me final instructions, the names and addresses of people to contact and, wishing me success, left the house.

Stanisław and his wife did not know that I was Jewish; Andretzky did not tell them and neither did I. They seemed to assume I was Volksdeutsch, because Andretzky and I had been conversing in German. After I had unpacked, Stanisław invited me into the kitchen and we chatted while his wife made dinner. He took out a bottle of *bimber* (moonshine) and two glasses, and asked me to drink with him. I refused politely, explaining that I had serious stomach problems and that it would be dangerous for me to drink. I was then only seventeen years old and had never tried alcohol before. He insisted I join him and said that it was customary to welcome a guest with a drink. He quoted the Polish saying, 'Guest in house is God in house', and I had no choice.

He toasted '*Na zdrowie*' and downed the whole glass. I just wet my lips, but the vodka burned, smelled and tasted terrible.

Maria set the table and started serving dinner. We had a kind of cabbage soup with homemade bread spread with butter and boiled potatoes sprinkled with fried onion. During dinner I mentioned paying for my board. Stanisław said that he had received enough money and he would not require any additional payment. He said that at his house, guests were always offered food and drink and that he considered me his guest.

I had expected some questions about myself, particularly about going to church the next day. Nothing was mentioned so I raised the topic myself.

'The church is in the village,' Stanisław answered in surprise, 'but we won't attend the mass. We're not churchgoers and we're not religious.'

'So why do you have such a huge picture of the Virgin Mary on the wall?'

'My wife's parents gave it to us and insisted we hang it on the wall for protection against bad luck and evil eyes.'

This made my situation much easier to deal with. We spent Sunday on a long walk in the forest, talking and resting, and I found Stanisław to be an intelligent man.

On Monday morning I looked out the window to see everything covered with a thick blanket of snow. It was stunning. Winter had arrived. After breakfast we jumped onto the train engine and travelled for about fifteen minutes to my new worksite. Stanisław knew most of the twenty workers already there and introduced me as the manager. They were all skilled woodcutters who had worked there before. First I took down their names and addresses and divided them into separate squads. Actually, they did it themselves; I only recorded the arrangement. The work progressed well and one of the workers volunteered as my assistant, which made my job even easier.

Stanisław returned around five o'clock to take me back home. At first he must have thought that I was a German supervisor because he addressed me in Polish as *Panie Kierowniku* or 'Mr Manager'. As time went by and our relationship developed, he then addressed me as 'Mr Siegmund'. For the next two and a half months, my job became routine. I had my lunch at home every day, rather than in the forest. Stanisław would come to pick me up and taught me to drive his engine, which was great fun, and he let me drive it whenever possible.

On 7 December 1941, the United States of America entered the war. This once again raised hopes that soon it would be over. That evening I discussed this with Stanisław while he poured himself a glass of vodka, claiming that such news was worth a drink. After work we spent long evenings together, talking or playing chess. Sometimes I helped him with some work around the house. We got on very well and he invited me to spend Christmas with him and Maria. I explained that I had already accepted an invitation to stay with friends in Starachowice-Wierzbnik.

On Christmas Eve I thanked my hosts for their warm hospitality, wished them a Merry Christmas and a happy 1942 and jumped on my bike. I rode for about two hours, travelling through deep snow and pedalling against strong headwinds, but the anticipation of my rendezvous with Rozka kept me going.

I arrived at her house and knocked eagerly. I waited a while and was disappointed when Rozka's youngest sister opened the door. I wondered why it had taken them so long to respond to my knocking – they must have seen me through the window. I received a frosty reception from the rest of her family, and saw Rozka disappear as I entered the room, leaving only Hanka to talk to me.

'Did you have a good trip?' she inquired politely. 'Did you come direct from Staszów?'

'No,' I responded. 'I came here from Bodzechów. I've been working there for the past two months.'

'Aha, I see now. We weren't expecting you. Rozka had written you a letter asking you to cancel your visit.'

'I've not received any letters from Rozka, or from anyone else.'

'Ah well, since you're here now, you might as well stay,' she said, shrugging her shoulders.

'What's going on?' I asked, becoming increasingly confused. 'Have I offended Rozka or someone in your family?'

'I don't know,' Hanka said, uncomfortable. 'You really should ask Rozka. She'll be here in a moment.'

'Has Moniek arrived yet?'

'No, I don't think he'll be coming. He's on duty during the festive season.'

Rozka slowly made her way back into the room, sporting a long face, barely saying hello. She still did not offer a hug or even a handshake.

'What's happened to you? Are you angry with me?' I asked.

'Nothing's happened. You might as well stay, unless you want to go to Busko-Zdrój to fetch Moniek.'

'Yes!' Hanka cried. 'Go to Busko-Zdrój and convince Moniek to come. We'll all have such a good time.'

To relieve the tension and show some chivalry, I agreed. Next morning, at huge risk, I rode to Busko-Zdrój during a blizzard – though perhaps it was the weather that saved me from being stopped by the police patrols that passed in both directions. After nine gruelling hours, I arrived in Busko-Zdrój not only exhausted but also hungry and soaked to the bone. Moniek was not surprised to see me – somehow the Laks family had let him know I was coming – and he was happy to accompany me back. He received permission to use the police truck for his private use but had to be back in three days. After spending the night at his house, we loaded my pushbike onto the truck and began the drive. I told Moniek about Rozka's strange behaviour and asked him what he thought about it. 'You'll never understand women,' he said shaking his head.

Just before we entered the house, I tied a piece of string onto Moniek's jacket button and jokingly led him in. 'Here he is,' I announced, noticing that the mood was more relaxed than the day before.

After much coaxing, Rozka admitted that she had felt offended because on my previous visit I had stopped at another girl's house before coming to see her. Guta Blas must have teased Rozka about this. I regarded the whole incident as immature and childish behaviour. In fact, the more I thought about it, the more I realised how stupid and absurd the whole incident was. It seemed so petty and Rozka's behaviour so silly. Moniek was right: I would never understand women! This incident made me rethink my feelings for Rozka, but I stayed with the Laks until the New Year then returned to Bodzechów.

Stanisław had slaughtered a pig for Christmas and there was plenty of food in the house. Ham and lard were stored in barrels filled with salt, in a deep underground cellar, meant to last for the whole year, or at least until Easter, when they would kill another pig. I never told Stanisław and Maria that I was Jewish, and they never asked. Perhaps they never suspected, because of the job I held, and my apparent freedom to travel.

Two weeks later I completed my assignment in Bodzechów and Mr Andretzky came to take me back to Staszów. Stanisław and his wife stood there with tears in their eyes. We had become very attached to each other. Maria gave me a bundle of food including a large Christmas cake. 'This is for your family with my best wishes for the new year,' she said. 'Your mother will like my baking. It's my grandmother's old recipe.'

'I'm sure she will,' I told her.

She stood there freezing, covered with a long woollen shawl. I kissed the back of her hand, as was customary in Poland.

Stanisław stepped forward and kissed and hugged me so forcefully that he almost crushed my ribs. 'You must learn to drink vodka, Mr Director,' he said. 'Next time I won't let you off the hook so easily. You will *have* to drink with me. In the meantime I wish you and your family a very happy new year.'

I thanked them for their hospitality and gifts and expressed my hope that we would meet again soon. I jumped into the truck and waved them farewell. It was Friday 16 January 1942.

CHAPTER 14

MY MOTHER WAS WAITING OUTSIDE THE HOUSE wearing her pelisse, a winter coat lined and trimmed with light-weight, high-quality fur. Somehow she looked different. The coat suddenly looked very large and baggy; her fur collar had gone, exposing the rough inner lining.

'You're looking at me wondering why I look like a tattered vagrant,' she said. 'Well, you've no idea how conditions have deteriorated. Ten days ago a large squad of SS-men and German police arrived and confiscated fur coats and ripped fur collars from Jews passing in the street. Over the next few days they searched all Jewish homes taking every piece of fur, boots and ski boots, yelling, beating, hitting and kicking helpless people, never missing an opportunity to steal something of value. This time we actually cooperated and unstitched the fur ourselves to avoid damaging the garments further. So this is how I surrendered my fur lining and collar.'

That campaign became known as the 'Fur Action' and was carried out among the Jewish population throughout the occupied Polish territory. The Germans needed warm clothing for their soldiers fighting the Soviet Union at the eastern front.

As I was still growing, my only winter shoes that fitted were the ski boots that I wore in Bodzechów. When I arrived back home my father spotted them and immediately took them to a shoemaker to have them remodelled. It was illegal for a Jew to have ski boots (if they hadn't been confiscated already) and the penalty would be death. In those days, ski boots were made from leather; they were square in form with grooves across the heels and as comfortable as any other pair of shoes. My new camouflaged boots had two major modifications: the front was reshaped into a rounded toe and the back was replaced with a grooveless heel.

The winter of 1942 was very cold. Temperatures remained below minus 15 degrees Celsius for almost the whole month of February. We kept relatively warm, having plenty of firewood, but we could not wait for spring to come. Throughout the winter I worked again with my father.

I still met my friends regularly, but now we contemplated ways of escaping the German persecution, rather than pursuing our studies. Polish Resistance activities in the area had increased. There were reports that the Resistance had executed a high-ranking German officer and successfully raided a local bank, and we tried to find contacts in order to join them. We knew of a young Polish woman with links to the partisans and she tried to help us but without success. The partisans did not want any Jews – despite the fact that we shared the same enemy, they too were hostile towards us.

Around Easter, tales of the 'deportation' of Jews generated enormous panic. At that time no-one believed that people were sent to gas chambers, despite persistent rumours. People needed to believe that they would be relocated eastwards, to the Soviet territories conquered by the Germans, and so they did believe it, but the fear and tension in the town intensified.

Jewish people ran around in a frenzied search for secure employment, called *placówka*, which might save them from being deported. The Judenrat, together with the German authorities, established some workshops to produce and repair uniforms and footwear for the German army. Many people tried to bribe the Jewish managers of the workshops to provide them with jobs. Mr Andretzky and other German managers were also approached and offered large sums of money. People paced about aimlessly, hitting their heads, pulling out tufts of hair, hitting their chests, wailing. 'What are we to do? Where can we hide? Where can we go? Oh God, help us!'

The third wartime Passover holiday was approaching. Family memories of past Seder tables caused longings and melancholy. During the festival of Passover, Jews reflect on the redemption of the children of Israel from the slavery of Pharaoh and the Egyptians; it was ironic that now, in modern times, the madman Hitler and the German people enslaved us. We so desperately needed one more miracle. There was no end to the raiding and searching, robbing and beatings.

Killings became more frequent and not a day passed without new victims. The authorities moved many Jews to a particular area of town and on 15 June 1942 the Staszów 'ghetto', which was until then still open, was closed off. To be caught outside the ghetto was punishable by death.

My mother experienced her third vision of the approaching genocide and cried for days. Others envied us for having secure jobs but we were miserable, humiliated and despondent. As hard as we tried to hold on, our world was slipping from us.

The Final Solution had started. During the months of May, June and July, sporadic deportations were conducted in surrounding towns and villages. The Germans approached the Judenrat in each community, demanding several hundred unemployed Jews to report for relocation. In order to lure their victims, the Germans ordered the distribution of a loaf of bread to anyone who volunteered. The people had become worn down and numb, and so were easily deceived, making the devil's work much easier. A few weeks later, mass deportation to the death camps sealed the fate of the European Jewry. By September, with the Jewish high holiday of Rosh Hashanah just a few days away, many people could not withstand the pressure and committed suicide, my Aunt Hela and Uncle Jerzy among them. Hela and Jerzy had found it difficult to cope with the turn their lives had taken since settling in Sędziszów and, after just a few months, they poisoned their little dog and then committed suicide together. They were still in their thirties. Others died of heart attack or stroke, not realising how 'lucky' they were.

On the eve of the holidays I could not face my parents: their red eyes were dark-rimmed and their faces were ashen and disfigured by pain and sorrow. Some people dug bunkers or built hide-outs, hoping to hide and survive. Others bought falsified Aryan identity documents and moved away. My father tried to secure such documents for us, but didn't have the right contacts. Everything was in turmoil and no-one knew what to do. There was no hope.

In Staszów, the synagogue had been burned down immediately after German forces entered the town, and it was the same in every city, town and village in occupied Poland. People who wanted to worship were forced to gather in private homes to pray for God's help. Rabbis called the community to convene and recite special prayers, to fast and light candles. The Almighty, however, was not listening.

In the middle of September, around Yom Kippur, a squad of uniformed Germans arrived in town and rounded up Jews who were in the street. They arrested and deported about forty people to an unknown destination. I later found out that they were sent to a slave labour camp in Skarżysko-Kamienna.

My parents attended the Yom Kippur service at one of the prayer houses in the morning and returned at dusk, having fasted from sundown the previous day. I had spent the day with my friends instead, but when I saw my mother and father holding each other I felt an overwhelming shame and guilt. I should have been there with them on the holiest day of the Jewish calendar. This feeling of guilt and regret was to stay with me for the rest of my life.

The deportations of Jews to the death camps were called *akcja* or 'actions'. Staszów's isolation and lack of direct railway connection had spared its Jewish population from these actions, for a time, but it was now clear that an action in Staszów was not far off. Parents who had babies or young children searched for Polish families willing to take their children in as their own. It was easier to place girls into these families and pass them off as Aryan than circumcised boys. The pain that these parents were prepared to endure in order to save their children is indescribable. Giving their children to total strangers, not knowing if they would protect and care for their precious innocent babies was more than some parents could bear. Some saw no other way out and took their own lives and those of their children. Others who had money bribed local peasants with all they had to take their child and promised them a handsome reward after the war.

We received a postcard from my aunt Regina telling us that Lunia had to leave her baby daughter with 'our family' in Kraków for a while. She explained that our 'uncle', Dr Nowak, would keep an eye on the little girl until Lunia returned. Dr Nowak, a gentile, was a close friend of my parents, but we did not know who the kind Polish family were. Regina had to be careful not to disclose their details to ensure her granddaughter's safety.

After Yom Kippur, the Judenrat announced the recruitment of 300 volunteers to work at the industrial centre of Starachowice-Wierzbnik. This was the chance we had prayed for and I fervently tried to convince my parents to volunteer. We were in a desperate state, trying to find a way to escape deportation and avoid the inevitable. We felt as if we were being swept along a fast-flowing river, battling to grab a branch to save our lives. I thought it was our last chance. At first they totally rejected this idea – only men would be accepted, and my father did not want to leave my mother behind – but then they decided to see what our cousins Samuel and Felix thought.

I had learned something about this area while living in Starachowice-Wierzbnik, and explained that the conditions there were not bad at all and that we should all register as soon as possible. I also suggested that the men should go first, and be joined later by my mother and Samuel's wife, Andzia. Both my uncles favoured this idea, but my father was not willing to separate from my mother. He was sure that his job would protect him and he would find a *placówka* at one of the workshops for my mother. It was decided that my uncles and my cousin Ludwig and I would volunteer while my parents would stay behind protected by their 'secure employment'. I also managed to convince many of my friends to join me.

The fact that I used to work at Starachowice-Wierzbnik spread like wildfire. People stopped me in the street for information about the working conditions in the factories there. I returned home one day to find a large group of people waiting for me in our tiny apartment. Our landlady asked the crowd to leave and threatened to call the police. Everyone wanted information. I explained that although I had worked there it was no holiday and that each individual had to make their own decision.

Samuel, Felix, Ludwig and I registered with the authorities the next day. In three days we were to report in, ready to leave. Samuel and Andzia's daughter Stefanie had obtained authentic Polish documents from the parents of a girl who had died in an accident. Stefanie volunteered to work in Germany as a Pole and left soon after. She was a beautiful fifteen-year-old girl. Tragically, her good fortune ran out a few days later. Even though she had shoulder-length blond hair and blue eyes, she was identified as a Jew and shot dead at Jędrzejów train station.

CHAPTER 15

FOR THE NEXT THREE DAYS OF WAITING we felt trapped like animals in a cage with no possible escape. I could not look my parents in the eyes, as we tried to believe that all of the rumours were just that. My mother had no tears left and my father, who was always able to care and guard us from harm, was mostly silent, deep in thought.

One afternoon he returned from work and tried to shake us out of our despair. 'Mourning won't help us at all. Let's be positive and prepare Siegmund for his journey.' He then asked me for my belt and, as bizarre as his request was, I did not ask why he wanted it. He said he had something to do in town and would be back soon.

As dejected as I was, I started to organise my clothes. Everything was neatly folded on the bed, keeping in mind that I could only take one backpack and had to leave room for my blanket. To save space I decided to wear as many shirts and pairs of underwear as I could; small items went into my pockets. I ended up wearing most of my belongings. My mother gave me my father's brand-new leather gloves that had never been worn.

'Take them with you, they might come in handy.'

'Why would I need such an elegant pair of leather gloves? I've a perfectly good pair of woollen ones that you made for me.'

'You never know. I really want you to have them. Please take them.'

I put the gloves into one of my pockets.

Two hours later my father returned carrying my newly soled shoes and my belt. The belt's well-polished brass buckle had been replaced by one made out of an old piece of wire of no particular colour. My father noticed the disappointment on my face.

'Do you remember the golden ingots that I hid in your shoes?'

'Yes, I do,' I answered.

'Well, I went to a goldsmith who melted them down for me to create this beautiful golden buckle.' The gold had been left unpolished after it had been heated and worked.

'But what is it good for?' I was puzzled.

'You never know, one day it may save your life.'

Understanding what he meant, I continued packing. I became very restless and impatient; my mind was racing and my palms were sweaty. That night I did not sleep at all and heard my mother sobbing softly. At last, dawn arrived. It was the end of September 1942.

In the town's main square far more than 300 young male volunteers lined up in rows of three. Each man hoped this was his chance to hold on to life, to survive. Many of my friends were there, including David Najman, who had run our study group meetings, Tusia Huzarski's brother and Heniek Nisenbaum. The Jewish policemen kept order and kept counting us. Our ranks were further swelled by parents, sisters, brothers and friends gathered around to say goodbye to their sons, husbands and fathers. Close friends who had decided not to volunteer came to the main square to say goodbye, and so did all the girls. People were standing around us, openly crying: for our departure, for our separation and for their own uncertain fate. I lined up with

Felix and a friend. Next to us stood Samuel and Ludwig. We wanted to keep close together.

Six large open trucks arrived carrying some twenty Germans in combat uniform. They jumped out of the cabins and rounded us up, ready to shoot. One of the high-ranking officers started to pull the weakest looking men from the line until there were only 300 of us left. The officer reshuffled us into six groups of fifty men and we began to climb onto the trucks, which were without tarpaulin covers, without seats and without rails. We wanted to sit on our backpacks but the Germans would not allow it. They wanted us to pile them in the rear of the truck to prevent us from escaping. I approached the officer and explained that, as we were volunteers, we had no intention of escaping and if each of us could sit on his backpack it would create more space. Scratching the back of his head he finally agreed.

We were now ready to board. I hugged my mother, kissing her and holding her trembling body. I looked at the bizarre shape of her fur-less collar and considered her surreal situation. Eva Siegreich was spoiled and indulged, first by her doting parents and then by her adoring husband. There she was, stripped of everything safe and familiar, yet still standing so proud and dignified. Now, both her children had been taken from her.

'Mummy dearest, please don't worry about me. I promise you that I will be all right. I am strong and careful and even the hardest work won't harm me.'

'I know you are, my darling,' she said as tears stained her cheeks. 'You will survive, because your guardian angel, one of the thirty-six, will take care of you. You must live, my darling. You must survive so you can avenge us all.'

A chill ran down my spine. I did not understand what she meant. At that stage our family was still intact.

'I'll do my best,' I said. 'Nothing will happen. We'll all survive this and be together soon.'

We knew that we were all doomed and yet we tried to reassure each other with banal clichés. We *knew* that entire Jewish communities had vanished. So many people had simply disappeared from the face of the earth. Even though we knew what lay ahead, we were unable to believe that such a thing was possible: it had to be science fiction.

My father placed his arms around me and tried to hide his despair by avoiding my gaze. We were locked together in this helpless embrace. He knew that he had to stay behind, to protect my mother and try to save her. 'I wish we could go together,' he said. 'Try to send word as often as you can and we shall do the same. Stay close to your uncles and help each other.'

I promised to do as he asked and reluctantly broke our embrace. I headed towards the waiting trucks. I looked back and saw my parents holding on to each other. My mother was sobbing. They looked so small, fragile and vulnerable.

At the last moment, just before we pulled out, two of my friends threw out their backpacks and jumped off the truck. As the convoy was set in motion we waved to the people left behind.

We were all very anxious, anticipating the unknown and sitting in silence bouncing from side to side as the truck drove along the country road. Except for a cold wind, the weather wasn't so bad. Passing through villages, some Poles threw us apples or pears while others made a cutthroat sign – most though looked at us with indifference.

Two hours later we passed Starachowice-Wierzbnik. I felt a sinking feeling in my gut. We had been deceived.

I cried out to my uncles. 'Where the hell are they taking us? We've been conned! Instead of going to Starachowice-Wierzbnik we're heading towards the Skarżysko-Kamienna hellhole.'

I could not believe this was happening. After another twenty minutes the column turned off the main road and veered left towards an enormous ammunition factory complex. We drove through huge open gates with a big sign above:

MUNITIONS WERKE HASAG
HUGO SCHNEIDER AKTIENGESELLSCHAFT
WERK SKARŻYSKO-KAMIENNA

PART III

SEPTEMBER 1942 – JANUARY 1943

CHAPTER 16

BY 1942, there were hundreds of labour camps in Poland whose purpose was to harness slave labour to assist the German war effort. We had arrived at Hasag Skarżysko-Kamienna. 'Hasag' was the name of a German company, Hugo Schneider Aktien Gesellschaft. At Skarżysko-Kamienna, Hasag's munitions factories spread over several square kilometres and comprised three different complexes – A, B and C – with a Jewish labour camp annexed to each of them.

Many years later, Rabbi Israel Fersztendig, a witness in the trial of Adolf Eichmann, would testify:

> I heard the opening statement of the attorney-general
> . . . When speaking of the concentration camps he listed
> the very worst, such as Auschwitz, Majdanek, Treblinka
> . . . but omitted one, which I believe should be included
> among the cruellest of them all: Skarżysko-Kamienna,
> Werk C. Any account of Nazi brutalities must include this
> camp. Whoever passed through Werk C will be haunted
> for the rest of his life.

The trucks drove through the gates and into a huge compound. Numerous large two-storey buildings were encircled by a web of roads and train tracks. We were ordered to line up in rows of three.

Guards carrying submachine guns surrounded us immediately. As they counted us, they noticed two men were missing from our truck. They searched for them and then questioned us. Not one person spoke up – no-one wanted trouble.

We were escorted in groups to the personnel building, where we had to line up to register. We had to surrender all our personal documents and were instead issued with a *Werks Arbeiterausweis*, an ID card giving personal data and an identification number, but no photos. This had to be shown whenever we passed through the gates of the camp and the work plant. During this process a dozen policjanten joined us. They were wearing the same black caps with a red band and the same belts and truncheons as those worn by the Jewish policemen in the towns and villages.

After registration, some twenty Ukrainian camp and factory guards called *Werkschutz* replaced the German guards. They wore dark grey uniforms, were armed with submachine guns and were under the command of half-a-dozen Germans in black uniforms. The Ukrainians were collaborating with the Germans, and assisted them in persecuting Jews. We were led into a large empty factory where we were told to line up in one long row.

A high-ranking officer stepped forward. 'You have come here to work and to die. How long you last is entirely up to you. You will be shown to the barracks where you will sleep and later you'll be assigned to the working commandos. First, you have to surrender all your money and valuables, including your watches and fountain pens. You shall drop them into the boxes provided. Those who will not comply with this order will be shot instantly!'

Then, at the officer's command, the policjanten paraded up and down in front of us. 'You bloody sons of whores!' they screamed. 'Hand it over! Give it all up!' The Ukrainians, who didn't speak German, shouted: *'Los! Los! Juden. Los! Los!'* ('Quick, Jews! Quick! Quick!')

The empty building amplified all the shouting, causing terror and confusion among the 'volunteers'. Both the Germans and the Jewish policjanten abused us and beat us with truncheons and rubber hoses while the boxes filled. One policjant thundered, 'Surrender everything!' then, with a soft whisper, added, 'Don't do it. Just give them the plague instead.' The four of us – my two uncles, my cousin and I – quickly surrendered our watches and some of our money. In the meantime, two Ukrainian guards removed three men from our group, escorting them outside, while the German officer declared: 'Those three men had money sewn into their jackets which they did not surrender. They will be shot immediately.'

There was complete silence. Then, from outside, three single shots pierced the stillness in the hall.

The response was immediate. People pulled out money, jewellery, foreign currency and other valuables from secret pockets and other hiding places. My uncle Samuel insisted that we comply. 'Give away everything,' he said. 'Don't risk your life.'

'I have my father's gold signet ring inside a ball of knitting yarn,' I told him.

'Give it to them.' My uncle was actually shaking with fear. 'Give them everything. We mustn't antagonise them and we have to protect each other.'

I untangled the ball, found the ring and threw it into the box.

Within two hours the Germans had collected a great deal of money and many valuables, including 298 watches, some of them made of gold. The German officer selected twenty men to load the heavy boxes full of confiscated goods onto a truck and then left, leaving us at the mercy of the Ukrainians.

The three men who had been shot suddenly re-appeared in the hall very much alive. They had been locked in the adjoining building and only released after the hoax was over.

More Werkschutz guardsmen came in and the looting began

all over again. Well-dressed people in better quality clothing were targeted and had their overcoats, caps and boots confiscated. Next we were ordered to empty our backpacks. Guardsmen took my boots, my heavy woollen pullover, two shirts, one pair of trousers and a terrycloth – something they had never seen before – but I still had many of my belongings in my rucksack when they were done. We were then taken to the showers and ordered to leave our remaining possessions in the adjoining delousing chamber. If we did not have any lice before, we certainly became infected now.

The spectacle lasted until 4 pm; we had not eaten or had water since leaving Staszów early that morning. Three trucks then arrived to take the first 150 men to their barracks. We were in the first group and travelled for about twenty minutes, deep into a thick pine forest. We could see a high double-barbed-wire fence and watchtowers. Before reaching the gate, the trucks were stopped by armed Werkschutz in front of a lowered boom gate. They checked the driver's documents, counted us three times, then allowed the truck to pass. Fifty metres further on, we went through the same procedure.

We had arrived at the infamous slave labour camp Skarżysko-Kamienna Werk C. At the *Appelplatz* (assembly square) we were ordered to line up – '*Raus, Juden! Schnell, schnell!*' – and were 'greeted' by about thirty Ukrainian Werkschutz. They emptied our backpacks and took whatever they chose.

Thirsty, hungry and completely exhausted, we were directed to yellow-greenish timber barracks that had just been built. Each barrack had three rooms; each room slept forty people on three-tier bunks. The four of us grabbed beds on the upper tier and had just managed to place our few remaining belongings on our bunks when the Jewish camp police ordered us to line up for soup. At last, something to eat.

As we came out to join the queue, we stared in disbelief at

the veteran Jewish prisoners. They were filthy, clad in rags, and their feet housed in wooden clogs dragged along the ground. The men were mostly unshaven and the women's heads were shaved bare and covered with a piece of cloth. They spoke a mixture of Yiddish and Polish peasant dialect.

They carried all kinds of containers – mess tins, pots, empty jam tins – and, of course, spoons. Some had wooden spoons, which they had made themselves. As newcomers we had no bowls or spoons. It had not occurred to us at all that we might need utensils when we volunteered.

The queue of about 2000 men snaked its way towards the small distribution platform. First in the queue were the veteran inmates who had just returned from work, followed by the newcomers. Some veterans advised us to put on head covers. We did not know why but took their advice. I put on a peaked work cap with earflaps.

I began to panic about not having eating utensils and on seeing one man who had quickly finished his soup asked him if I could borrow his bowl. He looked me up and down and hesitated but after I explained that I had just arrived he agreed.

On the platform were a dozen cauldrons full of watery soup. A man called Stanisław Kotlega, a grotesque oversized Volksdeutsche, stood there, ladle in hand, surrounded by a dozen Ukrainian Werkschutz. Kotlega was a cruel and vicious man with a simple and brutal method of punishing the workers. If the man standing in front of him did not submit his dish in a particular manner, holding it right over the cauldron, Kotlega would pour the hot soup on the unfortunate inmate's hands, burning him severely. If a person did not have a dish, the brute would pour the soup into his cap, and if the inmate did not have a cap, Kotlega poured the soup on the ground, ordered him to lick it off the muddy soil, and then ground the man's face into the dirt with his boot. At the same time, he would hit the men over their heads with his ladle, yelling abuse at them for the amusement of the Werkschutz.

I lined up anxiously, watching the others around us gulping their soup so fast they hardly stopped to breathe. I tried to imagine what the soup was like as my stomach churned and rumbled with hunger. The line of men was moving quite fast considering the number of inmates being served. Soon it was my turn.

I held up my dish in front of me when, all of a sudden, I felt a heavy blow to my head, accompanied by a guttural roar. 'You filthy Jewish bastard, you're lining up for more soup!'

Kotlega snatched the dish out of my hands and flung it across the yard as far as he could. He struck me four or five times until I fell bleeding to the ground. He must have knocked me out because I came to on a stretcher carried by two inmates. In my naivety, I had not thought to rinse the dish. As a result, I ended up with a big lump on my head, a blood nose and cut lips. While I went to sleep hungry, most of our group had received their soup in their caps.

*

Next morning while it was still dark, the policjanten woke us. 'Get out, every living soul. Line up for rollcall. Quick! Quick!' they screamed. Disorientated, confused and intimidated, we made our way outside. We had no idea of the time as no-one had a watch.

We were counted and recounted, but they were still two volunteers short. (One of these was Heniek Nisenbaum, whom I met again by coincidence some fifty years later in Melbourne's famous Scheherazade restaurant. After he had jumped off the truck he went into hiding and survived the Holocaust in a dugout bunker in the woods near Staszów. After the war, he lived in Israel and travelled to Melbourne to visit his brother David.) It took the policjanten another hour to realise that only 298 volunteers had entered the camp.

As I would later discover, even on a dry day the Appelplatz remained full of puddles and deep in mud. On one side was a communal latrine, forty metres long, double-sided and doorless, with an internal partition dividing the women and men. The sewage overflowed towards the square, producing an unbearable stench. Next to the latrine stood a communal washroom, also divided into two, consisting of two long cement troughs with a row of cold water taps running along the middle.

Heniek Eisenberg was a prisoner at the camp whom the Germans had chosen to be commander of the policjanten. He appeared before us wearing a cap with three stars. He was a good-looking man with a chiselled face. He climbed on a platform and addressed us. 'Don't fool yourselves. You have come here to work and to die. Don't have any illusions or try anything stupid, as no-one has ever escaped from this camp alive.'

As he stepped back, an exceptionally attractive woman came out of the administration barrack. She was about thirty years old with a stunning figure and an elegant demeanour, which was completely out of place in this godforsaken dump. Her appearance was immaculate while the camp was sinking in mud and excrement.

Komendantka Fela Markowiczowa, nicknamed 'Katarina the Great', was Jewish, and ran the camp for the Germans. The life and death of each prisoner depended on her mercy. She held a riding crop and wore highly polished knee-high black leather boots. Without uttering a single word, she paraded in front of us and examined us like a general inspecting his brigade on a military parade.

After this official welcome a group of komendanten – Jewish inmates who were appointed by the Germans as camp administrators – began sorting the newcomers into work squads.

The four of us were selected to the *Waldkommando* (forest commando) and, although we did not know what this meant, it sounded promising. Working in the forest couldn't be so bad. We were to be ready for work in one hour.

Before returning to my barrack, I paid a visit to the police command post to speak to Eisenberg, the head of the camp police. At the entrance to his office, a policjant on duty confronted me aggressively in Yiddish. 'What the fuck do you want here?'

I did not speak any Yiddish and answered in Polish that I wished to speak with Mr Eisenberg.

'Oh, what have we here?' He raised his voice. 'A *shminteligent* – a Polish speaker. Is it beyond your dignity to speak Yiddish, your mother tongue? You bastard!'

I was dumbfounded. 'I have an important private message for Mr Eisenberg,' I said politely.

The policjant knocked at the door, held it ajar and announced that somebody – a Polish speaker – wanted to see the commander. Mr Eisenberg saw me in the doorway and asked me in. The room was modest, with a window on the far wall that let in very little light. In the centre stood a desk with some manila folders and behind it a shabby wooden armchair. The room was thick with cigarette smoke.

'What do you want to talk to me about?'

I forced myself to smile to hide my fear. 'I have a problem. It's a matter of life and death.'

'What's so important?' he asked, raising an eyebrow.

'I only arrived yesterday and am in urgent need of a dish and a spoon so I can collect and eat my soup,' I said.

He must have been in a good mood, because he burst out laughing. 'It can be done. Do you have money?'

'Not yet, but I will. The money I had was taken from me. I hope to get some more soon.'

'Maybe you have valuables? Jewellery perhaps?'

'No, everything was taken from me, but I have an excellent pair of gloves made from the finest pigskin.'

'Show them to me,' he responded eagerly. I handed them over and saw a spark in his eyes. He had probably never held gloves like these before, particularly if he had grown up in a religious home. He tried them on and they fitted perfectly.

'OK,' he said with satisfaction. 'Come with me and I'll give you a dish and a spoon.'

To the amazement of the police guard, we moved out of the office and went to a nearby hut that was used as a storeroom. Inside the shelves groaned with everything imaginable: clothing and shoes, crockery, cutlery, bowls and irons. Blankets were piled up in one corner and one shelf had some tinned food. Eisenberg removed a simple spoon made of sheet zinc and a pot with two round handles placed oddly close together, used specifically for ritual hand-washing by religious Jews. I thanked him and he said that he would be happy to do business with me any time. He was sure that I was good for more valuables for him to loot. What extraordinary foresight did my mother have, insisting that I take those gloves?

CHAPTER 17

THE COMMANDO was already divided into two groups: a *Baukommando* or construction commando of 400 prisoners; and a smaller *Schiessstandkommando*, a commando of about forty veteran inmates who were building a shooting range that would be used to test the ammunition produced in Hasag's factories. We joined the shooting range commando, increasing their number by another twenty-five. Normally the job of the Jewish komendanten was to escort the prisoners to and from work inside the camp perimeter. We had been assigned to the shooting range outside the camp and so were escorted only up to the gate. Once there, about ten Werkschutz took over, swearing and yelling at us all the way.

We started to build a shooting range on a fresh clearing in the middle of a dense pine forest about three kilometres east of the camp. The Ukrainian Werkschutz guarded us. The working day started at 7 am and lasted until 5 pm. We lopped five-metre-long logs from pine trees and then erected them vertically in two rows, four metres apart. The space between the rows we filled with dirt – to create a protective wall. We started by digging foundations to hold the logs in place.

At eleven o'clock, we had half an hour break for lunch when the soup was distributed. This time our soup was delivered to us, doled out by one of the komendanten – Kotlega was ladling soup to the 400 inmates of the construction commando. The brew, of a non-specific colour and texture, was foul-smelling and tasted even worse. This dirty water contained pieces of white beet that sank to the bottom of the bowl. Most of the newcomers were unable to eat it. I sat next to Ludwig, who looked down at his own soup. 'I shall have to summon the waiter and register a complaint!' I said. We sat there in stunned silence before bursting into laughter.

'*Shiviys! Shiviys!*' shouted an inmate. This was the Yiddish word for the Pentecost Jewish holiday, also known as the 'green holiday'. I asked the person next to me why it was being used.

'Don't raise your head,' he warned in a hushed voice. 'He's coming! Work as fast as you can!' Then in a low voice he explained it to me: 'The guy on lookout uses *Shiviys* as a warning call to let us know that *he* is approaching.'

'*Who* is approaching?'

'Zimmermann. The German supervisor. He's a vicious and violent sadist. Beware of him. We call him *grine marnarke* – the green jacket.'

I saw a man walking towards our squad wearing a green forester-type jacket, carrying a heavy wooden club. Zimmermann ordered us to line up. He then selected three inmates who allegedly did not work fast enough.

'You filthy Jewish bastards,' he screamed at them, suddenly furious, 'I'll show you how to work! You parasites! We're feeding you, while you sabotage the German efforts. This is a crime against the German Reich and will be punished by death!' His face bright red and sweating, his breathing heavy, Zimmermann swung his club. He smashed their skulls in a crazed frenzy, transforming their faces into bloody pulp. I stood there bewildered and watched three men beaten to death. No-one moved. Everybody was frozen to the spot. Even the victims failed to react, even when they knew they were going to be killed: after the first one was slain, the other two stood there motionless, resigned to their fate.

I felt sick and with great difficulty stopped myself from throwing up, fearing for my life. The bitter taste in my mouth made me gag even more. Zimmermann then turned to me and, pointing his blood-soaked club, ordered me and two others to strip the corpses. Other men had to dig a pit in the forest. A third group dragged the bodies to the pit and yet another group covered them with dirt. Zimmermann ensured that each of us was involved in this gruesome activity. He then grabbed the discarded clothing and threw it at the men, watching with pleasure as they fought over it. Those young men were sons, brothers or husbands and their families will never know how they died and where they are buried.

As my two uncles, my cousin and I marched back to the barracks, an old-timer turned to me. 'You'll get used to it. This is nothing new, and it's happening daily now.'

We were scared, exhausted and distressed. Back in the barracks, we dropped fully dressed onto our bunks and fell asleep at once despite lying on bare and rough wooden planks. We used our clothes as pillows to alleviate our discomfort and to guard them from theft. Two hours later, loud whistles and screams interrupted our rest.

'All men out and line up at the Appelplatz. Out! Out!'

Within minutes we were walking out of the camp gates and towards the huge ammunition warehouses, some distance away, where forty railway goods carriages stood on a sidetrack. Huge lights illuminated the area. The Germans ordered us to transfer wooden crates full of ammunition from the warehouses and lift them high up onto the carriages. There was no platform or ramp for easy loading. They assigned two men to carry one box, which had two cord handles on either side, and weighed 54 kilograms

– the weight was printed on the side. We carried this heavy load while being beaten with clubs, sticks and bare fists. It was an impossible task.

After about three hours, the chief German commander decided that we were not fast enough, and ordered three men to carry two crates. My arms were coming out of their sockets with this Sisyphean chore. I needed to rest for a minute and disappeared between two coupled carriages.

On the ground I saw an abandoned stick. Surely this was divine intervention? A trimmed sapling branch around a metre long was to be my saviour. I joined another group of workers, now pretending to be one of the overseers. I was lucky enough not to be identified as a prisoner by the others – I was new to the camp and my clothes were still in good condition. I started running around screaming at those bowed under their load, 'Quick, quick. Faster, faster.' I shouted, but I didn't hit anyone. I just waved the stick around in the air. By this time many of the real supervisors had walked away, themselves exhausted after twenty hours.

Around 2 am the following morning, some thirty hours later, the job was finished. I dispensed of the stick and helped others walk back to the barracks. About a dozen men died from the brutal beatings, extreme exhaustion or both.

That night I decided to escape. I knew that my chances of survival outside were not much better than inside the camp, but if I were to die I would rather it be from a bullet as a free man than from starvation, exhaustion or beatings as a prisoner. That thought never left me.

The next morning was Monday 5 October 1942. We had missed the Sunday, which was normally a rest day, and were taken back to the site of the shooting range. I was miserable, scared and tired, cranky and angry: too many emotions welled up inside of me all at once, which in itself was driving me insane. I tried to overcome my frustrations by working hard and fast and planning my escape.

Zimmerman had found four more victims, except this time they were from the construction commando. He followed exactly the same procedure as before. We could hear him yelling, drowning out the screams of the dying men.

Somehow, Samuel and Felix seemed less affected than I was, maybe because they were older – they were in their mid forties. Ludwig seemed to be indifferent – he was only sixteen – or maybe he, like me, was just very scared. Or maybe the three of them were more immune to things around them because they had each other.

At the next rollcall, while we lined up at the Appelplatz and the komendanten counted and recounted us, Komendantka Markowiczowa walked along our line, carefully scrutinising each of us. She stopped from time to time, exchanging a few words with one of the inmates.

She stopped in front of me. 'What's your name?'

'Siegmund Siegreich, madam.'

'Are you a relative of Samuel Siegreich?'

'Yes, I am, madam.'

'I want to see you in my office after rollcall,' she said firmly.

She finished her inspection and returned to her office.

I became very nervous, not knowing what to expect from the komendantka. I told Samuel that she wanted to see me, and that she had asked me if we were related.

'What could she possibly want from me?' I asked him.

'Don't worry, I can assure you that she won't harm you. Go to see her, she can be a very nice woman.'

Some minutes later I knocked on the door of a large, white-painted barrack dubbed the White House; the other barracks were smaller and painted green to blend into the surrounding forest. A young Jewish policjant opened the door. 'What do you want?'

'Komendantka Markowiczowa ordered me to report to her office.'

'What's your name?'

'Siegreich.'

'Ask him in,' Markowiczowa called out.

Inside was a table serving as a desk, and behind it a very tall chair where Markowiczowa had just sat down. Two wooden chairs in front of the desk completed the office furniture. At the back, a door must have led to her private quarters. I was surprised by the lack of more sophisticated fittings. There was not a piece of paper, a file or pencil to be seen, but the simplicity of her office must have had a purpose.

'I'm here as you requested, madam.'

'Please, take a seat.' She pointed to a chair. 'So, you're Siegmund Siegreich and you're related to Samuel. What is the relationship?'

'He's my uncle.'

'I see. And where do you come from?'

'Originally I am from Katowice, but we left our home in 1939. I came here from Staszów.'

'Where have you been assigned for work?'

'I'm with the *Schiessstandkommando* at the shooting range in the forest.'

'You don't speak Yiddish?' she stated rather than asked.

'No, I speak only German and Polish.'

'I might be able to get you a better job than your current one. I'll let you know.'

'Thank you very much. I would be most grateful,' I said trying not to sound too surprised, and left her office. I never found out what her connection to my uncle was, and I soon forgot about the meeting, as nothing came of it.

*

Since the third day in the camp I had been hungry all the time. The Werkschutz guardsmen had taken my two cakes of soap, towels and razor blades and we had to line up at the camp barber's for the mandatory weekly shave. But the worst thing about daily life was the lack of toilet paper. Only on very rare occasions would we find old newspaper or some scrap to divide into pieces. We tried to wait until we were in the forest where we could use the foliage of nearby shrubs. Sometimes we kept some leaves in our pockets, though these soon became brittle.

Before long we turned into robots, walking, working and eating in silence. The rainy days and ankle-deep mud made us miserable. We became depressed. A rumour circulated that 150 sick, elderly and debilitated workers from Werk A and B had been slaughtered. They had been loaded onto trucks and driven deep into the forest where they were shot and buried. These rumours, later confirmed by our overseer Leon Kanarek, were our first awareness of 'selections', and we learned that they occurred at least once a month.

The Germans also had an ingenious idea not just to use precious bullets for killing people but to coordinate the killing with the testing of the ammunition. One day, around noon, while we were at the shooting range, there was a terrible accident in one of the main buildings. A huge blast ripped through one of the work areas where the inmates filled artillery shells with explosives. Twenty-five female inmates were killed and about thirty seriously wounded. The injured were later taken to the shooting range and 'mercy killed'.

Jews were not the only people killed in the woods at Werk C. There were also prisoners of war, Poles suspected of belonging to the underground, people arrested for peddling goods on the black market, those who had helped Jews and others black-listed by the Germans, and many who simply happened to be in the wrong place at the wrong time.

With my sister, Halinka, on my first day of school, 1 September 1930. I had a uniform, a cap, a new schoolbag and a cardboard cone filled to the brim with lollies. The other children teased me about my girlish curls and I went home crying, insisting I would never go back.

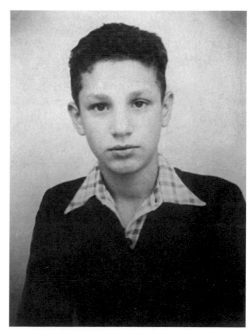

Me at age eleven, from a school ID pass.

Left: My mother, Halinka and me (aged ten), 15 April 1934.

Below: Me at age fourteen, with my friends at our family's timber yard, Katowice, May 1938.

With my family in April 1938. Left to right: my aunt, Father, Halinka, Mother, me (sitting on top of the car), our chauffeur, Stefan, and my maternal grandmother and grandfather.

My parents, Eva and Samuel David Siegreich, Bystra, August 1938.

Above: A family gathering at Ustroń, a Polish spa resort, July 1939. Left to right, around the table: Ignac Rosenzweig (Andzia's brother) and his daughter; my mother's sister Hela Manela; Andzia Siegreich (Samuel's wife); her son Ludwig; Ignac's wife; my mother; her sister Regina Reichman; and Sofie and Felix Siegreich.

Left: My maternal grandmother, Rachel Siegreich, her husband, David Siegreich, and their daughter Hela Manela.

Right: My sister with her boyfriend, Don Grünspan, in Kraków, 1939. Halinka and Don were about to announce their engagement when the war broke out.

Below: We had to communicate via postcards, as letters sealed in envelopes were not permitted by the German censors. My parents anxiously awaited postcards from Halinka and their arrival was cause for great rejoicing.

Left: With Hanka in Katowice, very much in love, March 1945.

Below: Hanka in Katowice, March 1945, enjoying the flowers I gave her.

Left: With Hanka and my aunt Andzia in the summer of 1945. Hanka had just told Andzia our happy secret: she was pregnant.

Above: With Hanka and our daughter Evelyne, just three months old, in 1946. This beautiful child of ours, this little miracle, was the first baby born in Katowice to Holocaust survivors, defying Hitler's promise to annihilate the Jewish people from the face of the earth.

Right: Me, Hanka, Halinka and Don with our babies in the prams and little Edward in front, Katowice, April 1946.

Above: With Hanka in Ustroń, 1946. *Below:* We never had an opportunity to get married under a *chuppah* – the canopy used in Jewish weddings to symbolise the home the couple will build together – so we decided to get 'remarried' on our fiftieth wedding anniversary.

One morning I bumped into a fourteen-year-old boy from Staszów who turned out to be the brother of my friend Sara Nojman. He told me that on 27 September he had been snatched from the street and dispatched to Skarżysko-Kamienna with another forty people.

'I'll be going home in the next couple of days,' he said cheerfully. 'Children up to the age of sixteen and men over forty are allowed to go home to their families in the ghettos if they wish.'

I was sceptical and said that that rule sounded suspicious. I told him that people in Staszów were now waiting for the final *akcja* – deportation to the extermination camps – and warned him not to go.

He did not listen. Three days later, the young Nojman boy and a group of some 300 other people were sent to the Skarżysko-Kamienna train station to join the final *akcja* of the local Jews to Treblinka.

*

On 11 October, a sunny crisp Sunday morning, we had our first day of rest. I went for a walk to check out the camp facilities and other installations. I saw a barrack marked no. 7; it was the infirmary, where there were no doctors, no qualified nurses and no medications, and where the dead and the dying, left lying next to each other, were covered with lice.

An unusual noise caught my attention. It was the clacking of wooden clogs, stop-starting, and accompanied by the shouts of the escorting komendant: march, stop, count, march, stop, count. It was a group of inmates, men and women, returning from the night shift. As they came nearer I saw a squad of marching yellow creatures. They had a human shape but looked like skeletons from outer space. They were clad in yellow rags, belted with string, to which they had attached their tin bowls and spoons, adding to the percussive noise. This was the worst commando in the whole of Werk C. This was the picric acid commando, known as the *Pikryna*.

Before the war this department was called *Elaboracja*. It was responsible for filling artillery shells with explosives. At that time, the Polish workers enjoyed special working conditions. Each shift lasted four hours with ten-minute breaks every hour. The workers were allocated one litre of milk to drink during their shift, which was believed to safeguard their health. They wore protective clothing with special dust-absorbing masks and had access to decontamination shower facilities, including special soap.

The Jewish slave workers, however, did not have enough food or any hot water or soap. They worked a twelve-hour shift, without any protective clothing apart from their rags and no masks. As a result their skin dried out and took on a greenish-yellow tinge, so that their hair, face, eyes, nails – even their tongues – were yellow. The yellow powder penetrated deep into the skin and, in time, everything around them tasted bitter, including drinking water. Their mortality rate, as would be expected, was very high. The situation was similar at the TNT department, the *Trotyl*, with the exception that those workers turned a shade of red. It became obvious to me that the German policy at the slave labour camps was extermination through hard work, starvation and maltreatment.

This terrible vision reinforced my decision to escape.

Later in the day, Samuel and Felix told me that they had been transferred to the power and heat commando (*Abteilung für Kraft und Wärme*). I asked if they could arrange a transfer for Ludwig and me but Samuel said that we were too young to pretend to be skilled plumbers or electricians. Ludwig and I stayed with the forest commando.

A week later Ludwig escaped. He did not tell anyone of his

plan, not even his father. We three remaining Siegreichs were totally traumatised and expected severe reprisals. Incredibly, nothing happened to us and no-one asked any questions. Kotlega killed two men that day and Zimmermann killed six more – probably part of their normal daily routine – but we were not targeted. We never saw Ludwig again.

The Germans concocted another scheme to extort more money from the inmates, announcing that prisoners could register to transfer to Palestine as part of a prisoner exchange program with the Allies, on the condition that they would advance the cost of transport to the authorities. On 9 November 1942 all those who, encouraged by the policjanten, signed up and paid for their fare, were executed.

I spent the following Sunday afternoon wandering between the barracks searching for friends. The veteran men's barracks were neglected, dirty and smelled awful compared with the women's, which were in much better condition, as were the women themselves. I stuck my head into the next women's barrack I passed and in the middle of the first room was a table covered with something like a tablecloth.

A girl my age called out my name and claimed to know me from Kraków. She told me her name but I could not remember her at all.

'Ah, yes. You are . . .'

'Mala,' she said.

'Oh yes, yes, Mala, of course. I remember well,' I said, although I still hadn't recognised her. 'Where did you come from?'

'I came with a group of 200 people from Wodzisław six weeks ago. My family settled there after we were deported from Kraków.'

I was happy to chat and found that we had mutual friends in Kraków. So engrossed were we in our conversation that we failed to notice a Ukrainian Werkschutz enter the barracks. All the other women had fled. The man was drunk and reeked of alcohol. He approached us, swaying from side to side. He began making lewd remarks to Mala, oblivious to my presence. When he continued with this I called out to him in German. '*Bitte lass das Mädchen in Ruhe.*' (Leave the girl in peace.) He stared at me with his glazed eyes, but did not say a word. It was obvious that he did not understand German so I repeated it in Polish. This time he understood.

He pulled out a knife and jumped on me. I tried to defend myself and to take the knife from him. We both fell on the floor and rolled from side to side. Suddenly he went still and I realised that he must have fallen on his own knife. Bleeding heavily from a wound below his shoulder, he lay prone on the floor.

'We must not panic,' I said aloud, trying to calm myself and catch my breath.

'Oh God. What are we going to do?' wailed Mala. 'We have to do something and we have to do it *quickly*.' She started to tremble and sob.

'Pull yourself together,' I scolded. 'No-one saw this, and no-one would dare come back while the guardsman's still here. Let's find a hiding spot for him and clean up the mess.'

'Cleaning up is no problem, but where can we hide him?' Mala asked looking around.

'I know! The building's on stumps so we'll hide him under the floor. We can't take him out through the door, but we can push him through the back windows that face the forest.'

'But how are we going to lift him up?' Mala whispered.

'Well, he's at least a head shorter than me. Come on, Mala, let's try.'

Mala fetched her blanket and spread it on the floor. We rolled him into the centre and, pulling the corners, dragged him to the window. We struggled, but we lifted him over the windowsill.

I jumped out of the window after him and dragged him under the barrack. I placed him face down, hid his knife under his body, and climbed back into the room. We cleaned up as quickly and as thoroughly as we could. Mala hid the dirty and bloodied blanket, hoping to wash it later. The whole process took only minutes to complete.

I suggested that she let the other women know that the guard had left. Mala hugged me and thanked me for saving her life. We made an agreement that if there were an investigation we would not admit anything. Mala was both baffled and surprised by the guardsman's behaviour. He had visited her barrack a few times before, sometimes bringing bread, and had never before been rude or aggressive.

I found out sometime later that the guard hadn't bled to death, as I had feared. He had woken up from his drunken stupor, unable to remember anything, and attributed his injury to too much alcohol. At the time, though, the incident terrified me and I was absolutely convinced that I must escape. Things were deteriorating at such speed that death couldn't be far away and I knew it was my duty to survive.

Back at my barrack Samuel was asleep while Felix was elsewhere. Not wanting to wake my uncle, I carefully took some things from my backpack to sell. I needed money and decided to go to the veteran's barrack where no-one would know me.

It wasn't hard to find someone who would buy my belongings from me. I cashed in enough to survive for at least two weeks and decided to escape the very next day.

CHAPTER 18

ON MONDAY 16 NOVEMBER I went to work as usual, very nervous and apprehensive, fearing the discovery of the dead Ukrainian under the floorboards. That morning I worked hard so as not to attract any attention. I tried to blend in and kept my head down.

Shortly after 11 am, out came the soup cauldron and our overseer, Leon Kanarek, began to fill the bowls. The prisoners liked to be at the end of the queue because the soup at the bottom of the pot was thicker than at the top. I lined up at the head of the queue, took my watery soup and searched for a tree stump to sit on. I could not find an appropriate one, so I ventured further away, deeper into the forest, gradually increasing my pace. I threw away my precious dish and spoon, paid for with my father's pigskin gloves, and then started to run. My body was pumping pure adrenaline.

I ran for about ten minutes thinking only of getting as far away as quickly as possible. I tried to stay in the denser part of the woods for extra camouflage, only leaving the forest when I reached the Kamienna River. In the distance I glimpsed the town of Skarżysko-Kamienna, the place I was heading. I looked for a bridge to cross the river but there was none in sight. While running, I kept repeating to myself, 'Life or death, but as a free man.'

I was aware that there were many opportunists ready to

denounce a Jew and condemn him to death for a bounty that consisted of a bottle of vodka and a kilogram of sugar. They were always on the lookout and were very good at spotting Jews. Nevertheless, I kept on repeating to myself, 'Life or death, but as a free man.'

I was quite exposed along the riverbank. All of a sudden I heard dogs barking and three or four shots fired. I looked over my shoulder but there was no-one there. My heart was pounding; it felt like it was trying to jump out of my chest. The barking came closer but I still could not see anyone. Maybe the wind was carrying the sound in my direction. I could not tell. Again, I heard a series of shots and the barking getting closer. I jumped down into a ditch and stayed there for what seemed an eternity. Finally the noise stopped and I began walking again.

Up ahead was a dark structure, which turned out to be the huge wooden wheel of an old dilapidated and abandoned watermill. As luck would have it, the mill had been constructed across the river, which enabled me to climb over it and reach the other side.

The town was still about four or five kilometres from the river, so I had to keep moving. As I drew close, I brushed myself free of mud and dust. I was wearing navy trousers, a navy three-quarter length overcoat and a traditional navy winter hat. The only thing causing me immediate danger was my scruffy beard. The men of this district used to shave only once a week, on Sundays, and this being Monday morning my priority upon reaching town was to find a barber shop. It was easy enough, and I soon found one.

'Good day,' I said casually as I entered.

On one side of the shop were three barber's chairs facing three mirrors and, on the other, a row of six chairs for waiting customers. On the wall was a rack with hangers for coats and caps. There were two barbers – only one was busy. No-one was waiting.

'Good day,' the two barbers greeted me in unison, and then one moved towards me. 'What can I do for you?'

'I think you can guess on a Monday morning with a beard like mine! Bloody hell,' I said, pretending to be annoyed, 'I had to work yesterday and didn't get to shave.'

'Yes, yes, certainly. But maybe you'd like a haircut as well?' the barber said politely, as only a Polish barber could.

'No, no. Thank you. Today I only need a good shave.'

I put my coat and cap on a hanger. The barber, swiping his towel across the chair, asked me to sit down and placed a white wrap around my neck. While he shaved me, I closed my eyes to prevent any conversation.

I paid him, put my overcoat on, grabbed my cap and moved towards the door. At that very moment my heart stopped.

Two Werkschutz from Werk C were about to walk in, evidently looking for an escapee. I was sure they had recognised me and were about to grab me when instead they stepped back to allow me to pass. I quickly raised my arm across my face to shield myself while putting on my cap. I could hardly breathe. My instinct was to run, to run as fast as my legs could carry me, but my brain told me to walk, to take my time and go slowly. I forced myself to walk to regain my composure. I paced around the town for a while, my gut in knots, contemplating my new situation.

I was getting cold. I made my way to the train station to warm up a little and to ask about the next train to Jędrzejów, which was not due for a while. The smell from the station cafeteria reminded me that I had not eaten since that previous afternoon. I ordered a knackwurst with sauerkraut and some bread and ate as if I was not hungry at all, pretending to be a local labourer.

I joined the ticket queue and stood behind a large woman holding a heavy wicker basket full of food. As we neared the cashier, I still could not see past this huge person in front of me.

It was her turn and she was arguing about the price of a return ticket. She turned aside to untie her handkerchief holding her money and as she did so I saw the little ticket office window.

On the other side of the window's bars was an old friend, Lucia Krakowski, a Jewish girl from my boarding school. We stared, both of us not daring to utter a single word lest we endangered the other. I presumed that she must have had false Aryan documents to get such a job.

It was my turn. I politely requested a return ticket to Staszów and then touched my lips with a finger, warning her not to talk.

'That will be eight zloty please.'

I handed her a ten-zloty bill. Leaning forward to take the money, she whispered that if I needed help at any time she would be there for me. I picked up the tickets and my change, which exceeded the price of the tickets tenfold. She winked and smiled at me. I walked away in total disbelief at this stroke of good fortune. My chances of survival had suddenly soared: running away from the hellhole of Werk C had been the right thing to do.

I boarded the overcrowded train. The carriage was dark and the heating was poor. I found a seat and stretched my legs out in front of me. The train conductor, accompanied by two German rail police, appeared with a lantern and I could see the other passengers. They were predominantly peasant women carrying baskets of foodstuffs for sale on the black market. The police inspected the identity cards and tickets of all passengers and, as my only document issued by Hasagwerke did not indicate my religion, I was not identifiable as a Jew.

I sat there trying to look unfazed and thrust my ID card at one of the rail police before he had a chance to request it. I was sure that everyone in the compartment could hear my heartbeat as it was deafening to me. The policeman looked me in the eye and then lowered his gaze to glance at the card. At that same instant his attention was diverted to his colleague, who was searching a passenger's luggage. Something took his fancy and he completely forgot about me.

The trip continued and the major topic of conversation in our carriage was to do with the Jews, with passengers praising the Germans for getting rid of them.

'Serves them right! They've been sucking our blood for years and now they're getting their own back,' was a common sentiment. To divert any suspicion I contributed just as enthusiastically as the others.

After midnight the train stopped at Chmielnik. Some people got off and two new passengers boarded. An elderly peasant woman sat down next to me, placing her basket between us, making it very cramped and uncomfortable. I offered to help her lift her basket onto the luggage rack above. She thanked me, covered herself with her large checked wrap and returned to her seat. The almost total darkness did not prevent conversation, in which I took a leading part. Despite there now being plenty of room on the bench, the peasant woman moved closer. I moved away, giving her more room, but she moved even closer. Then she moved again, squashing me right against the wall. I lost my patience. 'Why are you pushing me? There's plenty of room here for both of us.'

She leaned towards me and whispered, 'Sigi?' She looked like a typical Polish peasant but I instantly recognised her voice from our group of friends in Staszów.

Covering my mouth to stifle the sound I whispered, 'Yes, it's me. I know who you are. You're Hinda Jaskółka .'

'Yes,' she whispered.

We both continued our charade of pretending until the other passengers fell asleep.

'I fled just before the final *akcja* in Staszów,' Hinda explained. 'I was taken in by my Polish friend to stay at her farmhouse.

146

Two days ago I went to Chmielnik to pick up some personal items from my relatives. I arrived there during the final *akcja*, and barely managed to escape.'

She pulled the scarf tightly around her shoulders and pretended to look at the scenery, but all that was on the other side of the window was the black night.

I looked around to make sure that no-one was listening to us. We could be killed on the spot if we were discovered. 'I've just escaped from Skarżysko and am on my way to see my parents. Do you have any news from Staszów?'

'I hear that there aren't many Jews left there,' she said.

Suddenly I felt faint. What if my parents had been rounded up and deported? I did not dare think the unthinkable.

To get to Staszów I had to change trains once more and wait another hour in a dark, unheated waiting room. Hinda waited there with me. When we reached Bogoria, we parted, wishing each other luck.

I arrived in Staszów at 5 am. I walked into town, sensing a great unease. No-one was around and, fearing that I had made a grave mistake, I decided to head back to the station. I was too scared to ask anyone what had happened, and in my panic I decided to catch the train back to Skarżysko-Kamienna.

The trip itself would offer me temporary shelter; and the opportunity to sit, rest and maybe doze for a while was irresistible. Furthermore, Lucia had given me a return ticket and had promised to help me. I realised what an extraordinary thing she had done for me. Who would spare such kindness and show such generosity in these difficult times? What would my mother say about this? Who was this guardian angel? Was she one of the thirty-six? Did they appear in a female form? I must have been going crazy! With these thoughts going through my head, I fell into a deep sleep.

After travelling for many hours, half-frozen, I arrived back at

Skarżysko-Kamienna station. Lucia was nowhere to be found. Now it seemed my luck had run out. I was an outlaw, travelling illegally, an escapee from a labour camp, homeless and an easy prey for headhunters.

Commuters rushed from the train into town, hurrying to the factories and other workplaces. Only a few people lined up to purchase tickets out of town. They were sitting on the benches rugged up with gloves and caps with earflaps.

I sat with them pretending to wait for my train, and my angel finally appeared. I sighed with relief and slowly approached Lucia at the ticket counter. She smiled mysteriously and I 'purchased' another ticket, telling her that I might be back.

She understood. With her head bent and eyes lowered, she pushed another wad of notes towards me and whispered, 'Good luck.'

Half an hour later I was heading back to Staszów. Somehow I was convinced that my parents were still there and I was now determined to go home. At Jędrzejów I again changed trains. I stepped onto the platform and found myself staring into Wacek's face. I froze as I recognised the young railway thief from Staszów. He had grown taller and had started shaving.

'Hey! What are you doing here?' he called out. His voice had broken as well. 'Aren't you supposed to be in Skarżysko?'

'Yes, you're right,' I replied, smiling, even though I was petrified. 'I am in Skarżysko but received a few days' leave to visit my parents.'

'Don't bullshit me. You people don't get leave,' he snorted.

I waved my Hasag ID card, pretending it was my leave pass. 'It's true.'

'It's not possible,' he argued.

'Well it is. I am with the *Junaks*.'

I thought this was plausible: the Junaks were young Polish volunteers involved with public works.

Wacek gave me an exasperated look. 'Oh, all right then. Say what you will,' he shrugged. 'You just better stick with me.' It was clear he did not believe a word I said.

I was trapped. This young thief now had the chance to pay me back for everything I had done to him by turning me over to the Germans. He only had to shout the word '*Jude*' and I would be history. I had to be careful not to provoke him.

'While we're waiting for the train, let's grab some food from the cafeteria,' he said, pointing the way and waiting for me to enter first.

'I'm not hungry,' I said. 'I ate earlier.'

'Bullshit. Everybody's hungry, especially you. Where you came from there is never enough food,' he said knowingly. He led the way into the cafeteria, asked me to take a seat and went to the counter. He came back with two serves of steaming sausage with sauerkraut and two thick slices of ryebread. 'This should be enough for the time being. Come on, let's eat.'

We continued our journey together. This time there were only two other people in the compartment. We sat by the window, opposite each other, without exchanging a word. Wacck soon fell asleep but I only pretended to sleep – I was scared. I remembered how I used to chase him when he stole from the timber yard and was convinced that he would denounce me to the Germans to collect his vodka and sugar.

We pulled into the station in Pińczów and the platform clock told me that it was almost 1 am. Wacek woke up and suggested we move to the waiting room to warm up. The station was crowded with Germans in different uniforms. I told him I felt uneasy. 'Don't worry,' he replied. 'You're with me.' I hadn't yet recovered from my near miss at the barber shop and didn't dare ask him what he meant. We entered the cafeteria. The only food available at that time was a pea soup that had been simmering for hours. Before the war I would have thought it unfit for consumption. Hot and served with a slice of bread it was nearly a feast.

We arrived in Bogoria around five in the morning to find the whole town covered in a white blanket of snow. We had to change trains again and the fire in the waiting room had gone out. The room was not only freezing but gloomy and depressing. 'We've at least two hours to wait and I don't see why we should stay here and freeze to death,' said Wacek. 'In the village is a bakery where we can wait inside a heated room and, if we get lucky, we might even get a few *popłanki*.' He winked with a cheeky smile.

I became suspicious and decided that if he headed towards a police station, I would break away and run for my life.

We walked in silence. I stayed half a pace behind him, ready to run, but Wacek indeed headed to the bakery and everything was as he said. The smell of freshly baked bread was overwhelming and made me feel safe and somehow peaceful. It reminded me of my childhood, a feeling that I had not had since leaving Katowice. It was so warm in the bakery that we actually had to remove our coats. We ate hot *popłanki* (pizza-like onion rolls) and chatted with the bakers while they pushed dough into the oven with long spatulas. Before we left, the baker gave us a loaf of bread each and refused to take any money. Was I dreaming?

We arrived in Staszów at dawn. We left the station and walked towards the centre of town.

'Do you think that my parents are still in Staszów?' I asked Wacek.

'I really don't know,' he answered evenly. 'I wasn't in Staszów during the final *akcja*. First, let's go to my house and then I'll find out for you.'

CHAPTER 19

WACEK UNLOCKED THE FRONT DOOR and we went straight up to the first floor. There was no-one there, and no sign of anybody living there. He said that he lived with his mother but she spent most of her time elsewhere.

'I hate my mother, that German whore!' he hissed under his breath. I pretended not to hear. He gathered some kindling and lit a fire under the stove, placing the teakettle on top. He prepared a few slices of fresh bread and placed a jar of lard on the table. We ate the bread and drank the hot tea.

'I have to go out to do a few things,' he said, clearing up. 'I'll find out about your parents and bring back some dinner. You stay here and *don't* move. You can rest on my bed if you want but don't answer the door for anyone. Stay away from the windows and don't turn on the light. Don't add any firewood to the stove; just let the fire go out. I'll lock you in. When I return, I'll knock twice, three times. And don't worry; everything will be all right.'

At that Wacek left and locked the door behind him. I heard the key turning in the lock and remained seated, unable to move. I could not figure out his intentions. Would he summon the gendarmes to arrest me or could I really trust him? It was impossible for me to leave without attracting the neighbours' attention. I could do nothing and wait for the worst, or try to defend myself. From the kitchen drawer I removed the largest knife I could find and placed it on the table within reach. This calmed me down, so much so that I lay on Wacek's cot and fell into a deep sleep.

I felt someone shaking my shoulder and opened my eyes to see Wacek standing over me. 'Wake up! Wake up!' he shouted, shaking me vigorously.

I jumped up off the bed. 'What happened? What time is it? How long was I asleep?'

'It's three o'clock in the afternoon. You've had a good sleep,' he said, unpacking his backpack. 'I have some good news for you and a surprise.'

'I like good news but I don't like surprises.'

'The good news is that there are still some Jewish people left in town.' Wacek deliberately used the expression 'Jewish people' instead of the more common derogatory term, 'Yid'.

'Some legal and some illegal,' he continued. 'The Ömler labour camp is still here and some other groups like the brush-makers and uniform-sewing shops. Your parents are not here. Your father was deported with the *akcja*, unless he managed to flee and hide somewhere. Andretzky got drunk on the morning of the *akcja* and didn't turn up to claim his people.'

I was devastated to hear Wacek's news, but thought of my father's resourcefulness and determination. I was sure that he was safe, somewhere, somehow.

'Your mother, however, was sent with a small group of people to Ostrowiec and she is all right.'

He took a wrapped parcel out of his bag and handed it to me. 'I think this is one surprise you will like.'

I looked at him with some apprehension and slowly began to untie the knot of the kerchief. Inside was a medium-sized red leather lady's handbag. I was dumbfounded. I had expected a parcel of food. Why had he given me this bag?

I looked up at him puzzled.

'This is your mother's,' he explained gently. 'Have a look inside; her money is still in there. Someone gave it to me to give to you.'

'What do you mean, my mother's handbag?' I had a hundred questions for him and began to think that maybe he stole this bag in the first place. I threw him a suspicious look.

'If you think I stole your mother's bag, you're wrong. I didn't,' he said matter-of-factly. 'After dark I'll take you to the small ghetto where you'll find some of your friends and comrades. But first we eat.' He rubbed his hands with delight. 'I've got some real delicacies for us to have a feast.' This special dinner turned out to be sausages with mustard, bread and some substitute tea – it was like a royal banquet. We talked as we ate.

'May I ask you something personal?' I said.

Wacek nodded. 'Sure, go ahead.'

'Where had you been when we met on the train?'

'I'd been visiting my grandmother on her farm near Jędrzejów. She's the only relative I like and I keep in touch with her. Why?'

'Because it was so far from Staszów.'

After dinner Wacek gave me a small old rucksack to pack everything in. He gave me a loaf of bread, a few sausages, some smoked dry fish, two sets of underwear and two pairs of socks. To my surprise he also gave me some money and a watch, noticing that I was not wearing one.

At last I asked him why he was doing all this for me. He gave me a big smile. 'Because I like you. I always enjoyed teasing you when you chased me at the timber yard. It was lots of fun.'

I was undone by this explanation and burst into tears. He stood there silent for a while. 'Get your stuff and let's go,' he finally said. 'Here, take my scarf. Outside it's well below zero. We can walk together for a while but we'll have to separate. When we get close to the gate, I'll chat with the guard to give you a chance to sneak into the compound.'

'OK,' I said. 'Tell me, when will I see you again?'

'I don't know,' he replied. 'Possibly soon, maybe never.' He shrugged his shoulders and smiled. 'Who knows what will happen? But if we do it will be under different circumstances.'

I wasn't sure what he meant by that. The only thing I was sure of was that the most unlikely person had been so kind in a world that had gone completely mad. Wacek had helped and re-humanised me. He had given me hope when everything around was corrupt.

'Thank you, Wacek. For everything. Goodbye and good luck. You're an amazing young man.'

His face broke into a big smile but he made no reply. We left his house walking side by side without exchanging a word. We turned a corner and saw two men coming towards us. My heart sank to my stomach. I looked over at Wacek, anticipating his next move. He turned to me and for a split second I saw a familiar spark I had seen before but could not remember where. I felt a sense of elation and serenity even though the two men came closer.

Wacek whispered to trust him – to continue walking, to hold my head high and not to look back. For that moment, I felt indestructible. Wacek whistled to the men, who crossed to the other side of the street, completely ignoring me. He went up to them and the three walked towards the guard together.

I sneaked into the ghetto. I turned around to see Wacek once more but no-one was there. I never saw him again.

Throughout my life I have often thought about Wacek, wondering how an illiterate street kid around my age, a thief and the son of a prostitute, could show so much compassion and humanity while endangering his own life without asking for anything in return. And how did he find out about my parents and find my mother's handbag?

After the war I searched for him, even though it was still extremely dangerous for Jews to travel around Poland. I travelled to Staszów, but not only was I unable to locate him, I was unable to find *any* news about him. I did not even know his full name. To this day my debt to him remains unsettled.

CHAPTER 20

BARBED WIRE AND GUARDS surrounded the ghetto. I looked around for familiar faces but knew I needed shelter for the night. I approached a group of men standing at a poorly lit street corner. 'Could you tell me where I could find a place to sleep, please?'

'There are plenty of empty houses,' one of them called out. 'Are you legal, or not?'

'What do you mean?'

'Do you belong to a working commando?'

'No. I just came here from the outside and I need a place to sleep.'

The man went on to explain that those who were 'legal', meaning those who belonged to the working commandos, occupied certain buildings under guard. The 'illegal' inhabited the 'abandoned' Jewish houses, and changed them continually to avoid capture.

I went to a house that seemed to be empty, though I heard voices. I climbed the stairs but no-one was there. I climbed higher until I reached the attic. There the rancid smell of unwashed bodies hit me and made me flinch. The odour came from a grey mass of some fifty young people lying on mattresses. They had escaped deportation, but had no possessions. There was no water, electricity or heating.

It was dark in the attic and I did not recognise anyone, but that could have been because everyone now looked so different. I was reminded of the homeless French clochards from nineteenth-century literature. I asked if I could spend the night with them, in a corner, when a human shape moved towards me. 'Sigi! I recognised you by the way you speak. It's been a long time since I heard such perfect Polish.' I looked closely at the feminine face and hair but it was too dark to see the girl's features.

'It's me, Tusia Huzarski. We were once good friends.' My heart missed a beat. Here was someone I knew – someone from my previous life, who spoke my language and made me feel welcome. In a single moment Tusia made me feel at home.

'We still *are* good friends,' I said with relief. 'Actually I was with your brother in Skarżysko-Kamienna. I even spoke to him last Sunday morning. A Ukrainian Werkschutz had confiscated his boots. Last Monday I escaped from there, but as far as I know he's OK.'

If not for the stench I could have forgotten where we actually were in my excitement at finding her. I had always liked Tusia. She was very pretty, with black curly hair, sky-blue eyes, a winning smile and a good sense of humour. She offered me a space next to her – the first mattress I had slept on in months – and said that I could share her blanket. We were fully dressed and even slept with our boots on.

I woke refreshed and bombarded Tusia with questions. 'What happened here? Why are you in the attic? Who escaped the *akcja*? Have you seen or heard of my parents? Where are your parents?' I was babbling.

Tusia calmed me down and suggested first we have some breakfast. 'Afterwards I'll take you to a place where we can talk in private,' she said.

'Do you have any food?' I asked.

'Yes, I have some bread and a bunch of parsnips,' she said.

'Good. I have bread, some sausage and smoked fish. We can have a great meal.'

'No,' she insisted. 'We'll eat mine here and save yours for lunch.' After breakfast, we left the attic.

Outside the sky was blue and the sun was rising from behind the buildings. The streets were white with snow and some Polish children were building a snowman and throwing snowballs. It was a beautiful day. God must have been mocking us, or maybe he was preoccupied.

Most of the houses had been stripped of their contents and were eerily deserted. Once the Jews had been taken from their homes, the Poles pounced and stole their belongings. The backyards were full of feathers from pillows that had been slashed with knives in the hope of finding riches. Even though we had been tricked to believe that 'deported' people had been resettled, some escapees from the death camps had managed to spread the news that it was all a lie and that the Jews who had lived here were all dead – gassed and cremated hundreds of kilometres away. That *all* of them were dead – men, women, children, babies and the elderly. How was it possible to believe something like this?

We entered Tusia's house, which had been looted and vandalised and now stood empty. At the end of the hallway there was an almost invisible door leading to a secret chamber. Tusia took a key from her bag, unlocked the door and stepped into a tiny windowless room. Inside were a small wardrobe, a unit of shelves and a few wooden crates. Thanks to the camouflaged door everything inside was still intact. Tusia was trembling.

'It must be extremely painful for you to walk back into this house,' I said as we sat down on the crates.

'It is. But I have no choice. I feel like I'm at my own funeral, but I won't cry today. I don't know what to do, though. Should I stay here or go back to the attic? Being together with other people makes me feel safer. Since the *akcja*, I come here every day to cry for my parents. Here we can talk undisturbed, which isn't possible at the attic.' She stopped for a moment to look at me and smiled.

'Tusia, I have so many questions to ask you. On my way to Staszów I met Hinda Jaskółka on the train. She escaped the *akcja* in Chmielnik, posing as an old peasant woman. Are any of our friends here? And tell me, how did you manage to escape?'

'Actually, I did nothing. On the Sunday when it began, I mistakenly lined up in the wrong queue. Unintentionally I went to the end of the line of a working commando and stood there until the *akcja* was over. When the working commando marched away, I became illegal, one of many overlooked in the confusion.'

'What actually happened here?'

'In your wildest dreams you cannot imagine the terror.' And with that, she began to tell me about what had occurred on the evening of Saturday 8 November 1942. 'The whole township was surrounded by armed German gendarmes, Polish police, as well as Ukrainian, Lithuanian and Latvian SS units, to prevent anyone escaping. In the early hours of Sunday morning Jewish policemen ran from house to house ordering people to assemble in the main square by 8 am. We were forbidden to take any belongings and warned that anyone failing to obey this order would be shot on the spot.

'Although we knew the final *akcja* was inevitable, the absurd sense of relief that followed was quite bizarre, though most people still panicked. Cries and shouts as well as children's screams were heard everywhere. Some men even came out wrapped in their prayer shawls, wearing their *tefillin*, reciting their prayers aloud. The Germans and their henchmen searched the buildings, room by room, and shot whoever they found – the sick, the disabled, the elderly, all those who decided not to leave their beds.' Tusia took a deep breath and sighed. She continued in a quivering voice. 'They found and shot babies hidden by their parents who had hoped that their children's lives would be spared.' Tears ran down her pale cheeks. 'They also discovered about a dozen bunkers where Jewish families were hiding. They shot all the occupants instantly. The sounds of single shots and salvos were heard everywhere. In the main square, in front of the assembled crowd, the Germans shot the Judenrat president Ephraim Singer, his wife and a few other members. It was so shocking to see the president publicly shot. Families huddled together, trembling and crying. The gunfire did not stop for a moment and somebody was killed with every shot. The street gutters flowed with blood.

'I saw a child pick up a stone and hurl it at a German. The poor child was then beaten, kicked and trampled to death by three Ukrainian guardsmen.' Tusia stopped and stared at the ground, remembering. After a few moments she looked up at me.

'I saw a Polish peasant from a nearby village carrying a baby in one arm and dragging two little Jewish girls behind him who were holding hands. The girls were not wearing any overcoats or hats despite the freezing temperature. They were shivering with the cold and were silent and sad. The baby was crying. The peasant approached a German and I watched as the German pointed for the girls to join the group. He called a woman over from the queue and the peasant handed her the crying baby. The German then took a packet of cigarettes out of his pocket and offered the peasant one. With a big smile on his face, the peasant took one, bowed several times and smugly walked away.

'Even worse was when a young pregnant women fell on the icy cobblestones and went into labour. Women nearby surrounded her, creating some privacy, while others tried to help. This caught the attention of a uniformed German who drew his pistol and went to inspect. The women dispersed and I saw the young woman lying on the ground with her newborn baby between her legs. Without any hesitation the German shot the woman and the baby dead. It was then that I fainted. When I came to, I got up from the pavement and saw that the Germans had selected two hundred able-bodied Jews to join the work commandos. Another group of around fifty people was to join the main group where the work commandos gathered. This was Andretzky's group.'

I was feeling sick. This was my father's group. I couldn't wait any longer and interrupted her to ask if she knew anything about my parents.

'I know your father worked for Andretzky. During the *akcja* his group lined up among the other commandos, but Andretzky didn't turn up to claim his workers and so they had to join the others. At exactly 10 am, the commander gave the order and over five thousand Jews – men, women, children and babies – began to march. It looked like a gigantic black centipede meandering its way through the snow-covered landscape.

'The escort surrounded the long column from every side and as they passed Krakowska Street, the guards started shooting. Whoever fell or moved out of line was instantly killed. By the time the convoy reached the outskirts of the town, some 190 bodies had been retrieved from Krakowska Street alone. I do not know how many more bodies were collected from the backyards and houses, but it took the Jewish police a few days to complete the job. The group had more than forty-five kilometres to cover to reach the train line in Szczucin. How many bodies were left where they fell on that march is anyone's guess.' Tusia turned towards me and grabbed my arms. 'Where was God?' she hissed.

I looked at her with tears in my eyes. 'This insanity can't go on forever, can it?' I asked.

'It will only stop when there are no Jews left in Europe,' she said grimly.

'Tusia, do you know what happened to my mother?'

'She was working in a commando sewing uniforms for the German army. Five days after the *akcja* the Germans selected more than one hundred people and sent them to Ostrowiec. She could be among them.'

We sat in silence for a few minutes. My grief was so deep that, before I realised it, I was thinking aloud. 'We must not get depressed or despondent or become melancholy and emotional. We *have* to retain our hope. We *have* to think clearly because we must survive.'

Tusia agreed. 'Let's be pragmatic. Take some of my brother's shirts and anything else you may need. You're about his size.' I selected some shirts, underwear, socks, a sweater and a pair of gloves – items I could wear one on top of the other.

We spent more than three hours talking. At one point Tusia put her arms around my neck, hugged me and kissed me on my cheek. 'Just by being here you've given me back my will to live. I feel as if you've taken the place of my parents.'

'I feel the same about you,' I said. 'We're both alone and we need each other. We must not lose each other, Tusia. We have to survive.'

I wanted to speak to my old landlady, to see if she knew anything. I told Tusia I would be back in an hour and left my food with her, warning her not to light a fire.

*

I knocked on the door of the house at Kolejowa Street and a familiar voice answered. 'Come in, the door is open.'

'Good afternoon, Mrs Bigos,' I said politely.

She was peeling potatoes and lifted her head in total disbelief. 'Oh! Holy Jesus and Mother of God! What are you doing here? You were sent to Skarżysko-Kamienna.'

'That's true,' I said, 'but I received a few days' leave to see my parents. It seems though that I came too late.'

She tried to show some compassion. 'It is *terrible* what they are doing to your people.'

'Did my parents leave anything for me?' I asked.

'Sorry, no. They left nothing; they may have sold everything before they left.'

'Nothing? Are you sure that there is nothing for me?' I asked again.

'Oh, actually a postcard from your father arrived a few days ago,' she suddenly remembered. She fetched the card from the dresser and gave it to me. I thanked her and said goodbye – it was too risky for me to ask to go down to the cellar, where my father had hidden our family's few remaining valuables behind the loose brick in the wall.

Outside on the street, I stopped to read my father's postcard.

Dear Eva,
*   I am all right. We are heading in the direction of*
Bełżec-Rawa Ruska. I'm throwing this card through a
crack in the sealed cattle train. Don't worry, all will be
well. I am kissing and embracing you,
*   Yours David*
*   I beg the finder of this card to keep the money and to*
drop this card into a letterbox.

I was right! I knew that my father would find a way to escape. After all, he had sent us a message. I was sure that he would find a way back to us. Now I had to find my mother. I returned to Tusia, who was preparing our lunch. I showed her the postcard.

'So they were sent to Bełżec,' she said. 'This confirms it. Before there were only rumours that Bełżec is an extermination camp. Now we know that this is where they were sent.'

Tusia collapsed in a heap and wept. I was still clinging to my conviction that my father, who was only in his forties, was a resourceful man who would find a way out. But still I cried. We cried for our parents, our brothers and sisters, our people and for ourselves. We cried until all our tears dried up.

'I must go to Ostrowiec to find my mother, but I've never been there before. And *how* am I going to get there? The bus is too dangerous and walking would take more than two days. If only I could organise a bicycle.'

'Ha!' Tusia cried and clapped her hands. 'Turn around and look up.'

I did as I was told. There from the ceiling hung a beautiful black bicycle. It had been her brother's.

'That problem is solved,' she said. 'And when we get back to the attic, somebody is bound to know how to help you get to Ostrowiec.'

Back at the attic, we asked if anyone knew where to find the people from Staszów who had been sent to Ostrowiec. Three of the men argued about it and could not agree. As the discussion became more and more heated, I interrupted and said that I would accept all three addresses. With a bike there wouldn't be any difficulty in checking out all three. I wrote down the addresses and one of the men asked if I'd deliver a letter to his brother in Ostrowiec.

'Sure, no problem,' I said, 'providing you let me have a pencil and a few sheets of paper.'

He agreed and later handed me his letter and a five-zloty bill.

'What's the money for? I'm not a professional courier.'

'It doesn't matter,' he said. 'You're entitled to compensation for your time and effort, not to mention the risk. I insist. Besides, I know that you need money. As long as we're alive, we all have to eat.'

A few others asked me to take their letters as well and within half an hour I had some twenty letters in my pockets. They had also insisted on giving me money – some even paid ten zloty and did not want any change. I shared the money with Tusia, joking that we were now wealthy entrepreneurs. With so many letters to deliver I was confident about finding my mother – some of the letters' recipients must surely be able to give me her address. Tusia and I hugged and I asked her to keep my sleeping spot for my return.

CHAPTER 21

IT DID NOT TAKE LONG to find the Ostrowiec compound. It was a simple single-storey warehouse with very high windows and long skylights running across the roof.

Inside there were about 250 men and women sitting and working in front of rows and rows of sewing machines, which were operated by foot pedals that made loud clicking noises. Another group of workers was busy pressing garments with heavy irons, while yet another folded ready-made uniforms and placed them in large baskets. The place resembled a real clothing factory except that the room was unheated and the freezing workers sat in their overcoats with their scarves bound tightly around their heads.

A woman rose from her sorting table at the other end of the warehouse. She turned to another woman sitting a bit further away and pointed in my direction. My heartbeat intensified. I sensed rather than recognised that this woman was my mother. I ran towards her, not seeing or hearing anything around me. I hugged and kissed her and felt how frail she was.

The proud woman I had known all my life had vanished. The woman who had always helped others and who had loved life was now a broken person. It was not quite ten weeks since I had last seen her but she had aged dramatically and lost a lot of weight. My mother now looked out at the world through black-rimmed, sunken red eyes set in a pained face. She wore her green and black tweed winter coat – minus its otter collar and beaver lining – and it hung from her bony shoulders. Her cropped dark wavy hair now peppered with grey was tucked under her hunter-green felt hat.

'My Sigi, my dear Sigi, where have you come from?' She sighed then looked into my eyes in wonderment. 'How did you manage to find me?' Still we clung to each other, neither wanting to release our embrace. Her supervisor approached and suggested she take an early lunch. My mother thanked him and we moved to a nearby room. We sat on bales of fabric and my mother explained things.

'As you know, Daddy had a secure *placówka* with Andretzky but I didn't. Your father met a man who promised, for a large sum, to arrange a *placówka* for me in a uniform-sewing shop. We paid him all the money we had, but it was not enough. Father also gave him his leather wallet and his Leica camera.

'During the *akcja*, we were ordered to line up separately. I was in an extraordinary state of mind: all three visions of the massacre that I had came back to me in yet another dream. But what I saw was real. It was intolerable and impossible to describe. Dante's depiction of hell would pale by comparison.

'After the massive convoy of people left in the direction of Szczucin, only the working commandos remained in the main square and I could not see the Andretzky group. I began to panic. There was no-one to ask, no-one to turn to. We were being counted and recounted. I was in a trance – unable to register what was happening. The other women with me who had husbands with Andretzky were also confused. At first no-one suspected that they could have been deported. Then someone asked a Jewish policjant, who told her that that is exactly what had happened. After hearing this, my world collapsed. I broke down. I wanted to end my life, but did not know how to go about it. There was nothing left to live for.'

I cut in. 'Don't say things like that. Please. Don't dare think about taking your own life. You have plenty to live for! Please, Mummy, listen to me. I've just arrived from Staszów and have brought you a postcard from Daddy. Look, it's addressed to you.'

My mother squealed with disbelief, then squealed again. 'Oh my God! It *is* from him!' She held the card with both hands and kissed it, read and re-read it, and cried and smiled. Excited now, she jumped from one topic to the next in a tangled web of questions, apologising for her erratic behaviour. 'I'm unable to think clearly and I don't seem to absorb any of this. Please, my darling, tell me again.' She tried to regain her composure. I hugged her again.

'Shh, shh, it's OK. I'll tell you everything I know. First, though, tell me how you are and if you have enough food.'

'Yes, yes. I'm well. I've befriended a very nice woman who sometimes shares her food with me. We sleep next to each other in one of the vacant Jewish houses. But I was allowed only one carry bag and don't really have enough winter clothing,' she said shivering.

'We must be strong and not give up,' I said. 'After all, Daddy has given us a sign of life. He's strong and has always kept his head above water . . . And think of your beloved Halinka. Don is taking good care of her. Maybe you're a grandmother already; and your grandchildren definitely need you. I still need you too, Mother. I'm only eighteen years old and you are also still so young. I promise I'll look after you.'

My mother was sobbing and mumbled about how she must help her own mother. She was not aware that my grandmother had died, because we had kept it from her.

'Let's have something to eat,' I suggested gently.

'I'll just get my bag from my workbench. I've a little bread and can fetch some hot water. Maybe that'll warm us up.' When she came back she had a bright smile on her face. Her supervisor had given her the rest of the day off; it was practically a day of celebration to be reunited with her son.

'Now I have a surprise for you,' I said as I opened my backpack. 'I'm sure you're going to like this.' I pulled out the handbag and saw her eyes widen in astonishment.

For a moment, she was speechless, then: 'That's my handbag! Where did you find it?' She examined it carefully. 'I lost it at least six months ago. How did you get it?' She opened the bag and began to take out her personal belongings, one by one. 'Everything is still here – my lipstick, mirror, powder box, handkerchief . . . and my purse! All the money's still here. It's completely intact. My little notebook and pencil and even my shopping list is still in the bag. Who is the honest finder?'

'Later I'll tell you all about this amazing boy, Wacek.'

I removed two brown paper bags from my backpack. Inside were six sandwiches, prepared by Tusia. I knew how hungry my mother was. I watched her take out a small bundle wrapped in a kerchief from her bag and carefully unfold it. She kept her ration of bread from the previous night to help her get through the next day. She insisted that we share it; I agreed but felt terrible. She ate only one sandwich and wanted to save the other two. I begged her to eat them all and promised her more food the next day.

I gave her the woollen shawl Wacek had given me and we walked back to her quarters. My mother suddenly asked if I remembered Salek Warman.

'Of course, I remember him very well from Starachowice-Wierzbnik. He and his father were refugees from Włocławek or Płock. They ate with us for many months. I even remember that you gave them some blankets and sheets as well. Why do you ask?'

'He is now in charge of the whole camp and the working commandos in Ostrowiec. I asked him for help and at first he pretended not to recognise me. Then he said he knew who I was but still could not help me. I stood there and looked him in the eye before leaving the room without saying a word. We, who had nothing ourselves, shared our meals and possessions with him and his father and this is how he shows his appreciation! Oh, but never mind, this war brings out the ugliest side in people.'

My mother's quarters were similar to those in the attic in Staszów. She did not even have a towel; one of the local women had torn an old bedsheet into pieces for the needy to use. My mother's entire wardrobe comprised three items of underwear, two blouses, a jumper, a skirt, a pair of shoes, an overcoat, a hat and a pair of gloves. She wore all of it at all times.

I pleaded for her to lie down and have a rest. She was exhausted with all the excitement of the last few hours. I explained that I had to deliver some letters to friends' relatives. I covered my mother with her overcoat, kissed her on her forehead and left the house.

First, I found the headquarters of Komendant Warman and knocked on his door.

'Do you recognise me?' I said.

'No. Should I?' he snapped.

'How is your father?' I inquired politely.

'He passed away about six months ago. Why do you ask? Who are you?'

'I'm sorry to hear that. About a year ago you and your father were guests in our home in Starachowice-Wierzbnik and ate with us for months. Do you remember the story your father told us about a pickpocket on a tram who emptied your father's pocket full of diamonds?'

'Yes, I know the story. *Now* I know who you are! I saw your mother recently; she was transported here from Staszów with one hundred other women. I'm really very sorry, but there was nothing I could do for her.'

'My mother told me she came to see you.'

'Is there anything else I can do for you?' he said, indicating that this topic was now closed.

'Oh, yes.' I wanted him to do something for us but had to be careful not to antagonise him. This now powerful man could make life far more miserable for us. 'I'm looking for some relatives of friends who asked me to pass on their regards.'

'That can easily be done,' he said smugly. He wrote a note to one of his clerks explaining my request.

I thanked him and left the building with some redress for my anger; I had a full list of addresses.

The first ten addresses were easy to find. Each recipient gave me at least ten zloty and all of them asked me to take back replies to Staszów. I promised to collect the new letters the following day. One by one, I delivered all my messages, until I had just one letter left.

At the last house, I knocked repeatedly but no-one came to the door. As it was after the major *akcja* in Staszów, there were many empty houses, so I checked and double-checked its address. I asked a woman standing in front of the house if the number was correct. She insisted that an old man definitely lived there. I knocked again, but there was still no answer. She then suggested I try the attic. I went inside and climbed the stairs. The loft was dark and I had to stoop not to hit my head on the beams. I searched the attic from one end to the other, then noticed a tiny flicker of light through a small crack in the wall. I approached cautiously, put my ear to the wall and listened – all was quiet. I checked the area around the crack and saw that there was a cleverly constructed door, with concealed hinges and no lock or handle.

I knocked and waited. I knocked once more. I called out, 'Is there anyone there?' I called out the name on the envelope. Still there was no reply. Then I tried to open the door. I pressed and pushed it hard and it moved a little bit. I kept pushing and could see that a hefty oak wardrobe barricaded the entrance. At last I pushed the door open wide enough for me to slip through.

A very old man dressed in a long white nightshirt was sitting bold upright in an iron bed. He was shaking. His eyes were wide with terror and his sparse grey hair stood on end as if electrified. On his bedside table was a single flickering candle – the only light source – which made him appear ghostly, almost translucent.

I expressed my regret for breaking in, still a little startled myself. I made sure that I was talking to the addressee and handed him the letter. Only then did the old man come out of his trance and start to breathe normally. After reading the letter he calmed down enough to ask if I was able to take a reply back. While he took a few minutes to compose his response, I asked him why he was in the attic. He explained that he had decided to remain in his hiding place until the war was over or until the Germans caught him. He handed me his letter, paid me to deliver it and wished me luck.

I headed back to my mother's quarters amazed by the resilience of Jews. I thought about how those people left behind after the *akcja* had adapted to their changed living conditions. Entrepreneurs had set up small tables along the roadside with personal or household items and other bric-a-brac for sale – at any price. One had a handwritten sign hanging in a window advertising hot meals. The prospect of taking my mother out to a 'restaurant' for dinner excited me.

She was still asleep when I returned. I sat quietly on the floor and watched her. I had a strong desire to cling to her, to hug her and to be her little boy again. I fixed my eyes on her face and forgot the whole world. I watched her for maybe five minutes or maybe an hour, until she slowly began to stir. Opening her eyes, she smiled. 'It was not a dream after all. I'm so happy to have you here. I dreamed about you, that I hugged you like when you were a little boy in Katowice.'

'I was watching you sleeping. Your face is so lovely. I wanted to hug you too, but didn't want to wake you.' With a flourish and a formal bow I then told her we were dining out.

We walked the short distance with my arm around her shoulder and entered a ground-floor single-room apartment. Surprisingly the room was well heated, probably by the kitchen stove, since the door between the room and the kitchen stood open. A tantalising aroma wafted through and I noticed my mother's face begin to relax. The room was clean, with four or five small tables seating two and a larger table for six. The chairs didn't match and crockery was a medley of styles, shapes and sizes, as was the cutlery. The meal was a hearty potato soup followed by cabbage and potatoes, sprinkled with some crackling. Most importantly the food was hot; it was my mother's first hot cooked meal in many weeks.

The maître d' was a Jewish man called Yankcl, very friendly and obliging, and my mother regained some of her poise and elegance. She encouraged me to tell her everything that had happened since she and Father waved goodbye to me some two months earlier.

I told her almost everything as gently as I could. I had to omit that I had been bashed, the fight with the guardsman and the drama during my escape. But I told her everything about Wacek. My mother was fascinated by this story, while I confessed that I didn't understand his motives.

'I think I know why he acted the way he did.' She paused. 'The whole thing sounds quite . . . spiritual. You are lucky and very special to have met someone like Wacek. He certainly is not who he appears to be.' My mother whispered quietly, almost to herself, 'Lamed Vav! I think Wacek could be one of them. One of the thirty-six righteous men.'

'But why would he come to help me? The whole European Jewry is in mortal danger. Why me?' I tried to reason with her.

She sighed and nodded. 'I don't know, there must be a reason that you or I do not understand. They work in mysterious ways. But it is your destiny. God preserves the world because of the thirty-six concealed saints, even if the rest of humanity has descended to barbarism.'

*

Back at my mother's room she introduced me to her new friend, Ester-Rivka. They slept on adjoining mattresses, and looked after each other. I decided to go out again and brought back a blanket and a small pillow which I gave to Mother. It was getting late and I had to look for a place to spend the night, but my mother insisted I share her mattress and sleep next to her. I accepted eagerly.

At Werk C, lying on my bunk, I had dreamed of being a little boy again, clinging to my mamma in her warm bed. And it had come true. Now I realised the true meaning of happiness: lying on a stranger's mattress in a dark attic huddled close to my beloved mother. I listened to her even breathing and fell into a blissful sleep. It felt like being back home, in Katowice in my previous life. For a little while life once again was good.

CHAPTER 22

THE RIDE BACK TO STASZÓW was much more difficult than getting to Ostrowiec. For several hours it snowed and the wind blew the snow into my eyes. It took almost three hours of hard pedalling to reach the outskirts of Staszów. I thought about Tusia and what a good friend she really was. I was quite anxious to see her and ensure she was all right. I wanted to share my joy at finding my mother and hoped that maybe together we could find news of her family too.

I went to her house first, but she was not there, so I headed over to the attic. Everyone there welcomed me, but they told me Tusia had left that morning and had not yet returned. All her belongings were still there. They asked how my journey was and if I had delivered their letters. I said that I had and had brought them many replies. I distributed the mail and there was a buzz of excitement as the letters were read. Once again, everyone insisted on paying me for acting as postman.

It became dark and there was still no sign of Tusia. She hadn't mentioned going anywhere, only that she would wait for my return. The money I gave her was not enough to do anything with, so where could she be? I grabbed something for dinner and waited another few hours. I did not believe that she would risk being on the street after curfew, and now the earliest she could return was morning.

I set out early next day to deliver the rest of the letters. Back at the attic there was still no sign of Tusia. Concerned and worried, I went to her house. The front door was open but inside I could not see anything different since I was there three days earlier. The secret door was still locked. I knocked and called her name but there was no response. Then something flashed through my mind – the bicycle hook on the ceiling. Oh God! I had to break down the door. I should not have left her alone; she had been emotional, and depressed. I looked for something to pick the lock, then tried to force the door with my body – it did not budge. I was still reluctant to damage the door in case Tusia came back.

I ran back to the attic and told the others my worst fears. They persuaded me to wait until midday and then four of us went to her house. One of them had a skeleton key and after several attempts we opened the secret door. It took a moment for our eyes to adjust to the darkness; my eyes went straight to the ceiling. I thanked God that the hook was bare. But where was she?

Unfortunately Tusia never returned and no-one was able explain her disappearance. She was eighteen years old and life for her should have been full of possibilities. No-one knew where she was murdered or where her grave was. No-one was left to mourn this wonderful, kind and loving girl.

*

Towards the end of 1942, billboards across the country announced the establishment of a so-called Judenstadt in four or five different Polish cities. Those Jews who were hiding in forests, in bunkers, in villages with Polish families, or anywhere else, were called to move to these designated cities and were granted a four-week amnesty to do so. They were allowed to take all their belongings and use any means of transportation. A peaceful new beginning was guaranteed. No-one believed it, but they went anyway, because they were desperate.

The nearest Judenstadt to Staszów and Ostrowiec was the city of Sandomierz, situated near the Wisła and San rivers, where some 300 Jews had remained after the main *akcja*. The empty houses in the former ghetto area were made available. Soon after the announcement around 100 people were transported from Ostrowiec to Sandomierz, though my mother's group remained in Ostrowiec.

I shuttled at first between Staszów and Ostrowiec, gaining more and more letter-writing clients. In Staszów I slept on Tusia's abandoned mattress while in Ostrowiec I slept next to my mother. But when people from Ostrowiec, and later from Staszów, began arriving in Sandomierz, I had to increase my area of operation and incorporate three towns, and I started to catch the train between Ostrowiec and Sandomierz. Even though the journey was dangerous, travelling in a heated compartment was far more comfortable and faster than riding my bike. I had to remove my armband and replace it every time I entered a ghetto or a Jewish *placówka*.

One morning I arrived at the station to find the stationmaster waving a flag and blowing his whistle to signal the train's departure. There was no time to purchase a ticket and I simply ran and jumped on the train as it began to pull out. I found an empty seat in a crowded compartment where the usual conversation about Jews was taking place. I fell into the conversation, as usual, ensuring my opinions and comments were among the loudest. After a while the conductor and three German rail police entered our compartment. The conductor was a short, overweight man with an enormous red bulbous nose that betrayed many years of drinking. His duty was to check the tickets while the rail police checked identity documents and any suspicious parcels on the train. Conversation came to an abrupt halt as the conductor asked us to produce our tickets. Most of the commuters silently showed their weekly or monthly cards.

My heart was thumping and my palms were sweating. It was my turn. I stood up and slowly searched my pockets one by one, pretending to become increasingly anxious. The conductor sighed and asked me to hurry up.

I patted my pockets again. 'My wallet is gone! Someone has stolen my wallet. My money, my documents, my ticket, all of it's gone!' I sat down holding my head in apparent disbelief.

He looked at me for a moment. 'This is your problem, not mine,' he said. 'As far as I'm concerned you must buy a new ticket and pay a fine of three zloty for boarding the train without a valid ticket.'

'We know this man,' someone called out to my great surprise. 'He always travels with us.'

The conductor insisted that it did not matter; I had to produce a valid ticket. I had no idea what to do next when something incredible happened.

The man sitting next to me took off his cap, placed a coin in it, and proceeded to pass it around the compartment. I sat there speechless. He looked at me for a moment with shining eyes and a knowing smile, nodding his head ever so slightly. I sensed something familiar about him, yet had never seen him before. Enough money was collected for my ticket and my fine. I had been saved by the kindness of anti-Semitic Poles.

Since my escape I had tried to make a point of blending into the environment I was in by adopting a dialect or speaking the language of the people around me. In this instance, dressing and behaving like the locals made them believe that they had seen me on the train before. I had only made the journey a few times then, so there was no way that they should have recognised me as fellow traveller.

Half an hour later I arrived safely in Sandomierz and walked into the new ghetto. Abandoned and dilapidated houses that had previously been looted, ransacked and vandalised by the local Polish population were now awaiting their new tenants. I finished delivering my letters and collected new mail without any problems and was soon back on a train to Ostrowiec.

There was only one man sitting in the compartment. He recognised me from the morning's event and I recognised him: he was the one who took up the collection. 'I hope you have a ticket this time,' he said, extending his hand.

'I sure have,' I said shaking his hand. 'Thank you so much for this morning. I'm Zygmunt.' I used the Polish version of my name.

'My name is Franciszek but everybody calls me Franek.' He offered me a cigarette and winked.

'I'm so angry about losing my documents,' I went on, spinning the lie, 'but I'm sure my boss will help me as he's very smart and well connected.'

We smoked and started chatting: about politics, the war, the Jews and the partisans. Franek claimed that the SS had established a special unit whose mission was to identify Polish children with certain Aryan racial characteristics between the ages of five and eight. They were to be taken from their families, tested to match certain criteria and then sent for adoption to German families. Indeed, much later I heard rumours that more than 50,000 Polish children had been kidnapped, or even as many as 200,000. A thousand were sent to Germany for adoption while the rest were sent to Auschwitz.

I sighed sympathetically and declared that the Germans were destroying our nation and that Poland should wake up and do something. I also said that the *Jedrusie* (the Polish Resistance) in this region was not doing enough. Franek claimed that young people were now assembling into organised groups ready to fight.

'That's great news! But does the general population support this movement? Because if it doesn't there's no chance of success.' The idea had me genuinely excited.

'So far the urban population is very supportive,' Franek said enthusiastically, 'but the peasants less so. The armies have enough support from the exiled Polish government, though we need more support in infrastructure, provisions, shelter, intelligence and so on.'

'*We?*' I asked, taken aback at his admission. 'You don't know anything about me at all and you said *we* – that's dangerous and irresponsible.'

'You might be right,' he smiled. 'Nevertheless, I have a good nose for people, and besides, we must take certain calculated risks otherwise we wouldn't be able to recruit volunteers. I feel that you're an honest Pole and a good patriot. You don't look like a German, a Volksdeutsche or a collaborator to me.'

'You're right, I'm not. In fact I'm willing to join you, but I need some time.'

Franek said he understood and gave me his address in Zawichost. His codename was 'Szary' (grey) and his group was called Bataliony Chłopskie (rural battalions). We arranged to meet again later that week.

Outside the train window many Jewish people in horse carts headed towards Sandomierz. There were even more on foot. The convoy, which was guarded by the Polish police, struggled with the below-zero temperature, snow and strong winds that made the journey even more gruelling. I had a sick feeling that these people might have set out from Ostrowiec and hoped that my mother was not among them.

As soon as the train pulled into the station, I rushed to my mother's quarters and found her there, safe. It was such a relief. I told her what had happened to me that day.

'It doesn't surprise me at all,' she said. 'You will always meet extraordinary people who will help and amaze you. I think you should join the underground army because it'll offer you the best chance of survival. And, as I told you back in Staszów before you left for Skarżysko-Kamienna, you *will* survive.'

'I don't know yet,' I demurred. 'I'll decide after my next meeting with Franek. But if I do I've already got my alias. It will be Borgi.' When I had attended youth camps I had sometimes called myself *Gibor*, the Hebrew word for hero, so my new codename was waiting for me.

*

Early in the morning, I was once again off to Staszów. It was snowing heavily and I had to pedal very hard to move and stay balanced. I thought about my mother, someone who never hurt anyone and was always ready to help people. I recalled a story my aunt told me when I was little. She said that my mother had a childhood friend who could not marry because her parents were poor and she did not have a dowry. My mother somehow donated a large amount of her own money anonymously, enough for a wedding and a dowry. Her friend never found out who her generous benefactor was. My mother had also helped the first refugees from Germany. She took in several of them under her own roof and provided for them, not to mention working for numerous charitable organisations. So why did she have to suffer so much and endure such stringent conditions? What had she done to deserve such deprivation, humiliation and hardship, destitution and suffering beyond human capacity?

Who can help us? I thought. Where can we go for advice? We have absolutely no rights. We have lost our identity as human beings. Has the whole world gone mad? Does no one see what is happening to us? Where can we protest about this cruelty? About this injustice, this expulsion from the human race, why is it happening to us?

Why? I asked myself, pedalling faster. Where in this hell was justice? There had to be a reason for everything, yet I could not understand why all this misery was happening to us.

Why? I asked, pushing myself into a frenzy. Why are innocent people being killed? Who is the beneficiary of all this? Killing for profit? Killing to rob the victims of their property? An animal kills for food, humans kill from fear, from hate, and in pathological cases, for pleasure. What motivates the mass perpetrators to mass killing? And what happened to Poland? A large country with a population of 35 million and a strong army defeated – and in a matter of weeks? Was it a betrayal at the highest level, motivated by greed?

There were rumours shortly before the war that Poland's foreign minister, Józef Beck, was a German spy. Unfortunately, the Polish leader Marshal Józef Piłsudski had died in 1935, leaving behind a bunch of incompetent people who were unable to prevent this catastrophe. He certainly would not have allowed this to happen.

Piłsudski had been a very popular leader, loved by all, able to unite the whole nation. I recalled a story my mother told me when my parents met him in March of 1931, while holidaying with friends on the isle of Madeira. The Marshal had overheard them speaking Polish in one of the elegant salons of the hotel, and had dispatched his adjutant to invite them to join his table. I remember how impressed my father was with Piłsudski's views on world matters and his plans for Poland's economic development. After their return home, my parents received a beautifully handwritten letter from Piłsudski, thanking them for giving him the pleasure of their company. My mother was fond of this letter, showing it to family and friends.

CHAPTER 23

THE ATTIC IN STASZÓW was abandoned. I headed to a *placówka* to find out where everyone had gone. I learned that two days earlier Polish police officers had ordered everyone to vacate as the city authorities had seized the house. Some of the occupants had gone to Sandomierz and the rest did not know what to do. It was the same for the Jews everywhere – no-one knew where to turn or what decision to make.

I decided not to stay overnight and returned to Ostrowiec. The next morning I caught the train to Sandomierz and saw a couple of men from the Staszów attic. I asked them lots of questions as I was considering moving to this Judenstadt with my mother. Perhaps the conditions would be more comfortable if we moved quickly – it seemed obvious that everyone would be rounded up and forced to move here eventually. I asked them to reserve a room for my mother and me and they promised they would.

I still had some letters to deliver and at one address I saw a girl who looked familiar. I asked her where she was from.

'My name's Marysia and I'm from Będzin, now renamed Bendsburg,' she told me. 'I came here to find out what happened to our relatives. We've been worried.'

Marysia went on to tell me she could travel freely because she had excellent fake ID. She'd since learned that her relatives had been deported a few weeks earlier and was planning on returning home. I told her I was keen to go to Będzin as I had many family members there, though I wasn't sure if they were still alive.

'Your family will still be safe because there haven't been any *akcje* there yet,' she said. 'I know someone in the border town of Wolbrom who, for a fee, will guide us across the border to reach Olkusz on the other side.'

'I'll have to think about it,' I said, half excited and half scared. 'Can I let you know in a day or two?'

'I can wait. Let's stay in touch,' Marysia said.

I returned to Ostrowiec just before the curfew. Mother and I talked about escaping to Będzin and maybe reaching Olkusz, where she believed her parents were. Surprisingly, she then tried to convince me that I should go without her, that she was too weak for such a hazardous journey. For her, escaping and running at night through unfamiliar territory while being hunted by Germans was inconceivable. She had deluded herself that somehow she would be reunited with my father and that, once again, he would make all the decisions for her. Her conviction in this was unshakeable.

'It is out of the question,' I argued. 'I cannot and will not leave you behind. Either I stay with you or you must come with us.' How could I abandon my mother and leave her to face her fate alone?

The more I begged and tried to reason with her, the more unwavering she became. 'Under no circumstances must you stay here with me. You must escape and find a way to save yourself. If your father were here now he would back me up on this. Remember, whatever you decide to do and wherever you go, you will survive. If you choose to go to our relatives or join the partisans, it's up to you. I would only be a hindrance to you. It's better for me to join your father. I cannot go with you.'

I felt torn between the need to protect my mother and my impotence to do so. How far could I go to shield her? We were condemned to die and she wanted me to live. My mother needed to feel that she did her utmost to save me.

*

Early the next day I left for Staszów. I was in the ghetto delivering letters when two trucks, one filled with gendarmes and the other with SS-men, drove into town. The Germans spread out surrounding the ghetto. A menacing growl, amplified through loudspeakers, ordered all Jews not belonging to any work commando to collect their belongings and assemble in the little square opposite Ben-Zion Ryzenberg's restaurant.

I was trapped, but I understood that when the Germans ordered people to take their belongings with them, they would likely be transferred to some place nearby – the Judenstadt in Sandomierz perhaps. I was somewhat relieved, because when the German exterminators rounded up their prey they usually ordered them to leave behind their belongings. At that stage they did not have to pretend any more.

People started arriving in the square within minutes. I lined up with my pushbike and backpack. A uniformed German approached me and, without bothering to say a word, took the bike and loaded it onto his truck. I did not dare object.

Ben-Zion Ryzenberg was a big, athletic man, and he wore a policjant cap. He came out of his restaurant and ordered Jews to line up in rows of three. One of the guarding Germans noticed that he wasn't wearing his armband and began to scream at him.

'Oh, I forgot it on the table when I changed my jacket, sir,' Ben-Zion said hurriedly. 'I'll get it right away, sir.' He turned to go back into his restaurant for the armband. The German nodded to a nearby gendarme who, in a split second, took his Luger out of its holster and shot Ben-Zion from behind. He collapsed face down but was dead before he hit the ground. Blood gushed from

185

his shattered skull and fragments of brain lay on the white snow. A large red circle appeared around his head.

Within half an hour about 300 people stood huddled together. A new order was given for us to line up in rows of three and start marching. We marched through the narrow streets to the main square, where a line of about twenty horse carts was waiting. Ten to twelve people were assigned to each cart; women, children and the elderly were allowed to climb up first and the rest had to walk. Twenty Polish police officers escorted us to Sandomierz. The journey was long and the weather painfully cold. After an hour, the police officers nominated people to climb down from the carts so that they themselves could board. A few young people escaped the convoy as we passed through a dense forest. The policemen, who were cold, tired and significantly outnumbered, began to shoot in the direction of the escapees but without really aiming.

Three children and five elderly people did not survive the eight-hour journey. They probably fell asleep and, suffering from hypothermia, froze to death. Once we had arrived the policjanten showed us to our quarters and disposed of the dead bodies. Only now did I realise how tough it must have been for my father and the 5000 people who marched the forty-five kilometres from Staszów to Szczucin.

Relieved that I had reserved accommodation for my mother and myself, I rushed straight to the room and dropped onto my bed in complete exhaustion. Marysia, who was there, offered me a much-needed hot drink. I told her that I had decided to go to Będzin with her, though I fell asleep before I finished my sentence. Marysia woke me up the next morning and we started to plan the first leg of our journey, to Wolbrom. We would leave in two days' time.

The four-week amnesty was still in effect, and I could travel freely, so I caught the train to Ostrowiec to check on my mother and found her in her quarters. 'I heard people saying that we are all going to be sent to Sandomierz soon,' she told me.

'I'll take you there as soon as possible. I'll give you the details of the people who are keeping a room for us. But let's have something to eat first.'

We went to Yankel's eatery and he told us he was moving to Sandomierz the next day. He had decided to hire a horse cart and take all his stuff with him. During our dinner, we discussed the matter and decided that we too would move to Sandomierz the following day. I asked Yankel if he could hire a horse cart for us as well, and he promised to help.

When we returned to Mother's quarters we were greeted by a very loud and lively conversation. Everyone was talking at the same time and no-one was listening. Something important must have happened. My mother's friend explained that half an hour ago the manager of their workshop arrived and announced that the workshop had been closed down and the whole group would be transferred to Sandomierz the next day. Everyone had to be ready with their belongings by eight o'clock in the morning.

I was quite pleased, as we were now going to travel compliments of the German Reich. I helped my mother pack her few remaining belongings and within minutes we were ready to leave. I went out into the street in search of bread and a packet of sugar lumps but could not find any. I continued desperately searching for at least another hour and had nearly given up when a woman approached me in the street, wanting to know what I was looking for. When I told her, she said that she herself did not have any bread or sugar but knew where I could get some. I rushed to this place and finally managed to buy a packet at an extremely inflated price.

By the time I got back my mother was already quite anxious about my safety. I tried to apologise for being away for so long, and she said she wished to hold me for as long as possible.

I promised her that I would not leave her again that evening, not even for a moment. We sat down close together, clinging to each other. She had a smile on her face and tears were running down her cheeks. She told me that she was elated, feeling such an absolute happiness as never before. She remembered when I was a little boy, how she used to hold me on her lap and tell me stories, and how she sang songs to me about a little orphan whose only wish was that his dead parents would appear to him in his dreams.

I was her one last remaining precious possession. My heart was tearing, breaking into millions of tiny pieces, pieces that could never be joined together and mend. I trembled from my core and my throat closed up as I tried desperately to hold back my tears, but they welled up, blurring my vision till I could no longer see. Exhausted and still embracing, we fell asleep.

Next morning we were ready to go. My mother did not have much luggage apart from what she was wearing; only a blanket and pillow I had bought for her not long ago. She squeezed the pillow into her bag and folded the blanket over her arm to cover herself during the journey. I carried her mattress, believing it could come handy, if not in Sandomierz, then on the journey as a seat on the horse cart.

We arrived in Sandomierz early in the afternoon and moved at once into the accommodation I had reserved. I think my mother liked the room or maybe she just pretended to like it, as she actually seemed oblivious, almost in a trance. Nothing mattered to her now. She was unaware of her surroundings, as if she had given up all hope.

I introduced her to Marysia, who explained why she was in Sandomierz. I then told my mother that Marysia and I were planning to leave for Będzin the following day. I could see pain and sadness on her face but she said that she would be very happy when we arrived safely in Będzin.

I asked my mother to come with me to our room where we could talk privately. I promised that I would somehow find a way to notify her as soon as I had arrived in Będzin, even if I had to hire a special messenger. I also promised that if anything went wrong or I was unable to settle there, I would return to her.

I told her that if an *akcja* took place while I was away, she should put on as many layers of clothing as possible and wear my trousers instead of her skirt, as well as her overcoat. Suddenly I vaguely recalled a time, in another world, when I had watched my mother supervise our housekeeper as she was packing my mother's trunks before she left on a journey. Mother was taking with her the most beautiful dresses, blouses, skirts and underwear, as well as shoes, stockings, jewellery and toiletries, handbags, gloves and a special box for her hats . . .

I told her to pack all her pockets with slices of bread and lumps of sugar, because the journey could take two or even three days. My mother listened intently, saying that she was really looking forward to being 'sent to the east' – she had a feeling that she would be sent to where my father was waiting. For her the idea that my father had been murdered with 5000 other Jews from Staszów was preposterous. And what if she were right? Maybe 5000 Jews were transported to Bełżec and maybe none had escaped the inevitable death that awaited them there, but how could such a thing have happened to my father? My hero? It was much easier to believe the unbelievable.

The next morning Yankel told me that he and his wife would be ready to open for business in Sandomierz that very evening. I was full of admiration for this man's initiative, optimism and resourcefulness. Later that morning Mother and I ended up at the new eatery and I asked Yankel if we might have some lunch. He was happy to help and I made my mother promise me that she would come to Yankel's every day to have at least one hot meal.

Late that afternoon I hugged and kissed my mother goodbye. I begged her to take good care of herself, to eat well and to be positive and stay optimistic. I had no idea how long I would be gone other than indefinitely. I left her enough money to last for a while and promised to bring her more on my return.

*

On a mid December weekday in 1942 Marysia and I set out from our quarters. We had discussed precautions for the journey and decided that we had to keep visual contact at all times while walking separately. We would talk to each other only when no-one was present, otherwise we would behave as strangers. If one of us was stopped, the other must not be involved. And if we were forced to separate, we would make our way alone and meet in Będzin at Marysia's address, which I had memorised.

We arrived in Wolbrom shortly after 7 pm. It was already dark and the streets were blanketed by freshly fallen snow. People in the streets were in a holiday mood, carrying bags and parcels full of Christmas shopping. For them, life went on as if nothing had changed. Generally speaking, the Polish population benefited after the Jews were sent to the death camps. Most 'legally' obtained possessions were sold to the Poles for a notional sum but the greater part was 'illegally obtained' or looted, and looting was common practice for both Germans and the Poles.

Within minutes Marysia and I had reached the guide's house. I waited outside and soon she called me in. A man in his thirties with a trustworthy face greeted me in the entrance hall and led us upstairs to a small dark room with a simple iron bed, a large flowerpot and a small window. He told us we had to spend the night here and early in the morning he would take us over the border to the German Reich. He forbade us to turn on the light and then locked us in; the window was also locked and had a grille across it.

We were trapped in this attic room at the mercy of this stranger. We sat on the bed and noticed the stars shining in the dark sky. I was amazed how much light these few stars generated on a frosty winter's night. There was no chamber pot or bowl so I used the flowerpot; Marysia wet her pants. She was petrified that the guide would be angry with her and tried to mop the floor with her wet undies, wringing them out in the flowerpot. We sat on the bed and talked until finally, still dressed, we fell asleep.

The guide woke us up early, asking for his payment. We left the house half an hour later. We walked through almost empty streets to the outskirts of town, passing through fields and into a dense pine forest. In the forest a group of about twenty young people – mostly teenagers but also children – waited for us, carrying bags and backpacks full of food. These were smugglers who moved a variety of foods, like dairy and meat products, from the Polish-occupied territories into the German Reich. Our guide also carried a fully laden backpack. They knew exactly where to cross the border and told us the whole operation should take no longer than forty minutes. We started walking.

We were about halfway there when suddenly a dozen German border police rose in a half-circle formation from behind shrubs and bushes, their rifles aimed at us, and shouted, '*Halt! Stehen bleiben!*'

All of us spread out, running as fast as we could. Shots were fired from all directions and bullets flew around me. I ran for about three kilometres, not daring to look over my shoulder or decrease my speed. Only when I was away from the forest and standing in an open field did I stop for a moment. I still heard shots.

I returned to the train station as fast as I could. It was the main building in the village, and easy to find. I purchased a ticket and boarded the next train to Sandomierz. I kept an eye out for Marysia but she was nowhere to be seen.

On the train the main topic of conversation was still the Jews. This time, however, I did not participate but only listened in disbelief. The passengers discussed how Poles were now allowed to 'inherit' the possessions of their exterminated Jewish neighbours. One traveller described how his relative, who had moved into the former home of a wealthy Jewish family, had found a large quantity of jewellery, money and gold hidden under the floor. Another passenger spoke of a neighbour who had found great riches after ransacking a Jewish house. Similar incidents occurred in every Polish town, township and village from which Jews had been deported. A completely new 'industry' had materialised, specialising in seeking hidden treasures and resulting in the demolition of hundreds of houses, perhaps thousands.

After three hours dozing on the train, I was back in Sandomierz hugging and kissing my mother. She had still been upset about our separation twenty-four hours earlier when I arrived but now had a dazzling smile on her face, the likes of which I had not seen for a long time. I rejoiced in seeing my mother again and hugged her a little bit too strongly. 'Let us go to Yankel's and have a nice lunch.'

Yankel's premises were cosy and warm. The windowpanes were covered with frost that formed stunning floral patterns. I explained to my mother what had happened while we ate.

'At least you tried,' my mother finally said. 'Now that Będzin is out of the question, it's time you joined the partisans.'

'Yes. I'll go to Zawichost tomorrow to meet Franek. If I join them, I'll be able to keep an eye on you as they're not too far from Sandomierz.'

We finished our lunch in silence and went for a stroll in the streets. More and more people had arrived in the town and the houses were filling up. Rumours were circulating that the Red Army was having great success on the front, south of Stalingrad, so maybe, just maybe, a miracle would happen and we would be saved.

While I had been away, two women from Staszów, Mrs Gitl-Leah and her daughter Hela, had moved into the third room in our apartment, and now I heard their story. They had been hiding with a Polish peasant family who had promised to give them shelter and food for an agreed sum. In addition the women worked on the Polish family's farm. The farmer said he had heard rumours that the Germans would be searching for Jews that night and offered to take them to his sister's farm in another village for an evening or two. The women thanked him and the peasant brought them directly to Sandomierz, where he ordered them to get out of the cart right in front of the ghetto. Foolishly they had left their money and belongings at the peasant's house.

'Ladies, if you are both available, perhaps the four of us can dine together?' I said.

I took the women with us back to Yankel's. Later I asked them if they would look after my mother while I was away.

CHAPTER 24

ZAWICHOST IS A SMALL TOWN by the Wisła River, about fifteen kilometres from Sandomierz. I knocked on the door of a small locksmith's workshop. A tall man unlocked the door and I told him that I had come to see Szary.

'Oh, Szary,' he repeated. 'I'll see if he's here.'

Suddenly the door behind opened and Franek burst into the workshop. 'Welcome, my friend, I'm glad to see you,' he said with an outstretched hand. 'I wasn't expecting you today, but it's good that you came. Come in, I have a small office here where we can talk.'

Franek showed me to a chair. We talked about the undercover resistance movement in Poland and about the various groups operating in this area. He told me that his group was well established and was getting support from the local country people.

'We have enough food and there are no problems with emergency accommodation and safe houses. Are you ready to join us?'

'Basically, yes, but I still need a bit more time to get my documents replaced.'

'Oh papers! Don't worry about them. We can organise them in a few days. Just give us two photographs and you can have any documents you like.'

'All right then, but I've already applied for replacements,' I lied.

'That's fine too,' said Franek. 'In our line of work it's good to have spare papers. It can be useful.' He winked at me. 'So, just give me your name and your alias and we're in business.'

'My name is Kotlicki, Zygmunt Kotlicki,' I said using my maternal grandmother's maiden name. 'And my pseudonym is Borgi.'

'That's an unusual name. Has it any meaning?'

'My grandfather used to go hunting and his dog's name was Borgi. His shotgun was confiscated, but he kept his dog – a very good and faithful dog.' I made up the story as I went along.

'Good choice. I hope you'll follow his example.'

'I'll do my best. I'm not a hero but I have a few bones to pick with the Germans.'

'To start you won't have any field duties. I'll give you a Luger and you'll be in charge of receiving and distributing arms and ammunition to our soldiers. I'll show you the procedure and the safety system.'

'What's your military rank?' I asked. 'How shall I address you?'

'That's not important now. I shall call you Borgi and you will call me Szary. I've a feeling that we'll work well together.'

Szary bent down and lifted one of the floorboards, which released and opened a hatch, revealing a hidden staircase. The hatch had no handles or hinges. He climbed down the stairs, reappearing seconds later brandishing a handgun with one spare magazine.

'This will be yours. I'll give it to you next time, when you take over this post. Do you know how to use it?'

'Yes, I do,' I said proudly, having won an award for a perfect score in shooting at the Hanoar Hatzioni summer camp.

'In that case, I can only give you one piece of advice. If you have to shoot, then you must shoot to kill. Remember that the last bullet is for you. Never let yourself be taken alive. I shall see you here on Friday 8 January. In the meantime have a Merry Christmas and a Happy New Year.'

I returned to Mother and told her that I was able to stay with her for almost two weeks. She was pleased and said that she was going to take care of me. She asked me if I could organise a bar of soap, soda or any other laundry detergent.

'Make me a shopping list and I'll see what I can find,' I said.

I asked a number of people if they could help but everyone looked at me as if I was from the moon. I headed back to the house when someone stopped me. 'Hey, are you the crazy man looking for soap?'

'Yes I am,' I answered, hopeful.

'You know that soap practically disappeared the day the war broke out.'

'Yes, I'm aware of that.'

'I have some,' he offered. 'It's not much and it's home-made.'

'That doesn't matter. How much do you want for it?'

'I don't know. I have no use for it myself so I'll give it to you for free. I wish to make a *mitzvah* as I may need it.' A mitzvah is a good deed carried out for another without reward; it's written up in the book of life for your final judgement.

'No, I can't take it without paying. I'll give you some money and you may give it to a beggar and we'll both be satisfied. But how did you know that I was looking for soap?'

'I just bumped into my friend and he was laughing uncontrollably. I asked him what was so funny. He told me that a crazy youth was here looking to buy soap. He thought you must be insane and pointed you out to me.'

'Maybe I am insane,' I replied. I went with him and we exchanged his soap for my five zloty.

I returned to our room and held out the piece of soap triumphantly. 'Now you can take a bath!' The last time my mother had a proper bath would have been when we left Kraków three years earlier.

'I have no intention of taking a bath,' my mother said. 'I can't see a way to heat the water and there's only a small washbowl. All I want is to launder your shirts, underwear, handkerchiefs and socks.'

'That's a great idea, but the water's freezing. It's below zero outside and not much warmer here. I'll do it myself and you can watch me.' I didn't want my mother's hands to freeze in the cold water. I started to strip layers of clothing from myself, keeping aside the top layers – the least dirty – in order to put them back on, so as not to freeze to death.

My mother found some string, stretched it across the room and hung the fresh laundry up to dry.

Over the next fortnight more and more people moved into the ghetto, causing overcrowding. The policjanten squeezed up to a dozen people into one small room; I bribed one policeman, who let us get away with only six people in our room. He said that they had expected 3000 people in the ghetto but already there were more than 4000.

When the Germans became aware of this they advertised for volunteers to do some work, promising payment of a loaf of bread. Since everyone was hungry it was a tempting proposition and about 500 Jews lined up. The Germans selected only fifty lucky volunteers and ordered the policjanten to choose fifty more for the next day, and so on for a week or more. None of those selected ever returned, but people kept on volunteering. We were like sleepwalkers, stumbling on, not seeing, not wanting to understand. The volunteers were taken by trucks to a nearby forest, shot and disposed of in a mass grave. The Germans had never expected so many Jews to have been overlooked by the *ackje*.

*

January brought snow and temperatures ten below zero. After a tearful goodbye with my mother I left for Zawichost – for the day or longer, I didn't know – on 8 January 1943.

Szary was waiting for me. We went down to the basement. I stared at the rows of shelves and wooden crates full of ammunition for British Sten guns, rifles and pistols. There were crates full of hand grenades, sticks of dynamite, explosives, detonators and rolls of wire. There were handguns and rifles and three heavy machine guns with ammunition belts.

Szary picked up a file listing all the stock, which we then checked and counted. He showed me the procedure of receiving and distributing the goods. We both signed the document and went back up to the workshop.

Szary called to the locksmith then turned to me. 'Now I will swear you in as a full member of the Bataliony Chłopskie. Please come forward. Salute and repeat after me.' I did as he asked.

'In the name of the Father, the Son and the Holy Ghost, the Mother of God and the Queen of Poland, I, Zygmunt Kotlicki, pseudonym Borgi, solemnly swear that I will obey all orders given to me. I will defend my country and the Polish people to the best of my ability and, if necessary, I will give my life for my homeland. So help me God.'

Both men hugged and kissed me. 'Now you are an official member of the Bataliony Chłopskie. Long live Poland!' Szary cried. He then handed me a Beretta pistol instead of the Luger. 'This is more suitable because it's smaller and lighter. You'll work independently, but from time to time someone will come here to help you.'

Szary introduced me to the middle-aged locksmith who owned the workshop. The man was tall and athletic with a bushy moustache. He assured me that he would not interfere with my job and would run his business as usual. I was then shown my sleeping area and a spot where I could even cook a meal.

'I wish you luck and I'll see you again on Monday,' Szary said.

I chatted with the owner of the shop for a while, but he barely responded. He turned his attention back to his workbench and I went down to the basement. I wanted to familiarise myself with how the goods were shelved.

The cellar itself was more of a depot than a basement. It was a bunker with many branches leading deep underground. My knowledge of firearms, acquired while serving with the cadets at school, was limited to handguns, rifles and hand grenades. I was amazed by the huge quantity of mortars, heavy machine guns, landmines, explosives and ammunition. In fact, some of the wooden crates looked familiar. I examined the rough knotted rope handles on either side of the crates and checked my palms for the burning blisters that were no longer there. The memory of loading the wagons with crates of ammunition at Skarżysko-Kamienna Werk C camp for thirty-odd hours made me smile. These meticulously produced bullets wrapped in special greased paper and neatly stacked into wooden crates were now in the hands of the enemy – the partisans – who were waiting to use them against the Germans. Now I realised that the German army was not invincible. The devoted young people who comprised the underground army could seriously harm the enemy. It was a thrilling feeling, especially given that just weeks earlier I was incarcerated in a labour camp with little chance of survival.

The building had no running water and the lavatory was in the backyard. A small iron stove with a kettle of boiling water on top was the only cooking and heating facility. The single bed had a reasonable mattress, a pillow and two good woollen blankets. All together it was much better than the conditions in Sandomierz, Ostrowiec or Staszów. I decided to spend the night here.

I came up to the workshop and told the locksmith that I was going out to the village. 'While I'm out is there anything I can get you?'

'Yes, thank you,' he said. 'I need a packet of cigarettes and a flint stone for my lighter.'

Zawichost was a very small village with only a few hundred residents. There was only one main road and a small square with a church and a well in the centre. In the poorly stocked general store the shelves were almost bare. I bought a few things and was back at the workshop in a matter of minutes.

I gave the locksmith his cigarettes and flint stones and refused to take his money. He insisted that I have some of his wife's Christmas cake and gave me a large slice. We chatted some more. Soon after, the locksmith left for the day. He gave me the keys in case I wanted to go out and said that he would be back at seven in the morning. I decided to stay indoors. I wanted to keep the cake for my mother so I ate some dry biscuits. Then I lay down on my bed to rest.

Suddenly I was back in time, at my paternal grandparents' place in Będzin with my family during Passover in April 1939. Many of my aunts and uncles and more than a dozen cousins filled the rambling two-storey house that had lots of rooms, alcoves and hallways. The lush garden surrounding the house was just awaking from its winter sleep. Lilac had begun to bloom and the four bushes of white and violet flowers were bursting with perfume.

My grandmother, Rosa Schneier, had beautiful blue-grey eyes, which my father inherited. A strong and powerful woman, she ran her household of nine children with an iron fist and her grandchildren were extremely scared of her. Attached to the belt of her apron hung a huge fascicle of keys of all shapes and sizes.

As little children we used to play hide-and-seek, and once,

while hiding in her wardrobe, I discovered her spare wig resting on a head-shaped wooden stand. Ever since that day I referred to her as the grandmother who had two heads, one on her neck and the other in her wardrobe. (As a religious person, she always wore a *sheitel* to conceal her hair, as was expected of a married Jewish woman.)

Children's shrieks and laughter were heard everywhere. The little ones played games all over the house and skipped rope outside in the garden. The older cousins played chess and backgammon. Bolek, Halinka, Paula and I had trivial yet passionate conversations as only teenagers can.

This wonderful period seemed so distant and surreal, as if a different lifetime in a different dimension. Was there really a time when we all lived an untroubled life? Was there actually a childhood where evil and fear were only a part of a bad dream or a bedtime story that was soothed away by a mother's embrace or the protective promise of a heroic father?

I woke up feeling cold and hungry; the fire was almost out. I jumped up and put a couple of logs in the stove, hoping that it would still rekindle. I ate the remaining biscuits for dinner, checked the level of kerosene in the lamps and looked for something to read. I had almost no opportunity to read any more. I found a few newspapers; the latest edition was three days old, and contained a few reports about the executions of Poles for having aided Jews, as well as information about the Katyn massacre of April 1940, in which the Soviets had killed more than 20,000 Polish prisoners of war. When the bodies were discovered, the Germans immediately accused the Soviets, who were in fact responsible, but it took many years for the truth to come out.

When a noise at the workshop woke me up, I realised that I had fallen asleep again, the paper still in my hands. I heard the locksmith opening the shutters. I got ready and went up to greet him. He had brought me two large slices of freshly home-baked bread with pork lard and crackling. 'This is from my wife, especially for you.'

I thanked him and asked if they had any children.

'Unfortunately not,' he said with a sad voice. 'God is punishing us, but our priest insists that we must keep praying. He tells us to light a candle every Sunday. My wife also drinks a special herbal tea, mixed by an old woman who collects herbs in the forest and is well known for her healing powers. She saw the Virgin Mary in her dreams and she asked her to help others.'

It was not unusual for the villagers to believe in such things – they believed that sky-blue paint on their houses would repel evil spirits and that a four-leafed clover, or a horseshoe attached to a house's threshold, would bring luck. Country Poles were both devoutly religious and deeply superstitious.

That day I decided to return to my mother as I wasn't really needed yet. Later that afternoon, I packed my belongings and tucked my gun into the right outer pocket of my overcoat. 'I'll be back on Monday morning, as arranged with Szary,' I said. 'I'll pray for you at tomorrow's mass. I wish you a holy and restful Sunday.'

'God be with you. See you on Monday,' he said.

CHAPTER 25

THE GUN IN MY POCKET gave me a sense of freedom. I felt in control of my own destiny in a way I hadn't since the war began. The knowledge that they would not get me alive and that I had the choice of killing myself made me feel strong. I could not wait to tell Mother that I had been accepted by the partisans and that I had a gun with a spare magazine.

However, my excitement was short lived. An hour later, I was with my mother. We hugged each other and I noticed that she was in a very bad state. She had black circles under her swollen red eyes.

'What's wrong? What happened to you?' I asked. She embraced me but could not stop crying. I asked my question repeatedly but she was sobbing uncontrollably and could not utter a word. I held her tightly, stroked her head and tried to calm her down. We moved towards her bed and I sat down, still holding her tightly. Trembling and shaking, she buried her face in my chest. Finally, still sobbing, she began to compose herself.

'After you left I felt empty and sad. I was so upset, not knowing if and when I would see you again, so I decided to lie down and rest a little. I must have fallen asleep because I awoke to arguing and shouting. Do you remember Mrs Gitl-Leah's daughter, Hela? You know, the one who was betrayed by the Polish peasant?'

I nodded.

'Well, she was caught in an argument with a man who tried to occupy your bed. I got up and explained to the stranger that this bed belonged to my son. He jumped up and started screaming at me in Yiddish. "If you speak Polish, you don't belong here. Go back to your Polaks." I repeated that it was my son's bed, and I insisted that he take his bundles and please go somewhere else. Instead he abused me and called me names in the most insulting and offensive manner, things I am not able to repeat. I forced my way to your bed and tried to sit on it, to claim it, but the man attacked me with both fists. Only then did the other occupants of our flat come between us, and stop him from hitting me further. Never in my whole life have I been exposed to such brutality. He could have killed me. Look at the bruises on my arms, my shoulders and my chest.'

My mother carefully lifted her sleeves to show me her bruises and my stomach heaved in waves of nausea. She had been severely beaten. Never in her whole life had anyone lifted a finger towards her, let alone hit her. Hitting out at a defenceless woman was beyond my comprehension.

'Where is this brute, where is he now?'

I was raging. One of the most agonising things for a child is to see a parent being abused and not being able to protect or avenge them.

Mrs Gitl-Leah answered. 'He spent the night sleeping in your bed and then in the morning he took his belongings and disappeared. Thank God.'

I turned to my mother and asked her forgiveness. 'It was entirely my fault. I should not have left you alone. I thought you were safe with the two women.'

'I was more hurt by his insults. But what was worse was that the incident woke me from another nightmare of a mass killing. This time it was more vivid than ever. But now that you are here with me, everything will be all right,' my mother said with a look that implied that she really believed it.

Now that she had begun to calm down, I insisted on putting cold compresses on her bruises to ease her pain. Then I told her in detail about my visit to Zawichost and that I was now in possession of a pistol. She insisted that I show her the gun, which I very discreetly did.

'I am very happy and proud of you,' she said. 'You are courageous and brave. You managed to escape from Skarżysko-Kamienna Werk C. You undertook an extremely dangerous job, risking your life, handling and delivering mail, and you joined the Polish underground army. You are resolute, bright and smart, so I *know* that you will survive and avenge us all. I really believe that one of the Lamed Vav will guard you.'

I hugged and kissed her. 'You're exaggerating, I'm not a hero and not courageous at all. In fact, I'm scared most of the time. I'm just trying to survive and help you as much as I can. I promise you that I'll do my very best to fulfil your wishes. We will both survive and shall find Daddy. Our life will go back to normal once this war is over. Halinka and Don will return home and we'll be happy again. Who knows, maybe you're already a grandmother. We only have each other here and you must survive this with me, because I need you and no one can replace you. I love you with all my heart.'

For a fleeting moment, my words sounded so reassuring – maybe there really was a future to believe in and to hold on to.

I approached one of the women, asking her to prepare some tea for us all, and invited them to join us for an exceptional feast. I unpacked the cake given to me by the locksmith and laid it out on my mother's bed. The aroma of the home-baked cake transported us back to a time when afternoon tea was served in the drawing room. Cake was served on a porcelain stand that matched the tea set. White linen napkins folded on a silver tray rested next to the cups, saucers, cake plates, silver teaspoons and cake forks. A little silver dish held the thinly sliced wedges of lemon and next to it was a sugar bowl with a silver spoon in the shape of a serpent. As a child, I was fascinated by this snake-like handle and loved to play with it.

Having afternoon tea on mother's bed was very different from the elegant surroundings of our drawing room, but the healing effect of this banquet was so precious. This little bit of normality helped to calm our nerves. Later, when it was quiet, I asked my mother to get ready, as we would soon be going to Yankel's for dinner, and we asked Mrs Gitl-Leah and Hela to join us.

On the way there we saw soldiers on some of the rooftops. They wore strange uniforms, different from the SS or gendarmes or any other German organisation. They were armed with long-barrelled rifles with strange bayonets. At Yankel's we waited for a table and the atmosphere was thick with tension; people were nervous and spoke very loudly. Someone said that we should expect an *akcja* very soon.

Returning to the house we saw more soldiers on the rooftops and the policjanten were marching in groups. We asked one what was going on. He told us that the ghetto had been closed, that no-one could enter or leave it and that hundreds of Lithuanian soldiers had it surrounded. We heard gunshots. People began to gather on street corners. Gitl-Leah and Hela started to panic; nothing could pacify them. My mother, however, was unexpectedly composed and a strange smile played on her face. I began to feel trapped. I *had* to get back to Zawichost.

After taking my mother and the others to their room I went back outside. I walked towards the main gate of the ghetto to see if the rumours were true. On the roof of one house I saw a soldier taking aim at a target in the building opposite, and I turned my head to see what he was aiming at. In a dormer window was a man's silhouette. I imagined that he was trying to see what the commotion was all about. Then a shot pierced the air. As if in slow motion, the bullet hit this innocent person. The bullet hit and the head exploded, the brain splattered and blood sprayed out. Seconds later the headless body collapsed out of sight.

I retched. In an instant a life was extinguished. Who was he? Would someone mourn him? Was all that remained of his existence now the memory of a seventeen-year-old stranger who witnessed his murder? I had seen many killings, but this time I broke down. I started crying and shaking ferociously. I was terrified.

The ghetto was now completely sealed off from the outside world. I returned to my mother with the news I had heard on the street: an *akcja* was to take place in three days and we were going to be 'deported'. My mother was composed, her face serene. She was looking forward to being reunited with my father, certain that we would be deported to where he was waiting. She was worried that she would have difficulties in finding him, but I reassured her that he was surely searching every new incoming transport and would find us instantly.

We prepared for the trip. It was so cold we decided to wear most of our clothes. I still had my belt with the golden buckle that my father gave me in Staszów. We stuffed rations of sugar and bread in our pockets. It was far easier to believe that we were going to be re-settled to the east rather than taken to an extermination camp. I decided not to take my backpack with me, as it would restrict my movements. Into my pockets, I stuffed only the most necessary items, including my pistol.

My mother lay down and I sat on the edge of her bed discussing our plans for the *akcja*. The minutes became hours and the night was dragging. We could not wait for daybreak.

'In case we are separated, you need to be very careful at the station not to slip on the snow,' I told Mother. 'When you board the train make sure you get a spot next to the opening, because it will be easier to breath there. I will try to find you, if not on the actual journey, then at the destination.'

I begged her to try to sleep a little as we were facing great hardship and needed all our strength. She closed her eyes, pretending.

At dawn, shots were fired in the ghetto. It was Sunday 10 January 1943. A voice through loudspeakers ordered everyone to assemble in the main square immediately. Anyone disobeying would be shot on the spot. Women and children lined up on one side of the main square and men on the other. The policjanten issued orders in Yiddish repeatedly. The Lithuanians and the Ukrainians screamed, '*Alle raus!*' ('Everybody out!')

I suggested we remain in our room for as long as possible. It was well below zero outside and who knew how long we would have to stand in the open? I prepared hot drinks for Mother and me, when Hela asked to join us.

'Of course. There's enough water for everyone.' I then asked them to help my mother as much as they could, as I would be separated from her. They told me that they had already decided to do so. I assured them that when we reached our destination, my father would be very thankful and look after all of us. My mother backed me up and promised them that her beloved David would make sure that we would never have to suffer like this again.

I sat on my mother's bed, holding and kissing her hands.

'I can't wait to see your father and am full of joy for the moment we're reunited,' she whispered.

'Let's go, it's getting late,' urged one of the two women. 'We're the last ones left and they'll come and shoot us right here thinking that we're trying to avoid being deported.'

'Just a few more minutes, please.' I took my mother in my arms and squeezed her so hard she could hardly breathe. She was tearful but so serene that she almost glowed. I released my grip and kissed her cheeks, then her forehead, her eyes and lips, whispering into her ears, 'Please, don't cry. Try to be happy. You are finally going to meet up with Daddy and you should be pleased that the long wait is finally over.' I held her face in both my hands. 'Please, don't cry. Let me see you smile. I want to remember your cheerful happy face. Please, please.'

Blinking, my mother smiled through her wet eyelashes. 'I am happy, my dear son. My tears are tears of joy. I'm not really crying.' She placed her arms around me and kissed me, holding me tight. And I knew and she knew that we were both participating in a farce where the impossible was possible and the possible was impossible. Slowly we relaxed our embrace, unable to let go completely, and held our hands for one last moment.

'Listen to me carefully,' I said. 'You must be extremely cautious and try to be patient. The march to the loading ramps of the waiting cattle train will be very gruelling and the Germans will look out for the weak and feeble. Make yourself as inconspicuous and invisible as you possibly can. Do not give them an excuse to single you out. Make sure you do not become separated from Mrs Gitl-Leah and Hela. They will watch over you. I promise I will see you as soon as it is possible.'

'I will,' she assured me. 'And it is equally important that you adhere to your own advice and make sure that you arrive there safely too.'

Slowly we made our way to the assembly point. Still holding on to my mother, I could feel a lump in my throat. The sun rose over the rooftops and its reflection from the snow hurt our eyes. There was a complete silence. Not even a child's cry could be heard. The only sounds that pierced the silence were the shouts of the Germans and gunfire. More and more people poured into the main square. Couples and families were forced to separate. There were heartbreaking scenes of children who did not want to be parted from their fathers or couples with children clinging together. The Germans dragged them apart, hitting them and threatening to kill them. And indeed, seconds later, at point-blank range, a gendarme shot a woman whose husband and child had tried to protect her; the German then shot both man and child in the back of their heads. The woman was left to bleed to death on the pavement.

Now we too were forced to separate. 'The Lamed Vav will guard you,' my mother whispered in a final hug before moving to the women and children's group. I moved towards the men's side.

In the middle of this mayhem, one of the black-uniformed officers announced over the loudspeaker that 300 men were needed for work in Skarżysko-Kamienna. Those who wished to volunteer should assemble at once in the next street, inside the ghetto.

Here was my chance to get back to the partisans. I turned to signal my mother but was met with a sea of tormented faces. I was searching for her when a sudden opening in the cluster of women momentarily revealed her face before she was obscured once again. I heard her calling out to me. 'You must survive. Run! This is your chance, this is your destiny.'

PART IV

JANUARY 1943 – APRIL 1943

CHAPTER 26

MEN, YOUNG AND OLD, stampeded to the designated area. We formed three lines and waited. I couldn't see back to the main square but heard Germans shouting and shots being fired. An hour later two platoons of SS-men replaced the Lithuanian guards and the selection began. Whoever was touched with the officer's crop had to leave the column, run down the street and turn left back to the main square. Every time someone was singled out and turned the corner, a salvo of submachine gunfire followed. Finally, there were no more than 300 Jews left in the line.

We were ordered to march back towards the main square. As we turned the corner we confronted a huge, bloodied mass of flesh. Corpses had been thrown together in a mound of blood and guts, their arms and legs intertwined, spilling from the footpath onto the road. The blood in the gutter had frozen in the sub-zero temperature. We marched forward, heads bowed, averting our eyes in case we recognised someone's brother, uncle, father or friend.

In the main square only a few scattered dead bodies remained. The policjanten collected them and threw them on the pile. There were only a few local Polish people around but one onlooker drew my attention. It was Marysia. She was dressed in an overcoat with an extravagant fur collar and blended very well with the Poles in the crowd, who had openly begun to wear looted Jewish clothing. I was so pleased to see her and know that she was still alive. We exchanged glances and, outwardly, she managed to look serene. I never saw her again.

As we stood there freezing, the policjanten and the Germans searched the houses in the ghetto, dragging out the last of the forgotten. One policjant believed so strongly that the Germans really were re-settling the Jews that he offered to reveal the hiding place of his own parents. So convinced was he that he was saving their lives that he grabbed a large pick and went off with German gendarmes. Half an hour later the same gendarmes led around twenty people to an unknown destination to be executed.

A convoy of military trucks finally arrived to take us to Skarżysko-Kamienna. We quickly climbed into the covered trucks and clung to each other to preserve our body heat. I grabbed a space on the side of the truck, next to a side seam of the tarpaulin. When we started to move, I took a penknife from my pocket and secretly cut a few stiches of the seam, behind my back, so I could look out. I still had my gun and hoped that something would allow me to escape and return to my post in Zawichost. It was a three-hour journey and maybe we would crash or the truck would overturn on the icy road. I had to stay alert.

But nothing did happen. I peeked through the hole in the tarpaulin and realised that we would soon arrive at the gate of the Hasag ammunition factory. I took out my penknife again and slit the canvas alongside the edge of the tray. In anticipation of the search conducted by the Germans on entering the compound, I pushed my gun through the slit – just in time.

The truck driver, who wore SS insignia, ordered us to get out and line up. I weaved through the group and placed myself in the back row, hoping not to be recognised as a former inmate and escapee. While waiting we began to talk to each other. Minutes later the truck driver reappeared, this time red-faced and enraged. 'Who the hell damaged my tarpaulin?' he barked, waving his whip. 'Who did it? If you don't come forward, you will *all* be shot.' No-one said a word. He began slapping our heads, abusing and threatening us. For a moment I sympathised, knowing that he would have to answer to his commander for the damage to government property.

A high-ranking Werkschutz appeared. He counted us, signed a few documents and shepherded us to a large empty building. This time the registration process was more sophisticated and efficient. We lined up in a long corridor that had a door at either end. Through the first door one gained entry to the main hall, where there were at least thirty tables, each with three Werkschutz. People entered the hall, undressed, were body-searched by the Werkschutz, and had their belongings searched and all valuables confiscated and placed into crates.

The men came out in their underwear, carrying or dragging their remaining belongings behind them. While still waiting my turn in the corridor I started undressing. Instead of going into the search hall, I decided, I would wait for a chance to sneak along the corridor towards the hall's exit and slip into the line of the men leaving the search area. This time I had money from my courier work and I wasn't going to let it be taken. Suddenly a shot was fired inside the hall and the Werkschutz who were guarding us ran to the noise. This gave me the opportunity I had hoped for, and I slipped into the other line.

The next hurdle was to register under an assumed name. If I was recognised, I would not just be shot, but interrogated, then beaten, tortured and, finally, hanged from the guard-turret in the middle of the Appelplatz with a sign across my chest: 'I escaped from this camp'. It was the standard procedure, intended to warn and discourage potential escapees. But I could not think of another name. I asked the person next to me what his name was. It was Morgen, and I used it. Zygmunt Morgen. I kept my real date of birth so I could remember it, even under stressful and difficult conditions.

During the registration, there was a commotion at the front of the queue, followed by three shots. Two men from our transport were shot dead, both of them from Chmielnik. They were singled out because they had created some kind of disturbance – it wasn't really clear exactly what had happened. By this stage, though, we had become so desensitised, utterly indifferent, that this event had absolutely no impact on us, as if it were happening to someone else, somewhere far away on another continent. We had involuntarily retracted into a place where there were no emotions or expectations, where each one of us functioned like a robot. It must be a subconscious reaction to ensure self-preservation. All we longed for was water and a place to rest.

Hours later, when the registration was completed, we were told that the whole group would be transferred to Werk C. We would spend the night here at Werk A and tomorrow march to our final destination. No-one else reacted to this announcement except for me – I became dizzy and almost fainted – because I knew this *was* a death sentence. But I also had the evening in Werk A to think of something. I felt a spark of hope and an idea came to me.

After a short march under guard, we entered the slave labour camp of Werk A. Two hundred and ninety-eight men were herded like cattle into an empty barrack which had once been a stable. This *koński barak* (horse barrack) was big enough to hold just eighty people. As a consequence we were only able to sit upright; those who were lucky enough to have some sort of backpack or bundle sat more comfortably. At least we were under cover and somewhat protected from the elements.

I knew that my uncle Samuel's wife was somewhere in this camp. I asked some women if they knew Andzia Siegreich but everyone wanted to know where she worked and in what department. I had no idea. I tried to describe her, when a very young woman asked, 'Does she only speak Polish?'

'No, I think she also speaks German and French.'

'But not Yiddish?'

'Possibly not,' I answered hopefully.

'I know who she is.' She directed me to an enormous building named 'Ekonomia', after the street it was on. She said I should look for Andzia in the hall that housed the inmates from Suchedniów.

I raced upstairs climbing two steps at a time and there she was. 'Andzia! I'm so happy to see you.'

She was an elegant blonde in her early forties, well groomed and of solid build, who wore her powder and lipstick proudly, not seeing her circumstances as sufficient reason to neglect her appearance. 'Sigi, what are you doing here?' she asked in wonder.

'I've just arrived,' I said and made a sign of silence. The building was centrally heated and the room was warm. I wanted to stay there but instead persuaded her to go outside where we could talk privately. We walked around the building, trying to keep warm.

'I know that you escaped with my Ludwig. Did you come here together? Is he here as well?'

'No, I'm sorry. Ludwig escaped from Werk C five days before me and I haven't seen him since. I went back to Staszów but he wasn't there. Did he have any contacts, anywhere he could find refuge or help?'

'I have no idea,' Andzia said. 'I only know that he had exceptionally good Aryan identity documents. I wish he'd send me a message to let me know he's all right. Have you seen your parents or Zahava and her husband?' she asked as we continued walking side by side.

'When I got back to Staszów after the main *akcja* I managed to trace Mother to a camp in Ostrowiec. She told me that Father had been "deported" to Bełżec together with five thousand of the town's Jews.'

I looked into my aunt's face to see if she had grasped what I was telling her. Could 5000 human beings have actually disappeared into thin air, and among them my father? The idea was inconceivable. We looked at each other with a surreal detachment, confirming that we both understood what fate had befallen them, but we were unable to face the enormity of the situation and suppressed our feelings, to be dealt with at some later stage, and continued our conversation.

'Did you see or hear anything from Stefanie?' Andzia anxiously inquired about her daughter.

Again I was forced to tell her that I had no news – but now we were running out of time, and I was anxious. I turned to face her. 'Andzia, please listen. I have a very serious problem and I need you to help me.'

'I'm sorry, but I have no money,' she said apologetically. 'My means are very limited and I can't rely on anyone to help me either.'

'Please, just hear me out,' I begged. 'I don't need your money. My life is in danger. Today's transport from Sandomierz has been assigned to Werk C, starting tomorrow. As soon as I'm recognised back there I'll be used as an example to stop other escape attempts. Can you see that under no circumstances can I go back there? Maybe you know someone with connections who could arrange something for me. I'm able to pay for this favour. Please, Andzia, I beg you. Please help me.'

Andzia understood at once and took me straight back to her room to introduce me to the wife of a man who had business dealings with Samuel. 'Apparently he's got good connections with the authorities inside the camp and at the factory. He's a good man and I have known him for many years. I'm sure that if he can help he will.'

I sat quietly on her bunk while she spoke to this man sitting with his wife. He listened carefully, shaking his head. I felt sick with anxiety. Moments later, he took Andzia under the arm and they walked over to me.

'I am Wolf Zylberfuden,' he said, his hand outstretched ready to shake mine. 'I'm from Suchedniów and know your uncle Samuel very well. We had a lot in common before the war and apart from being good friends, we did business together.'

He led me back outside to talk and we huddled in the doorway, rubbing our hands to keep warm. 'I'll arrange for you to remain here in Werk A and for you to be assigned to the best working commando. Unfortunately, it will cost you, as I'll have to bribe some people. I'll spend as little of your money as I can, but regrettably these bastards always profit from the misfortunes of others. And of course this matter, and that of your name, remains completely confidential.'

I could hardly believe my ears. Could my problem be overcome so easily? *This is not possible, I must be dreaming*, I thought. Was this another divine intervention? Maybe it was true, just as my mother said – *one of the thirty-six* . . . We walked together to the internal camp administration office and he introduced me to Eljasz Albirt, known as 'Pinie', the Jewish camp's chief komendant, whom the Germans had nominated as *Lagerältester*, or 'camp elder'.

'This man, Zygmunt Morgen, arrived here today from Sandomierz and will remain in Werk A,' Mr Zylberfuden told him. 'Morgen is a skilled toolmaker and can work in the toolmaking department of the steel tempering subsection. Please register him and allocate him a place to sleep, preferably in the Ekonomia building. I will notify Mendel Wajntraub.'

I wanted to hug this man in gratitude but instead held out my hand, shook his, and told him that I was indebted to him for the rest of my life. I returned to Andzia and we both spoke warmly of Mr Zylberfuden. Andzia helped me further by giving me her spare bowl. My new life had begun.

*

The first task of the next day was to go to the communal latrine, located in the middle of the camp. The thirty-metre-long barrack could not cope with the traffic, and there were long queues on both sides of the building. This meant I missed my morning 'coffee' – not a big loss, except for the precious warmth it provided.

We lined up in rows of five and were counted at the gate and escorted to work. I was assigned to the Werkzeugbau Härterei Abteilung or steel tempering subsection, but before entering our workshop area, we were counted again. Our group consisted of around 500 workers, and more than half were women. Komendant Mendel Wajntraub walked in front of our line-up swinging a rubber truncheon, looking out for new faces. 'Who joined my squad today? Who is new here?' he shouted. I raised my arm. 'Are you the one who arrived yesterday?'

'Yes, that's me.'

'What's your number?'

'Eight thousand and eighty-seven.'

'What is your name?

'Zygmunt Morgen.'

'Next time answer *eighty, eighty-seven*. That's how we call out the numbers. Are you a relative of Mr Albirt?' He assumed that I must be related to receive such special treatment.

'Not yet. Maybe one day I might be – that is, if he has a beautiful daughter,' I joked. Everyone who heard my answer laughed.

Wajntraub made a few notes in a file and dismissed the squad.

People began to move into the building, but I was waiting for further instructions. Wajntraub ordered me to follow him. He pointed to a large two-storey building, one of many that housed the huge Hasag ammunition factory. 'This is the toolmaking factory, division A.' The windows, located high up and running the length of the building, were reinforced with steel-wire opaque glass. Only the upper floor, where the draughtsroom and offices were located, had normal windows. A network of roads and rail tracks linked all the buildings.

We walked into an enormous hall full of machinery but with a clear passageway through the middle. There were small and large lathes, milling and planing machines, grinding and polishing machines, and many more specialised tools. On the left was a row of about fifteen semiautomatic lathes. The machines and tools looked familiar to me. When I was small, I had often visited the factories owned by my family. The ELTES company, run by my uncles Felix and Samuel, had a huge department full of all kinds of machinery, and I used to spend a lot of time there, asking questions.

The whole of division A manufactured tools that were used to produce infantry ammunition for the Wehrmacht, such as stencils, stamps, rammers and reamers. In the middle of the hall there were offices, a work distribution centre, storerooms and lavatories. On the other side there were more machines but these were gigantic. This was the toolmaking factory's division B, which made tools for the production of artillery shells, mortars and mines.

To the right there was an opening leading to a hall. A sign above read *Härterei* (tempering department). This department worked for both A and B divisions and was my new workplace. Wajntraub spoke briefly to the manager, then left. I stood waiting for instructions. The manager, a tall, blond man, looked me up and down, asked a few questions, then told me to start work.

I looked around the well-lit room. It was about ten by thirty-five metres in size. At one end was the manager's office, a small room with a large window facing into the hall. Just to the left of the entrance in the middle of the room, a woman was sitting at a desk working on a measuring instrument called the Rockwell Hardness Tester. She was extremely well dressed and did not look like an inmate, though I later found out she was. I wondered how she looked so smart while everyone else looked as if they had crawled out from under a bridge. For a moment she reminded me of my mother.

Along one wall were about twenty special electrical furnaces of various shapes and sizes. On the opposite wall, some four workbenches with fifteen more furnaces were positioned. In the middle, between the two rows, were many large, open containers filled with different oils, and one with constant running water. At the other end of this hall was a storeroom where, behind a glass wall, one could see metal cylinders of various lengths and diameters, and sacks and crates full of empty cocoa pods, used to harden steel.

Two young Jewish men – slave labourers – were busy at the workbench, preparing steel tools for the hardening process while two Polish technicians operated the furnaces. I was sent to a workbench where Abramek, a thirteen- or fourteen-year-old inmate, showed me how to tie up the unfinished tools with soft wire, each piece separately attached to a shank.

We worked until eleven o'clock, when the siren announced the lunchbreak. Abramek, a cheeky young boy, told me to follow him to receive our soup. I took my bowl – my most precious possession and one I carried with me at all times – and went through the main hall up to the main entrance. Outside there were cauldrons full of soup ready to be distributed to 500 people.

Deputy komendant Yosel Patac was handing out the soup using a large tin attached to a long stick as a ladle. I remembered how Kotlega at Werk C wanted the dish to be held, above the cauldron, so when my turn came I held it in the same manner. A huge yell escaped from Yosel Patac's small throat. 'Look at how you're holding your bloody dish!' After filling my dish with the watery soup, he swung the nearly empty ladle up over my head, not really scalding me but causing the soup to dribble down and stain my jacket. (No matter how hard I tried, I never managed to get it clean again.) Abramek thought the whole episode was hilarious.

At five o'clock the siren sounded the end of our shift. The night shift arrived ten minutes before we finished and took over from us without any furnaces being turned off. The plant continued production twenty-four hours a day. We then lined up in rows of five in front of the building, where we were counted, recounted, and marched to the gate to wait once again. There were hundreds of people in front of us and many more arrived from other departments. We waited for at least an hour before the gate from the factory compound opened and had just started crossing the main road towards the camp's gates when the counting began afresh. This time they counted us as we passed through. I kept close to Abramek. We could not yet disperse, having to line up for the evening soup and collect our bread rations. Everything became very hectic, as hundreds of people moved around in deep mud. (How was it that the mud *never* froze, even though temperatures were well below zero? Maybe it was because thousands of feet were trampling in it repeatedly.)

I went to tell Andzia about my day. While we chatted I saw my saviour, Mr Zylberfuden. I told him about my day too, and as we began to chat about all sorts of things, I realised how much I missed my father and the intelligent and informative discussions we used to have. It was tremendous to talk and to listen to Mr Zylberfuden. He was softly spoken, perceptive and knowledgeable, like my father, and had a thorough understanding of the camp and its functions. I asked him if he could teach me more about how things were run in Werk A. I did not want to be treated as a greenhorn, tormented by other inmates, and wished to blend in as fast as possible.

'Of course,' he replied. 'You're Samuel's nephew and we're like family. I'm happy to help.' He took a breath. 'I came to this camp with my wife Hela and two sons and two daughters. We were brought here from Suchedniów. It's important to remember our camp is not only surrounded by a double razor-wire fence and several watchtowers, it is run according to a long list of rules and regulations. Firstly, you must remember that the true chief commander, Anton Ipfling, a high-ranking SS officer, together with his henchmen, is master over our life and death. It is *essential* that you avoid him,' Mr Zylberfuden warned. 'If he comes near you, keep your head down and make yourself invisible. Next there are the Werkschutz and the internal Jewish administration, who make sure that our life is unbearable.'

'I know,' I nodded. 'I've already had some experience with these people.'

'The Werkschutz guardsmen are usually Ukrainian, Kalmyk and Tatar collaborators and they're armed with submachine guns, rifles and whips. They patrol the camp perimeter *inside* the double fence and guard the gates. They also escort the inmates to and from work, capture runaways, conduct spot checks and body searches, arrest inmates and carry out sentences when individual inmates are to be flogged or executed.'

Alarm bells rang in my ears. 'Do the Werkschutz from Werk C camp come to Werk A for duty? Is there any association between the two camps?'

'No, I don't think so, though I understand your concern,' he said with compassion. 'As far as I know all three camps are separate entities. You're lucky, you have an excellent job here and I'm sure that you'll be safe.'

Mr Zylberfuden then touched on the Jewish administration, explaining that Pinie Albirt, the Jewish camp komendant, was the camp's official representative in dealings with the German authorities. He was in charge of all internal administration and was not to be trusted. Mr Zylberfuden added that most of the authorities, regardless of their position, were sadists and extortionists who never hesitated to use their rubber truncheons. Then there were the policjanten, responsible for security and order inside the camp. The Jewish police ran the morning and evening rollcalls; escorted the inmates, together with the Werkschutz, to and from work; and guarded the camp's gates from inside. Their commander-in-chief was Lejzer Teperman and his two deputies were Josef Krzepicki and Gilek Goldfarb. These men ordered the arrests of inmates for crimes and issued their punishment, usually lashing. They also appointed new policjanten by selling the jobs to the highest bidder. Much of this was similar to Werk C.

By now it was getting late. I thanked Mr Zylberfuden effusively and we planned to continue our chat the following day. Exhausted after a long, hard day and quite overwhelmed by Mr Zylberfuden's account, I went to my sleeping quarters, for which I had paid a handsome bribe. I lay flat on my bare pallet, put my head on some of my clothes, covered myself with my overcoat and fell into a deep sleep.

I was woken by loud whistling and yelling. As I was already fully dressed, I ran to the latrine to be one of the first. I could hardly walk and my muscles were stiff and hurting. This time I managed to get some 'coffee', a brew made from roasted, or rather burnt, beetroot that smelled bad and tasted even worse. However, it was wet and hot.

I found the second day's work easier and Abramek tried to be funny by singing frivolous songs. I could not wait to see Mr Zylberfuden, though, and my eyes were drawn, all day, to the slow-moving hands on the big factory clock. At last, after gulping my soup, I was in his company again.

'Hello, Zygmunt,' he greeted me warmly. 'I'm glad you came because I have something for you.' He reached into his pocket and unwrapped a packet that contained a slice of black bread. He handed it to me, smiling, and asked me about my day.

I told him that the day was without problems and that, although grateful for the offer of bread, I couldn't accept it. I was, in fact, embarrassed.

'Don't be shy, take it,' he said. 'No-one has too much bread in camp. You're practically on your own and I feel I owe it to your family. I'm sure that if the situation was reversed the Siegreichs would look after my children.'

I took the bread with thanks and tucked it into my pocket for later.

'Yesterday I told you about the policjanten,' Mr Zylberfuden said. 'They are exempt from work and can move freely between the camp and the plant – they're even allowed to go into town if escorted by Werkschutz. They're entitled to special quarters where they may live with their wives or girlfriends, and receive special food rations the rest of us can only dream about. As you know, there are also the Jewish camp administrators – the komendanten – who have the same insignia as the policjanten but wear green armbands. A number of them are in charge of inmates' accommodation at the Ekonomia building – and the much worse *ogolniak barak* (common barrack) that is part of it. They nominate people to cut the bread and the cleaners and the caretakers responsible for the heating.'

'Heating? I haven't seen any heaters. In my room hot-water pipes run along the walls for heating. Exactly as here, in your room.'

'That's right, but other barracks and huts don't have these facilities. They have very primitive sawdust heaters.'

Mr Zylberfuden continued. 'Milsztajn, the komendant who is in charge of a horse cart, has perhaps the most important job in Werk A, transporting the bread from the bakery into the camp each day. Bread distribution to each barrack is entrusted to Eljasz Szajbe.

'Now, next Sunday being a day off,' he finished up, 'I'll take you around the camp and show you what's what. You'll get to know everything in no time.'

On my guided tour Mr Zylberfuden spared me nothing. A few days later we walked past a huge crate located next to the horse barrack. 'Is it for garbage collection?' I asked naively.

'No, this is a kind of a morgue. Dead bodies are kept here until collected for cremation at Werk C.'

As we moved closer, chills ran down my spine. The crate was full of human skeletons covered with thin grey skin. *This is where we all will finish up*, I thought to myself.

'Mr Szafran and Ewa Krzepicki distribute second-hand clothes brought here from Bełżec and other death camps. These clothes were left by their owners in the changing rooms next to the gas chambers and later collected and sorted. The Germans send the finer garments to Germany but the rejected rags are supposed to go to needy inmates. These are stored in a hut surrounded by barbed wire. Szafran and Ewa Krzepicki operate the distribution centre for their own personal gain, exploiting those inmates who can afford to pay, leaving the needy to walk in tatters or even worse, wrapped in empty cement paper bags.'

'If this clothing belonged to people who were murdered,' I cried out, 'it could have also belonged to my father and the five thousand Jews sent to Bełżec from Staszów last November.'

'Possibly, but clothing is brought here from other places too,' Mr Zylberfuden added gently.

'But what if I accidentally find *his* clothes here?' I said, my voice rising in panic.

'Don't worry. Your father's clothes were of the finest quality and fashion and would have been sent to Germany.'

Mr Zylberfuden quickly changed the subject. 'The health department is run by Dr Saks and a few nurses. The doctor can excuse a sick inmate from attending work, providing that his or her temperature reaches at least 38 degrees Celsius, or if they have funds to pay for the privilege. The infirmary has only one thermometer, a limited stock of aspirin and a small quantity of calcium permanganate that is used as a disinfectant. The hospital is also the responsibility of Dr Saks but he never sees it from the inside. Its day-to-day running is in the hands of Lola and Mojsie Finger, a couple happily engaged in lucrative work. Two male nurses, Safirsztajn and Zylberfuden, no relation, assist them. The bathhouse, which has showers and a delousing chamber, is also a part of the health department's responsibility and is run by a man called Najman. Six barbers deal with all shaving and haircuts and Majlech Sobol is their komendant. You will have seen for yourself that there are far too few barbers, resulting in endless queues. But bribes allow for a backdoor entry, just as they do everywhere else. And a fellow called Morcin is in charge of the latrines and sanitation.'

Once again I thanked Mr Zylberfuden for his time and information. I had become increasingly fond of this man and now felt much more alert to what went on in the camp.

CHAPTER 27

THE WORKERS OF THE TOOLMAKING DEPARTMENT were under orders to report for work clean-shaven, because of regular visits from German personnel. This meant I had to line up every second day at the camp barber, while the majority of inmates only had a weekly shave – an exception were those wealthy enough to pay for extra shaves. The process was primitive and sloppy. The barber's barrack had a door at either end. After queuing outside for some time, one entered the room, sat down on a long bench along the wall, and waited one's turn, sliding along each time a shaving chair became vacant. When you sat down for your shave, the barber quickly brushed on a thin layer of lather, barely covering the beard, then shaved your face with three simple strokes before you were shoved out the door. Some of the inmates' faces remained covered with soot, except where the razor had cleaned off the dirt. If you could wash your face after the shave you were lucky, otherwise you stayed like that until the next time you were anywhere near water. When I could, I bribed the barber to soap my face a little bit longer, to soften the bristle for a less painful shave.

*

Over the next few days I collected some fine wood shavings that had been lying near some packing crates in the storerooms at work. I lined my pallet with them for a more comfortable night's sleep. Then, a couple of weeks later, I walked back to my bunk after work to discover a stranger occupying my pallet. I woke him and told him that he was in my spot.

'From now on, *I* sleep here,' he stated boldly. 'This spot has been assigned to me.'

'There must be some mistake. I've been sleeping here for the last three weeks,' I said, indignant. 'I was told this is my bunk.'

'If you don't believe me, go and ask the komendant yourself,' he said with a sneer and turned his back on me.

It was time for our evening soup. I could ill afford to miss any food, but so worried was I about my bunk and not wanting to waste time that I ate while running. My barrack komendant, who was responsible for three or four barracks housing around 200 inmates each, could be anywhere. I had to find him.

I passed the latrines and saw Morcin, the latrine and sanitation komendant. He was bending over a bucket filled with water holding something. At first I thought he was holding a cat and drowning it in the bucket when I heard a shrill little cry and realised that it was a newborn baby held by its ankles.

I moaned aloud and ran as fast as I could, shaking my head trying to rid myself of this macabre sight. Later, I visited Mr Zylberfuden and mentioned it to him. 'The world we once knew has ceased to exist,' he explained. 'We strive always to live another day but the life we crave is slowly eroded by the struggle to stay alive. When a child is born in this godforsaken place, its fate is sealed. Morcin is not only responsible for the maintenance of the latrines and washrooms but his duties also include the disposal of newborns.'

At last I found the barrack komendant and told him about my dilemma.

'Albirt instructed me to remove you from there,' he answered, emotionless.

'But where shall I find another place to sleep?' I asked.

'I don't give a shit. Go to the ogolniak or the horse barrack and find yourself a hole and crawl into it, you *shminteligent*,' he said with disdain.

I went to Albirt's office but he threw me out, yelling, 'Just be damned thankful that you're here at all and not with the rest of your group in Werk C.'

What had caused this sudden change? He who bribes last, wins. Albirt himself was an inmate after all, despite his position of power over us, and worried about his own survival. It was obvious that he had been offered a bribe and his greed overtook his decency and compassion for a fellow Jew. It did not seem to matter that I was without a place to sleep, without a safe refuge.

I had to find a new place to sleep as soon as possible. I collected my belongings and went to Mr Zylberfuden asking for help. This time, unfortunately, he could not. Apparently he had argued with Albirt and since I was Mr Zylberfuden's protégé, I was punished. He did, however, promise to find a solution, but right now I had to find somewhere to sleep.

The ogolniak was a very large hall in the Ekonomia building where five-tiered bunk beds had been constructed to cope with the influx of Jews. Over 2000 men and women slept here, usually in two shifts, elbowing each other for space. Actually, no-one knew how many inmates there were. Those who found a spot considered themselves lucky as many slept outside. Although the bunk beds were very low, it was difficult to climb up to the fifth tier, but the advantage of sleeping on the top tier was that no-one could urinate on you. It was also impossible to sit up in any of the bunks except the top one because of the inadequate height between the tiers.

I climbed up and down the bunks, carrying my bundle, but every space was taken by a wretched inmate trying to sleep.

I climbed a final time up to the fifth tier when someone called, 'Hey! You over there.'

'Who me?' I turned.

'Yes, you. Are you looking for a space?'

'Desperately.'

'Look to your left. Someone just left and moved to another spot. Hurry up and grab it.'

I shouted my thanks and rushed to the vacant pallet. Out of breath I lay down on the rough planks and did not dare move. I was so glad to be undercover – outside it was still below zero.

Ogolniak inmates shared their sleeping space with those who worked the opposite shift. Sometimes when shifts were changed, inmates had to sleep together. Conditions were worst on Sundays when there was no work; those who returned exhausted from Saturday's night shift wanting to rest couldn't. Everyone was tired and short-tempered with the overcrowding and fights often broke out.

As more Jews arrived almost every week, the conditions in the camp worsened. Many people slept in the lavatory shed and even under the open sky.

Several large metal containers, like cut-down 44-gallon drums, were placed alongside the bunks for urinating during the night. By morning they were full of faeces and overflowing. The stench penetrated your every pore, making it almost impossible to sleep. The constant fighting, screaming and yelling only compounded the inhumane conditions. Not once did I see any of the komendanten enter the ogolniak.

At night all I wanted was rest and sleep, but sleep was a rare gift. There was the incessant hunger and the bitter cold, the noise from other inmates and the nightly rollcalls. Further, as our food was mostly liquid, my bladder was always full. Fighting for each minute of sleep, I tried to ignore the painful pressure but the urge to pass water would force me to clamber down from the fifth tier and queue at the end of the long line to relieve myself in the already overflowing containers. One of the worst jobs in the camp was to empty these vats, which had to be carried to the latrine and emptied each morning. The barrack komendant mostly chose the inmates at random, though sometimes this chore was used as a punishment. I only had to haul this putrid container across the compound to the latrine, a distance of around 100 metres, once. The containers had two handles and the two of us had to stop every few paces to rest and free our clogs from the grasping mud, a problem that was exacerbated by the weight we carried. With each step urine splashed onto our trousers and into our shoes.

*

The first few weeks in the camp had the most significant influence on the fate of an inmate. If you became apathetic you were condemned to die, but if you looked after yourself and stayed clean and positive, your chances of survival were good. Generally the women in the camp were stronger, more resilient, suffered less from hunger and had a much better rate of survival than the men.

I was depressed and became increasingly indifferent to what was going on around me. I only kept contact with Abramek, Andzia and sometimes Mr Zylberfuden. I kept my head low, trying to avoid beatings and abuse. I did not speak Yiddish and because of this was ostracised by the other inmates and discriminated against and abused by the komendanten and policjanten. I was dubbed *der shminteligent, der Pojlisz redder* (the Polish-speaking intellectual), an expression of contempt and 'inferiority'.

At least once a week there was a 'selection'. The sick, the weak and sometimes the elderly, which meant anyone over the age of thirty, were singled out, loaded into vans whose exhaust pipes were redirected back into the sealed compartment, and transported to Werk C. By the time the vans reached their destination the passengers had been gassed to death by the poisonous fumes. Mass graves had been prepared in advance to receive the dead.

Learning of this was my wake-up call. I knew that if I did not take better care of myself I would die. I began carefully observing the camp's routine, the relationships between the different groups – men and women, workers and the authorities, policjanten and komendanten – hoping to find my niche.

A rumour circulated that half-a-dozen inmates had escaped. We didn't know if they were successful, but the next morning we endured an exceptionally long rollcall. After the day shift marched off to the plant, we remaining inmates stayed in line. We were counted and recounted several times and then buckets full of red paint were brought and the komendanten started marking our clothes; on the back they painted a wide stripe from the neck to the waist, and a narrower stripe on each side of our trousers or skirts.

One day during a day shift in early February, Kalata, the manager of the work distribution office, approached me. 'After lunch, collect your belongings and wait in front of my office. You're being transferred to Werk C.'

Swallowing hard, I asked why.

'There is no *why*!' he barked. 'Just be there.'

An inmate standing some distance away had seen the exchange and bounded over to me. 'What did Kalata want? Are you in trouble?'

He was softly spoken and had an honest face.

'Who are you?' I asked.

'I'm Goldberg. I work in department B, just nearby on the large lathe, the first one in the row behind the entrance.'

'No, no, there's no trouble, everything is fine,' I said.

'I think you have a problem. I know Kalata, and maybe I can help. Don't be afraid.'

I wondered if this man knew I had been in Werk C. I looked directly into his eyes. 'Well, there is something, although I'm not sure what it means as I'm new in the camp. He said that I would be transferred to Werk C. What is it, Werk C?'

'Werk C is the worst camp of all three camps here in Skarżysko-Kamienna!' he exclaimed.

We talked for a while longer and I said I'd be grateful if he could help stop my transfer.

Goldberg thought for a moment. 'I'll try, but I can't promise anything. Let me talk to Kalata, I know him quite well. I'll try to find out what this is all about. Give me a moment, I'll be back.'

I couldn't figure out if Goldberg knew that I had escaped from Werk C, but I suspected now that he was going to blackmail me. My body responded to this stress with painful stomach cramps and diarrhoea. When I returned from the latrines Goldberg was waiting for me with a helpless smile on his face – an indication of trouble.

'I spoke to Kalata but he said that it was not up to him to overturn this decision. The order came from a high-ranking Werkschutz officer and only he has the power to reverse it. But Kalata said he would try to bribe him, which of course will cost you.' He pursed his lips into a mournful expression.

My suspicions had been well-founded. Should I give in to this blatant extortion or risk gambling with my life? Then again, there was no guarantee that after my money had gone I would not be sent to Werk C anyway or, worse yet, placed on the selections list. I decided to try and buy more time.

'And how much would I have to pay?' I asked.

Goldberg answered without blinking an eye. 'One thousand zloty.'

'What! And who has such money in here?'

The going price for a loaf of bread in the camp was sixteen to eighteen zloty, but outside it was two-thirds cheaper. Most inmates had no money at all. Those who earned money in the camp were tradespeople, servants to the *prominente* (the top rung of inmates) or those who secretly produced or stole items for sale.

'You'd be surprised,' countered Goldberg. 'People pay five thousand zloty for a case like yours. This is a bargain, considering that Kalata has to pay off a Werkschutz and make a few zloty for himself. A real bargain.'

I was unable to comprehend how an inmate, a Jew no less, himself in a similar predicament as a slave to the Germans, would collude with our common enemy. *This is a bargain!*

'Sure, I appreciate this, but I don't have that much money at the moment. The most I can scrape together is two hundred zloty.'

'What do you mean "at the moment"?'

'That's all I have right now, but I'm expecting more money soon.'

'I have to ask Kalata if that would be acceptable. When do you expect the rest of the money?'

'I don't know exactly, maybe a week or ten days,' I bluffed.

Minutes later Goldberg returned with the news that Kalata agreed and that the money would be paid back to him in weekly instalments. 'He is really a good man, but you must pay the two hundred zloty right now.'

I did so, and during the days that followed Goldberg frequently visited our department. He pretended to have business there, though I was sure that he came to check up on me. He always spoke to other inmates, ignoring me completely, yet when it was time for the next instalment, Goldberg appeared minutes before the lunchbreak.

'Your payment is due today!' he announced. 'Do you have the money?'

'No, not yet. It's been sent, but my contact hasn't had a chance to see me. It might take another two or three days,' I lied. 'I'm sorry, but you have to be patient.'

Goldberg looked irritated. 'I'll be back in three days. Make sure that you have the money. Should you get it earlier, you know where to find me.'

My problem was escalating. I had heard people say that in a case of blackmail no amount of money could save a Jew's life. After the victim had been totally exploited and when there was no chance of extracting any more money, he or she was disposed of. I had to continue to play for time. Maybe something would happen and somehow the situation would resolve itself. I felt I had no-one to talk to or seek advice from. I did not want to stress Andzia. Abramek was just a kid. The only one left was Mr Zylberfuden, but it was too dangerous to implicate him, as he knew my predicament and could become a victim himself. I was too embarrassed to ask him for help and started to avoid him. I had to manage this on my own. I was completely alone.

Three days later, as soon as we arrived at the plant, Goldberg turned up, hissing through his teeth, 'Payday's today!'

'I know,' I said, miming a bright smile. 'I'll pay you at lunch.'

As soon as the siren signalled the lunchbreak, Goldberg appeared. He took the money without a word, his face set in anger. My death sentence had been postponed for another week.

After a long rollcall during a heavy downpour, standing in ankle-deep mud, I was angry and depressed. I decided to visit Andzia, feeling a desperate need to talk, and was greeted with a bright smile. 'I saw Samuel today,' Andzia told me. 'He came over with a group to take their monthly bath and delousing. I even managed to speak with him for few minutes. He's trying to get a transfer to Werk A and may have made the right contact. He might be here in a few days!'

I was very happy to hear this and it proved to be true. On Monday, when Andzia and I started our night shift, Samuel finally arrived, carrying his small suitcase. I rushed to see him at Andzia's quarters. He looked surprisingly well and healthy. He explained that Felix wasn't planning to transfer as he had a good job in plumbing and heating and a good German boss. His position meant he could move freely around the camp, provided he carried his tools with him, and he also had limited contact with the outside world.

Andzia was overwhelmed by Samuel's long-anticipated arrival, hardly able to concentrate or to take part in our conversation. She stroked his arm and looked at him as if he might disappear should she take her eyes off him.

'Have you had your work placement and your sleeping quarters allocated yet?' I asked.

'No, not yet,' he answered. 'In half an hour I have to report to Camp Commander Ipfling. But tell me, did you see Ludwig or Stefanie when you were on the outside, after your escape from Werk C?'

We talked some more about family and then I asked what had happened after my escape. 'Were there any repercussions? Did they single any of you out because we're related?'

'No, we weren't hurt, but your squad was punished.'

I told Samuel the story of Mala and the guard and that I had no choice but to escape. I apologised again.

Andzia turned to Samuel. 'I think you have to report to Ipfling now. Since no-one has a watch any more, I really don't want you to be late. Please go now.'

We walked Samuel to the gate and watched as a Ukrainian guard escorted him to Ipfling's office just outside the camp. As Mr Zylberfuden had explained to me, the German camp commander, Anton Ipfling, oversaw all three camps at Skarżysko-Kamienna. We saw Samuel enter the building and returned to Andzia's room to wait. We waited and waited. We never saw my uncle Samuel again. Samuel Siegreich was a man of honour and integrity, an upstanding member of the community who was also a devoted son, a loving husband and a doting, proud father. He was a successful industrialist who had provided jobs for thousands of people and Ipfling killed him. We never learned why.

CHAPTER 28

ANDZIA WAS INCONSOLABLE at losing Samuel. Nevertheless, we had to pretend nothing had happened; to choose to feel, to cry and mourn our loss would have meant our own death. I implored her to pull herself together, for her own children as well as for me.

We went to work. We were counted and recounted and we came back. We went to work again and again and we were counted and recounted, but Andzia was only there physically. Her spirit was broken. I visited her each afternoon, trying to comfort her, chatting, asking questions about the work she was doing. Andzia's department mass-produced small ammunition detonators for rifles and handguns. The detonators were later inserted into the base of the shells before they were filled with propellant. She supervised the machines and reloaded the raw material – steel rods – into them. The work was rather easy and the supervisors were relatively humane. To get a job in this department required lots of luck or a substantial bribe.

My next instalment was due though I fobbed Goldberg off for nearly another week. Then I tried a scam of my own: I made sure I was a few zloty short and, using small denominations, divided the notes into all my pockets. When we arrived in the toilet block, I started to count the money into his hands, bill by bill. I pretended to search my pockets, slowly pulling out the bills, one by one. Goldberg pursed his lips in frustration. As for the shortfall, he just barked irritably, 'Remember to pay me the balance with your next instalment.' It worked. Now I would try and delay the next payment for at least two weeks.

*

The cold slowly eased a little and the temperature climbed back to zero, but I did not feel well. I had a headache and felt feverish. Perhaps it was due to all the trouble of the past few weeks. I went to the camp infirmary and spoke with the duty nurse, Mrs Kanencukier.

She listened to my complaint and told me that she would be happy to help me, but the only medication available was aspirin and that was only to be administered if my temperature shot above 38 degrees Celsius. She touched my forehead and took my temperature, complimenting me on my Polish. We chatted about where I came from and then she asked how old I was.

'If I survive till my next birthday, I'll be nineteen on the sixteenth of May.'

'You look much older,' she said, 'more like a grown-up man. Where are your parents?'

I told her they had both been deported in separate *ackje*. We talked a little more.

'I'm sorry,' she said. 'Your fever is only 37.8, which means you're not sick enough to get an exemption from work or to be given aspirin.'

'I don't want you to excuse me from work, but I do want something to relieve this headache.'

Mrs Kanencukier reached behind the curtain and fetched two tablets. She took my dish, filled it with water and held out the aspirin, telling me to take them at once. 'You know we have typhus in the camp now. Hundreds of people are infected every day and we cannot cope with the situation at all. We have one doctor, insufficient room to accommodate the sick and no medication. In the infirmary, which is in the horse barrack, the sick are lying on bare pallets, squeezed together like sardines, with some lying on top of others. I truly hope you'll be spared. My only advice is to drink a lot of boiled water. Can you do this?'

'At work, I can. That's no problem,' I said. 'Where I work there are many furnaces, but here in the camp there's nowhere to boil water.'

'Then go to the coffee kitchen and drink as much as you can,' she suggested.

The next morning the first thing I did was get the hot brew then join my work commando. At work I drank a lot of boiled water. Back in the camp, after collecting my food, I went straight to the infirmary for more aspirin. There was a line of more than fifty inmates waiting to be seen but Mrs Kanencukier noticed me and called me straight in, saying she was expecting me.

'How do you feel, Morgen? Do you still have a headache? 'Did you drink a lot of boiled water like I told you to?'

'I did, I drank a lot, but my headache is worse today.'

'Let me take your temperature and examine your chest.' She inspected my chest very carefully, pressed on a few spots with her finger and said with a slight frown, 'I can't see any spots, so maybe you just have influenza. Your temperature is a little higher than yesterday, but still not the critical thirty-eight degrees. See me again tomorrow after work, and take these two aspirin with a lot of water.'

The next morning I was unable to stand properly but forced myself to go to work with everyone else. By midday, though, I became dizzy and passed out. Someone gave me water and notified the German manager. He expressed concern and insisted I go back to the camp. 'You're not well and you need to rest. I don't want you to come back until you're well and fit for work.

One of the komendanten will take you to the infirmary and I'll give you a note for the doctor.' He hastily wrote a note and handed it to me. I was adamant that I did not need a doctor, that I was just a little tired after a sleepless night.

'I am *ordering* you to report to the infirmary,' he insisted. 'I don't need sick people here. Besides, it could be contagious.' Szlagbaum, the komendant on duty, took me back to the camp and demanded to see the note the manager had written for the doctor.

'The note is not for you,' I told him. 'Anyhow, it's written in German. You don't speak German.'

'So tell me what he wrote,' he insisted.

'I don't know. I don't speak German either,' I lied.

'You do speak German. I know you do.'

'I'm telling you that I *don't* know. Please, leave me alone. I have a terrible headache.'

'You'll keep,' he warned. 'I'm not done with you yet.'

Szlagbaum was such an unpleasant man. He was cunning and greedy, and often extremely violent. He was short and obese with large protruding ears, small piggy eyes and a high-pitched voice. He walked me straight up to Dr Saks at the infirmary, bypassing the line of waiting inmates.

The doctor, dressed in a white coat, turned away from the patient in front of him, looked at Szlagbaum and me and snatched the manager's note from my hand. He read it and ordered me to undress. Dr Saks pulled open the front of my shirt using two wooden spatulas. He glimpsed at my chest and uttered 'typhus' to a male nurse standing nearby. 'Take care of him.'

I wanted to ask some questions, but Dr Saks had already turned back to his patient. Mrs Kanencukier was not around and I did not know what to do next. The male nurse asked me to follow him. He took me to a room that was the domain of Majlech Sobol, the chief barber. Sobol didn't mince his words.

'If you have money, we can place you into a *separatka*, a room with no more than eleven people. Josef Krzepicki, the second-in-command of the policjanten, has been just admitted in there and we have one more place left.'

In pre-war Poland, some barbers were also paramedics and some doctors used them as assistants – to apply cupping glasses or leeches, perform enemas and such like. As Sobol and Saks were from the same town, they probably used to work together, and now the doctor used the barber as an agent.

'I don't have access to my money right now, but I have pure gold which is worth a lot of money,' I said, and removed the golden buckle from my belt that my father had given me. I handed it to Sobol.

'This doesn't look like gold to me.'

'It certainly *is* gold, and even twenty-two or twenty-four carat. It's been cast from pure ingots,' I insisted.

He left the room, taking the buckle with him. Minutes later, he returned, nodding. 'It is gold. You can be admitted.'

The male nurse took me to a room on the second floor of the Ekonomia building, where four bunks were erected in one row, each with three tiers. There was one empty pallet on the upper tier waiting for me. All the pallets had thin straw-filled paillasses and pillows and thin blankets. I was thrilled to sleep on something resembling a mattress. I undressed, peeling off layers of clothing but keeping one shirt on. I tied up all my possessions into a bundle and hung it from a beam on the ceiling, above my head, where I could see it at all times.

My usual allowance of bread, soup and coffee was brought to me. The other patients in the room were the *prominente* and they enjoyed extra luxuries: there was always someone from their family or a friend who delivered extra food, drinks and, most importantly, medicine. I never envied anyone their food or even their medication, but I was jealous of them being cared for by family or a friend, being given a drink or having their forehead wiped with a wet cloth. All I wanted was to hold someone's hand or for someone to utter a comforting word to me. I tried to send word to Andzia, but didn't hear anything. I suspected my message had not reached her; perhaps she was sick too. Again I faced the reality of how hard it was to be alone. This loneliness drastically reduced my chances of survival.

On the third day in the room, my temperature rose to forty degrees Celsius. Mrs Kanencukier suddenly turned up and gave me two aspirin and a dish of water. I wasn't sure if I was hallucinating or not, but I felt so pleased that someone had come to see me and ask how I was feeling. It must have been rewarding for her as well because, according to Jewish belief, one of the most charitable deeds is *bikur holim* (comforting the sick). My mother was involved in this work. Maybe she sent Mrs Kanencukier to visit me.

Where is my mother anyway? I thought. She left home this morning and hasn't returned. It is getting late and we are going to have a beautiful banquet tonight. We are going to have all my favourite food tonight. What are we celebrating? Is it my birthday? I must speak with my father about my boarding school. Where is Mother? Oh, she went to speak with Wacek. He returned her handbag and all its contents intact. What a miracle!

I lay semiconscious, hallucinating, for at least six days. I slowly came to and then became delirious again. When I came to a second time, I asked where Krzepicki was and the nurse replied that he had been discharged. I realised then that my bundle, including all my money, had disappeared. I burst into tears and soon lost consciousness again.

Days later two male nurses half led, half dragged me across the Appelplatz in the direction of the horse barrack. I noticed that I was barefoot and wore only a shirt. The bright sunlight pierced my eyes. In a voice so weak it sounded as if it belonged to someone else, I asked why they were taking me to the horse barrack.

'We've kept you much longer than what you paid for. Now that you've become a *muselman* the komendant ordered us to evict you.'

It was true. I had become a muselman. This was the German word the Jews at the camp used to describe the weakest and most starved of all inmates. The type most likely to die.

'And where are my belongings?' I asked, feigning indignance.

'We don't know, there was nothing on your pallet.'

I hoped I was still hallucinating. I am going to fall asleep soon and Mrs Kanencukier will bring me my tablets again, I thought. If only my feet would stop burning. Why am I having such trouble trying to walk? I cannot move my feet properly.

'We're nearly there,' said one of the nurses, jolting me back to reality. The horse barrack, which had only one entrance, was at least fifty metres long. It had no windows and only small vents in the roof that cast a dim light inside. Outside, next to the door, was the crate containing the bodies of those who had perished during the night. During the typhus epidemic the crate was collected up to twice a day for cremation at Werk C. As we neared the barrack, three emaciated naked bodies on one stretcher were carried out of the building and tipped into the crate. One of the men pointed. 'You see? They're making room for you!'

The other nurse burst out laughing. 'There's a scam going on in there,' he said. 'There's lots more corpses but the staff keep the dead to collect their food rations, then sell them to those inmates who can afford to pay. They only remove the dead bodies of those who have relatives, or if someone is visiting or inquiring about them.'

The other nurse nodded. 'Mojsie Finger, who's in charge, told me that bodies lie there for days, their faces half eaten by rats. The rats attack those still alive too. There are hundreds of these rodents and they're as big as cats.'

We had arrived.

'We've brought you a new prospect, a potential corpse,' one of the nurses said to Lola, Finger's wife.

A terrible stench hit my nostrils; it was far worse than that of the camp's latrines or the ogolniak. It was the smell of death. My eyes became accustomed to the darkness and, as I couldn't stand on my feet, I kneeled, then slowly collapsed onto the floor. Two rows of three-tiered bunks rested against the walls. Many sick inmates, some covered with rags, were packed onto them. They mostly occupied the lower tiers – the upper bunks were impossible for these skeletal human beings to reach.

Moaning, unanswered calls for water and cries for help came out of scores of throats. Between the two rows of pallets in the middle of the room were three sawdust ovens. At one end was a small area, divided by a screen, with a small table and two benches; here, Lola, her husband and three male nurses were based. At the other end was a shabby curtain, but it was too far and too dark to see what was behind it.

Some inmates were being looked after by relatives or friends. They fed them, wiped them down and consoled them. The vast majority, however, were alone.

'Your name?' Lola asked.

'Morgen,' I whispered.

'Number?'

'Eighty eighty-seven.'

'Find yourself an empty pallet and a rag to cover your ass, if you can,' Lola said in a no-nonsense voice. 'You piss into the barrels next to the pallets; the shithouse is at the other end of the barrack. Don't shit on the pallet, there's no-one here to clean you up. Ignore the rats – as long as you stay alive, they're harmless.'

I crawled along the floor, a mixture of mud and excrement, looking for an empty pallet. In some places, people lay on top of each other, while others remained on the floor, too weak to climb onto the lowest tier. I turned around to search the opposite side of the barrack when Lola walked up. 'I'll find a space for you. Wait here.' She called out to her nurses, 'Pull out the dead body from here and take it to the end of the row, next to the shithouse, then come back and help Morgen up to the pallet.'

I inherited the dead man's straw, a piece of rag that had served him as a blanket and a clean white bedsheet, neatly folded beneath it all. I also found a bundle containing dirty trousers, a shirt and a vest, which the dead man had used as a pillow. I lay down on my back and covered myself with the rag.

After some time, certainly weeks later, I finally woke up, disorientated. The roof of the barrack had been blown away by a storm and rain poured in. I was wet and my blanket was soaked. As I became more conscious, I felt sharp pain around my lumbar area, on my hips and on my palms. I called for a nurse and eventually Lola and Safirsztajn came. They removed my blanket and inspected my body. Both my hands were covered in ulcerated open wounds.

'What's this then?' Lola looked closely. 'Your blood must be very sweet because the lice like it very much and there are plenty of them. Don't worry, you won't die from this. We'll wash the lice away and take care of the wounds. Do you have anybody who can organise some bandages, dressings or just plain clean cloth for you?'

'Yes, my mother or my father will provide for me. Just let them know and they'll bring everything we need. They always do.'

'Yeah, yeah. Your mother and father. Very good. Now turn around. Let's see your back.'

I tried but Lola and the nurse had to roll me over. 'You've a lot of bedsores on your back from lying on the pallet for a long time. But you won't die from this either.'

'How long have I been here?'

'I don't know exactly, around two months,' she said.

My open sores were where the bone had rubbed the skin away, exposing bare flesh. Safirsztajn brought some water, and Lola washed the lice from my wounds. I cried and groaned and they tried to calm me down. In the meantime, another nurse brought me some soup and I tried to feed myself. Unable to hold a spoon, I drank from the tin, then held it out and asked for more. The nurse told me that I could have more, but that I had to pay for it.

*

Loud hammering woke me. A squad of workers was busy rebuilding the roof. Lola and Mrs Kanencukier were standing next to my pallet, embroiled in a fierce conversation. When they saw me open my eyes, they stopped.

'I brought you some soup and two aspirin,' Mrs Kanencukier said. 'Take them straight away and eat the soup. We thought that we had lost you. You've slept for the last twenty-four hours. Your crisis is now over. It's time for you to get well.

'Thousands of people have died from the epidemic, and are still dying. It's not over yet. I came to visit many times, but you were unconscious. You've spent more than two months here and it's only thanks to Lola you survived. I'll be back tomorrow with something to eat and to take care of your wounds.'

Lola brought me a fresh blanket. 'Don't worry, between Kanencukier and I, we'll get you on your feet very soon.'

I gulped my soup and slept some more. I found myself in my old bedroom at home, my mother sitting on the edge of my bed holding my hands. I heard her gentle, sweet voice. 'Don't worry, my darling, you're in very good hands. One of the Lamed Vav will care for you. Now, go back to sleep until I come back.' She kissed me on my forehead and left the room, vanishing through the closed door, though the scent of her perfume lingered.

I was woken by shouting. 'Who wants to go to the shower room?' From all over the barrack, voices cried out: 'Me!' 'Me!' 'Take me!' 'Me too!' Inmates crawled from their pallets towards the door. The nurses selected the fittest, sending the weak back to their bunks. People were crying, begging to be included and trying to push themselves towards the exit.

The next day Kanencukier came with a tin of soup and a small slice of bread. I told her about yesterday's commotion. 'I hope that you'll go to the shower room soon,' she said. 'It'll mean that you've survived.'

Six days later I did go to the shower room. Kanencukier told me that almost everybody in the camp, including the policjanten, the komendanten and the Werkschutz, had been affected by typhus. The sickness lasted anywhere from six days to three months, depending on the individual. In our micro-world it was a pandemic – somewhere between 8000 and 10,000 inmates died from typhus. But there was some good news: because of the heavy losses of workers, the Germans temporarily discontinued their weekly selections and killings.

CHAPTER 29

WHEN I CAME BACK AFTER MY SHOWER, Lola helped me dress. I put my few items, including my wet shirt, into the blanket from my bed and tied it up as a bundle. I asked for her to help me to the administration barrack. As before, I sat by the doorway there, waiting to be allocated a new bunk. While I was waiting, a policjant was ordered to take me and two others to get a haircut and shave. My beard was at least a few months old.

I asked the policjant to carry my small bundle for me, as I didn't have the strength to do it myself. Even walking was beyond my abilities; I held onto a wall or crawled. The policjant stared at me, but after hesitating briefly he took my bundle, proving that he still had some humanity.

I sat on the chair in front of Sobol, the chief barber. He did not recognise me. He attempted conversation while lathering my face. 'Where have you been all this time? Your beard looks months old.'

'I just came out of the hospital, where you put me,' I said.

'Me? I've nothing to do with the hospital. I'm just a barber – not a doctor, not even a nurse.'

'But you helped me like a good friend to get in. I'm indebted to you for the rest of my life.'

After he had shaved me, he peered at my face but still did not recognise me. 'What's your name?'

'Morgen.'

'I don't know any Morgen. I still don't know who you are.'

'You must remember. You liked the buckle of my belt very much and, as a good friend, I gave it to you.'

'Ah, uh, yes, yes.' I saw embarrassment on his face. He fell silent for a moment, then said abruptly, 'I suggest you have your head shaved as you'll lose your hair anyway. After typhus everyone loses their hair temporarily.'

'No. Please cut it very short, but don't shave it.'

'You know, I really liked that buckle, but unfortunately I've lost it. But I have something else for you.' He turned around and out of a drawer took my leather wallet and handed it to me.

'I found this after you were moved from here and kept it in case you survived the epidemic. To be honest, I didn't believe you would. But miracles do happen.'

The policjant took us back to the administration building, where we were told to pick out any unoccupied pallet at the ogolniak – there were now plenty to choose from. I chose a pallet on the lowest level and as close to the entrance as possible. I fell exhausted on top of the pallet and took out my wallet. I checked the inside pocket, hoping that maybe, just maybe, Sobol forgot to take the money. He hadn't. Then I took out the half-a-dozen family photos and held them with both hands, remnants of a once loving and cherished family, as tears filled my eyes, distorting the images of my dearest ones, and ran down my cheeks. I could not control myself and surrendered to waves of convulsive sobbing. Only later, when we were called to collect our food ration, did I begin to calm down. My tremor slowly abated, but I still trembled from time to time.

Later, I tried to remember small details about the photos. Where were they taken? Who was there and what did we do at the time? They transported me back to events long forgotten, to things that had happened in another lifetime. These photographs became my most treasured possessions, even more valuable than bread, the most important commodity in the camp. I fell asleep, clutching the wallet with the photos tightly in my fists.

When I awoke I went to see Kanencukier at the infirmary. She touched my forehead and felt my pulse. She checked the wounds on my wrists and the bedsores on my back, washed them in a solution of calcium permanganate and replaced the pieces of sheet used as dressings. 'You're just a bag of bones. You *must* gain weight and return to work as soon as possible,' she warned. 'You don't want to be sent to Werk C, do you?'

'Of course not, but everything's been stolen and I've no money to buy food.'

'I can't solve your problem, but I'll see what I can do.'

'There's something else. My gums are bleeding and my teeth are becoming loose. What do I do about it?'

'You have scurvy, which is caused by vitamin C deficiency. Eat fresh vegetables and fruit – anything raw will do. If you can make your way to the camp kitchen where they have sauerkraut, beg them to give you some. And if you have access to salt, dissolve some in water and rinse your mouth a few times a day. See me tomorrow at the same time,' she ordered and gave me two slices of bread. The following day, Kanencukier gave me another slice of bread and a portion of soup as well.

Slowly I regained some strength but was still disorientated and too weak to resume work. I started looking for scraps of food in the bins behind the kitchen but I was not the only one looking for food. Others were quicker and more cunning than me.

I had heard somewhere that death from starvation began with swollen feet. Mine began to swell and I started to panic. I had spasms of panting, which Kanencukier explained was due to hunger seizures. In desperation I began to beg for food. Sometimes people gave me a crumb or two, which was unusual, as people had very little compassion for the muselman. I looked so destitute, my hand bandaged in rags, stooped by my infirmity and humiliated at the demoralising need to beg. The pain of hunger was so intense that I was totally inert, though my eyes constantly searched for food, hoping to find something that someone had dropped.

Around this time Jewish scientists in the Warsaw ghetto clandestinely researched the process of death by starvation. At the onset, the pulse weakens, the heart slows and blood pressure drops. The next symptoms of starvation are dryness of the mouth and increased urine production. A rapid loss of the layer of fat beneath the skin occurs and the victim has a constant desire to chew something, even inedible material.

As the process progresses, the victim feels general weakness, lapses into sleep, and constantly feels the cold. Starving people in the ghetto weighed as little as half of what they had before the war. Their skin turned pale or brownish and became fine in texture.

In the final stage, people's faces turned grey and their body temperature dropped one degree below normal. Prolonged malnutrition causes metabolic changes in body cells and tissue. Vital internal organs shrink and muscles atrophy. The organs that deteriorate most are the heart, liver and kidneys; the brain deteriorates relatively little.

A week after being discharged from the hospital I was still not ready to work, though I knew I had to get better. If I didn't I would be selected. I was sitting on the steps of the entrance to the Ekonomia, my face and arms out to the sun, when a well-dressed woman and a group of policjanten approached. I strained to remember who she was, as she looked very familiar.

The woman stopped in front of me and spoke. 'Siegmund

Siegreich!' she exclaimed. 'Good God, what are you doing here? Is it really you?'

I racked my brain but still didn't know who she was. I looked around in panic, worried that someone had heard her call me by my real name. All of a sudden it clicked. This was Markowiczowa, the komendantka from Werk C, accompanied by her deputies.

'Mrs Markowiczowa!' I said with false enthusiasm. 'You look as stunning as ever.' I did not know what else to say. 'Would you please call me by my first name only? I'm known here only as Zygmunt,' I awkwardly added.

'What's happened to you? You look terrible. If it weren't for your eyes, I wouldn't have recognised you at all.'

I explained I was still getting over typhus.

'That's awful, but I can see that you are on the way to recovery. Come and have lunch with us.'

'Thank you very much. I'm delighted to accept your invitation,' I mumbled quickly, scarcely able to believe my luck.

The party proceeded up the stairs and through the door. I crawled on all fours, determined to get to the top: a meal was a powerful incentive. The room was divided by two rows of bunks and in its centre were a table and two benches. They sat around the table and I took my place on one of the pallets opposite Mrs Markowiczowa. They spoke in Yiddish, mixing in a few Polish words from time to time. One of the komendanten took my tin can, filled it with homemade barley soup and handed it back with a generous slice of buttered bread. I finished my soup before the others had even started and was too embarrassed to ask for more.

Mrs Markowiczowa said that she and her party were in Werk A for at least a week and that I was invited to have lunch with them every day. In fact, I had lunch with them only once more. I never found out why Mrs Markowiczowa came to Werk A. It's quite possible that she didn't visit at all, and that this is an imagined memory caused by my sickness; it's true that intense hunger can cause vivid hallucinations. But I'm inclined to believe that it was real. That this was another small miracle of food being offered when I needed it most. A few more days and I was declared fit to return to work.

CHAPTER 30

Mrs Kanencukier got me a jacket from the camp storeroom in readiness for my return to work. I was transferred to the shift led by Szlagbaum, who told me that my place at the steel tempering department had been given to somebody else. I was now allocated a new job in a stockroom containing steel and non-ferrous metal rods. I joined three other inmates who had worked there since they arrived at the camp. One was a rabbi from a nearby village whom we called Rabin, the second was Chaim, a skinny but very strong man, and the third was Mendel Feldman, whom I befriended. Our supervisor, Majewski, was a Pole in his fifties with grey hair, a bushy moustache and black-framed spectacles. He lived in Szydłowiec, a small village nearby, and knew Mendel and his parents from long before the war. They had been neighbours.

I was still very weak and not much help to my workmates. We handled heavy metal rods and bars, carrying them from one place to another, loading, unloading and placing them on shelves. Fortunately, my coworkers were considerate and helped me a lot. Since I was competent with paperwork, I translated German orders for Majewski, though he would never ask for my help if someone else was around. First he would send the other workers out, then ask me to read out the order, pretending that he could not see the small print. He always argued with me about the pronunciation of some German words. I tried to explain the differences, but he didn't want to listen and yelled that he had been a storeman for more than thirty years and knew better. Otherwise he was not a nasty man.

Partly because of hunger, partly because of the lingering effects of illness, I had a number of recurring dreams. In one I sat down to a magnificent meal. I could smell the delicious aromas of cooked food, my mouth watered in anticipation, but I would wake up just before the food landed on my tongue. The second dream was quite different. My brother-in-law Don took an active part in the liberation of our camp with the help of the Russians. I saw him lead a battalion of tanks into the camp. He stood on top of the first tank, holding a huge bunch of white lilac in his hand, and shouted, 'You are free! You are free!' I could smell the strong scent of the freshly cut lilac. A slight variation on this had him arriving on a white horse, still with white lilac, shouting, 'You are liberated! Go home!'

*

Rumours spread that an SS *Sonderkommando* or special command group had arrived at Werk C with up to 100 condemned prisoners taken from the Gestapo district prison in Radom. These men were forced to open all mass graves in the forest, exhume the corpses, burn them in a makeshift crematorium and scatter the ashes in the woods – that is what we heard. We saw smoke rising from the nearby forest and, when the wind blew in our direction, smelled the odour of burning flesh. At the same time there was heavy traffic into Werk C: airtight trucks were laden with prisoners who were dead on arrival and whose bodies were quickly cremated. And Majewski told us that the Germans were killing Russian, English and American prisoners of war in the forests around Skarżysko-Kamienna and burning the bodies at Patelnia. (Patelnia was the nickname for the crematorium at

Werk C.) In the meantime, people still died from starvation.

I was still a muselman and kept a low profile. I walked as close to buildings as I could with my head down and my eyes avoiding the stares of others. When I walked through the gates to and from work I tried to keep in the middle of the group to avoid being hit. The only time I relaxed a little was during my shift. Once I was sent to deliver a few steel rods to the distribution centre at division B. I passed Goldberg's lathe. We looked each other in the face. Goldberg did not recognise me or pretended not to know me – but if he did, he now knew that he could not squeeze anything more from me. I breathed a little easier.

Typhus and the mass deportation and extermination of Jews from towns and villages meant that the Germans had very few replacements for their much-needed workforce and stopped selections for a time. As a result our food allowance had been increased slightly while I was sick. I benefited greatly from this as I recovered. The additional weekly ration consisted of 50 grams of sugar and 100 grams of black pudding, but because of problems in distributing the sugar, it was added to the soup once a week. Many of the inmates could not tolerate the sweet soup or the black pudding. It tasted bad and it was not kosher, so many who could afford to buy other food did so. I was in heaven. Rabin and some other inmates passed their extra allowance on to me, which practically saved my life. The swelling of my feet slowly receded and I regained some strength, but lost all my hair, as Sobol had predicted.

The temporary amnesty did not last long. As soon as the Germans could get new workers the selections resumed. Some smaller camps were liquidated, like those in Piotrków, Radomsko, Pionki, Trawniki, Poniatowa and Staszów. Their inmates were transferred to Skarżysko-Kamienna to replace recently selected prisoners.

Among those from Staszów was my old friend Heniek

Nisenbaum's brother, David. David was a very handsome man, well mannered, softly spoken and polite. I sought him out because I wanted to know what happened to Heniek after he jumped off the truck just before we left Staszów. David told me he had heard that Heniek was living in the forest working for the partisans.

David had been a policjant in Staszów. He had kept his uniform and was appointed komendant of some female barracks in Werk A. As such, he was in charge of distributing bread and the once-weekly portion of jam. He promised to help me as much as he could and immediately filled my tin can with jam, approximately half a kilogram's worth. He continued to do this for me every week until the end of June 1944, a period of more than a year. With this asset I was able to barter for bread and sometimes for soup or even a cigarette. This generosity greatly improved my situation. It not only speeded up my recovery but I was no longer looked upon as a muselman and people stopped bullying me.

*

A few days before Easter 1943, a Werkschutz guardsman appeared at our storeroom and exchanged a few words with Majewski, who in turn called Mendel Feldman and me.

'You two go with this guardsman for some special duties. After you finish, report to me. Understood?'

We both answered in unison, 'Yes sir, Mr Majewski.'

The guardsman led us to the side gate of the factory and escorted us through. We found ourselves in an open area between the factory's high brick fence and the house of Egon Dalski, the general manager of Hasag Industries in the Generalgouvernement. We walked through the back entrance into a huge garden surrounding Dalski's residence. The two-storey house had large French windows framed by white-painted wooden shutters. It reminded me a lot of my grandparents' house in Będzin where the whole family would gather during the holidays.

The guard left us in the yard while he entered the building through the back door. Moments later an elderly Polish woman appeared wearing a long grey apron over her multicoloured striped skirt. She was the housekeeper. 'Over there you will find ten geese,' she said, and pointed to an enclosure. 'Slaughter and pluck them, then cut them open, gut them and bring them into my kitchen. In the corner is a tree stump with an axe in it which you can use.'

Mendel and I looked at each other.

'We've never done this before, but I'm sure we can manage,' I said.

'You need to dig a hole in the ground and let the blood flow into it. When you've finished, cover the hole with dirt.'

The guard left and the housekeeper waddled back into the house. We walked across to where the geese were making a hell of a racket; it was as if they knew their fate. We struggled for about five minutes trying to catch our first goose. As soon as we bent down to grab it, the bird flapped its wings, quacked and honked and jumped about creating total mayhem. Finally, Mendel managed to hold one by its wings, while I quickly grabbed its feet. The goose was almost as strong as we were and we struggled, with feathers flying everywhere. We tried to place the bird's neck on the stump, but it simply refused to comply. We really needed an extra pair of hands. We wrestled the goose for a few more minutes, without much success.

'I'll hold the wings still and you grab the goose's head with your left hand, holding the axe in your right hand,' I said to Mendel. 'Then place the neck on the stump and chop off its head.'

'No. I'll hold it and *you* chop off its head,' Mendel argued.

'But I've never killed anything in my entire life.'

'What? And you think I have?'

'I don't know,' I shrugged. 'But the only geese I've seen in Katowice were stuffed and roasted on a platter on the dining room table. I'm *certain* that in Szydłowiec they were running wild in the street,' I teased.

'Ha. You think you're so funny. Why don't we toss a coin?'

'OK, toss a coin,' I said.

'I don't have one,' he answered.

'Neither do I.'

We both burst out laughing, nearly releasing our grip on the goose.

Mendel then grabbed the axe and chopped the poor goose's head off in one strong swing, but it refused to die. It jumped up and down and ran around headless, splashing blood everywhere. Mendel pointed at me and said how funny I looked with spots of blood all over my face and clothes.

'Have you seen yourself?' I retorted. 'If anyone could see us now, they would die laughing. Now I understand how in 390 BC the geese saved Rome.' I had studied Livy's *History of Rome* in college.

'Who is Rome?' Mendel asked.

'Never mind,' I said. 'Let's get back to work.'

Before long we had become quite expert at slaughtering geese – but instead of letting the blood flow into the hole as instructed by the housekeeper, we filled up our containers. We reckoned that it would be a good source of protein which we badly needed. The blood would coagulate and we could mix it with soup or bread and have a nutritious meal.

By midday we had almost finished with the killing, just as a Werkschutz arrived on pushbike, bringing with him a ten-litre cauldron full of sweet soup for our lunch. What a dilemma we had. We needed our containers to drink the soup, but they were full of blood. We couldn't drink the blood as it was, as we'd vomit it instantly, and we didn't want to spoil the soup by mixing it in. We emptied our containers into the hole and filled them with the soup, which contained noodles and was exceptionally good. It must have been brought from the kitchen that catered for the Poles and delivered to the big boss's house. We ate and ate but despite our great hunger were unable to finish all ten litres. We filled our containers and left the rest in the cauldron, cursing the fact that we did not have larger tins.

We finished the slaughtering and were contemplating how to go about plucking the geese when the housekeeper called us inside. The woman, seeing our bloodstained hands and faces, called for us to wash up in the next room. What a surprise awaited us. Real soap. And even a proper fresh and clean towel.

We emerged to see the kitchen table was set for two people, with proper crockery and cutlery. The woman served two bowls of beef broth with noodles and two plates with boiled beef and potatoes. We could not believe our eyes. We had not seen such a grand meal for a very long time. The cruel irony was that we were full and could not eat at all. Here was all this wonderful hot food and we could not fit in another morsel.

I had an idea and explained that we'd just eaten but asked if we could finish our work and return for the meal afterwards.

'But everything will be cold,' the housekeeper protested. 'I can't warm it up again later.'

'Don't worry, we're used to eating cold food,' I said convincingly. The woman raised her shoulders in defeat and left the room.

We went back to work and started to pluck the geese, not knowing where to begin. The woman brought us a sack to put the feathers and the down in and showed us how to go about it. Around five o'clock we finished our work and, to the chickens' delight, we emptied our soup into the henhouse's feeding trough. We walked back into the house, filled our tins with noodles and potatoes, wrapped the meat in old newspaper and carried it back to the plant in our pockets.

That was by far my best day in the camp.

PART V

MAY 1943 – MAY 1944

CHAPTER 31

O<small>NE</small> <small>MORNING AROUND</small> 10 <small>AM</small> the camp commander, Anton Ipfling, ordered a rollcall for all inmates. We were shaken out of a brief sleep soon after our return from the night shift. We dragged ourselves outside and lined up, but were not counted. After twenty minutes, two Werkschutz appeared, flanking an inmate. His hands were tied behind his back and two lengths of rubber from an old tyre dangled around his neck attached to a placard, which read:

> *I am a thief.*
> *I stole from the German Reich.*
> *I deserve to die.*

The Werkschutz paraded him up and down in front of us. Then, at the watchtower, they stopped. One of the guards selected the tallest and strongest-looking inmate, whose name was Weisberg, and ordered him to hang the condemned man. The Werkschutz gave Weisberg a noose and showed him how to knot it. Poor Weisberg begged to be relieved from this task. One guard punched him hard in the nose and shouted at him. '*Du verfluchter dreckiger Jude! Wenn du es nicht tust, dann gehst du mit auf dem Galgen.*' ('You damned filthy Jew! If you don't do it, you'll go with him to the gallows.')

A ladder was brought and the other Werkschutz fastened the loose end of the noose, which Weisberg had knotted, to the watchtower. Weisberg then placed the noose around the inmate's neck. The condemned was then forced to climb the ladder. At a signal from one of the guards, Weisberg had to kick away the ladder. At that moment the body fell, the noose tightened. Legs kicked out wildly trying to find a foothold; the neck broke. The body swung and fluttered a few times, then stopped.

The body remained hanging there for twenty-four hours before being cut down. Weisberg was inconsolable for months.

Not long after this a new transport of several hundred Jews from the Łódź ghetto arrived. The barracks and Ekonomia were now fit to bursting, which resulted in more frequent selections. Luckily, I had gained weight and was getting stronger. A new working group of several hundred inmates had been created to build a new camp at Werk A. Some inmates thought this indicated that we had a future; others believed it was to be built for English or American prisoners of war and that we would be exterminated.

One day, as the day shift finished and the night shift arrived, armed Werkschutz herded the fresh workers into the huge central yard of the plant. I had finished my shift and was on my way back to the camp, but the gate was closed and the guard did not have the authority to open it. From my position at the gate I watched what was unfolding in the main yard.

A scaffold had been hastily erected in the centre of the yard and a dozen black-uniformed Germans led a man towards it. He was handcuffed from behind and wore two placards. On his chest: *I helped Jews with food and money*; on his back: *I aided my enemies and am a traitor. I deserve to die.*

A steel wire noose hung from the scaffolding. An SS officer placed it around his victim's neck and ordered him to climb onto a simple wooden chair. The German kicked the chair away and the Pole cried out, 'Long live Poland!' The noose almost cut through his neck.

The Werkschutz then fired into the air to subdue the crowd. The next day posters appeared all over the plant, inside and outside the buildings and on official billboards, stating that the SS and the police commander hereby granted amnesty to all current offenders but those caught in the future committing a similar crime could expect the same fate:

Workers! The management appeals to your conscience. Remember when the Jews exploited you and sucked your blood. Remember the Bolshevik barbarians in Katyn. 12,000 Polish officers murdered. Everyone knows this was the work of the Jews. Anyone helping the Jews, the murderers of your brothers and comrades, is a traitor.

The Polish underground had apparently stepped up activities in the area and Poles at the plant told us this had led to increased reprisals from the Germans. We later found out that the Germans had actually executed four Polish partisans accused of sabotage and anti-German activity. Three of them were hanged publicly at the main square in the town centre, while the fourth, Tadeusz Nowak, had been transferred to the Hasag plant and hanged in front of us. The Germans were using Nowak's execution to intimidate, to frighten and to discourage the Poles from helping and aiding Jews.

*

One morning in May I woke early. The sun was already up and a cloudless sky heralded a beautiful day, which in itself was unusual. I went to the latrine while it was still almost empty. Only two or three men were at the other end so I didn't have to queue. I was keen to go back outside, lured by the clear morning.

Suddenly a ray of sun bounced off a bright shiny spot in the eternal mud. I was intrigued and bent down for a closer look. With two fingers like tweezers I picked up a small stone. It was a diamond the size of a large pea. I held it between my fingers until I was back on my pallet, where I could take a good look. I'd never seen a loose diamond before and had no idea of its authenticity or value. I wrapped the stone in a scrap of newspaper, which I always had in reserve, forming a tiny envelope, and put it right at the bottom of my pocket. I was sure it was worth a lot of money and, if I could find a buyer, it would help me survive.

Some people smuggled jewellery and money into the camp and made a living from it, but I didn't know where to go or whom to trust. I kept checking my pocket to feel the stone between my fingers. I thought of the things I could buy: bread, margarine, a piece of sausage. First, though, I needed new trousers and shoes. I knew Mendel Feldman had a relative in the camp with some connections but was not sure if I could trust him. Then a thought came to me. Perhaps Rabin, the rabbi from my work group? He was bound to know someone, and if I could trust anyone surely it would be a pious person?

I saw him in the latrines at lunchtime and I asked outright if he was interested in buying a diamond from me.

'I don't know,' Rabin stammered, surprised. 'I'd have to see the ring: see if it's set in platinum or gold, the quality, the size of the stone and the way it's set.' He spoke like an expert. 'Can you show it to me?'

'Yes, of course. But this is a loose stone, not a ring.'

He removed the diamond from its envelope, placed it on his palm and examined it thoroughly against the light. 'Where did you get it?'

In my naivety, I told him.

'I'll sell it for you for the best possible price, but I need two to three days to locate my contact and finalise the transaction.'

That was all fine by me, though I was puzzled that Rabin, as a man of God, didn't first suggest that I try to find the owner and return the stone.

I saw Rabin the next day. He did not say anything and I did not ask anything. On the third day, as soon as we arrived at the storeroom, he called me aside.

'That stone you gave me has caused me great embarrassment, you glazier,' he said with a sneer. 'The buyer who is a jeweller derided me and says that it's a complete fake. It's just a piece of glass.'

'It's a real diamond,' I insisted. 'Who would cut facets in glass and how else would it have such a brilliant polish? If you can't sell it, give it back to me.'

'I haven't got it. I threw it away.'

I didn't believe him and chastised him for throwing something away that wasn't his.

'What do you think, I would carry a piece of glass in my pocket?' he answered aggressively. I had told him that I found the stone in the mud, in front of the latrine – that I was not its rightful owner. Perhaps he felt this absolved him of his dishonesty. He never returned the diamond and from then on we avoided each other.

*

A few days later, on 16 May 1943, my nineteenth birthday, I was transferred from the storeroom to a job in another section of the toolmaking department. I was assigned to help a Polish master turner at his lathe. His name was Biernacki. A tall blond man in his late twenties, he lived in Skarżysko-Kamienna with his parents. He wore navy overalls, white sneakers and a grey cycling cap. He had started there as an apprentice at fourteen and had become one of the best of his profession.

He hardly looked at me, but pointing to the machine in front of him he asked; 'Do you know what this is?'

'Yes sir, I do. It's a lathe.'

'Have you ever worked on a lathe?'

'Never, sir.'

'How old are you?'

'As a matter of fact, today is my nineteenth birthday, sir.'

'Where did you work before the war and what did you do here at this factory?'

'Before the war broke out I was still attending year nine at high school. Here at the plant I started work at the tempering department and later, after recovering from typhoid, I was transferred to the raw material storeroom, where I am still working, sir.'

'Can you read a technical drawing?'

'Yes sir, I can. Although I don't have any technical education, I studied mathematics, trigonometry and geometry. I know what sine and cosine are as well as pi, tangents, parabola, radius, diameter and circumference.'

'Excellent. I'll teach you turning and if you do well you'll have a secure job.'

He showed me how the lathe worked, explaining all its functions, then encouraged me to operate it. After an hour or so observing me he was confident I wouldn't have any problems. A few days later he allowed me to work independently. He only supervised me when there was change of product or tools. Sometimes, when he skipped a day or two of work, I was left on my own. I enjoyed the job; I was learning a lot about the tools and parts we produced, and was curious to know where the finished products ended up.

Biernacki was reluctant to show any support for inmates, especially after the public hanging a few weeks earlier. On rare occasions, though, he would take my dish and collect the so-called Polish soup (carefully checking over his shoulder), then place the dish into the drawer of his tool cabinet and disappear – he was too scared even to watch me eat the soup. From time to time, he gave me his cigarette butts and once a whole one. He even brought me a pair of worn-out overalls to replace my paper suit. Generally, Biernacki was a good man. A month or so later he failed to come to work and I never saw him again. Some said that he was arrested, others that he had joined the partisans. As more and more Jewish inmates were assigned to the department to replace the Poles who were abandoning Hasag en masse, I took over Biernacki's job, and became a foreman in charge of a dozen lathes. I had some freedom in the factory and whenever I could I visited other departments to learn where the parts and tools we produced were used and for what purpose. Before long I gained a thorough understanding of how ammunition for military rifles and machine guns was produced, and the processes involved.

After the final annihilation of the Jews in ghettos, towns and villages was accomplished, it was difficult to obtain new Jewish workers. The administrators of some commercial entities, including ours, which depended on this low-cost workforce, resorted to bribing those in charge of concentration camps, or simply bought Jews. Sometimes they even kidnapped large transports of Jews who had been sentenced to extermination in the gas chambers.

In June about fifty people arrived from a small slave labour camp in Radom that had been shut down. By a fortunate 'error' these Jews landed in Skarżysko-Kamienna instead of Auschwitz. About ten men from this group were assigned to work under my supervision and one of them, Yumek Kielman, would become my good friend.

Later that same month a transport of 2500 Jewish men and women arrived from Majdanek concentration camp; they had all been sent there after the Warsaw ghetto uprising was thwarted. They too were destined for Auschwitz but were instead kidnapped and brought to Skarżysko-Kamienna, allegedly by a special military unit cooperating with the armament industry. Weeks later another transport arrived with a further 500 prisoners. Two thousand new inmates were allocated to Werk A, and a thousand sent to Werk C. They all wore concentration camp uniforms – a blue and grey striped shirt and pants called *pasiaki*, with the letters *K* and *L*, large and red, painted on the back, and wooden clogs called *holenderki*.

I watched them line up at the Appelplatz and searched for familiar faces in the crowd. Someone called out, 'Look at the letters *K* and *L* on their backs. They're *ka-el-niks*.' The name stuck. The *K* and *L* stood for *Konzentrazions Lager* or concentration camp, and henceforth the men were known as *kaëlniks* and the women *kaëlankas*. They arrived without any belongings or valuables, having been robbed, dehumanised and deprived of their dignity in Majdanek, and as such they provoked the anger of the Jewish camp administrators. They were classified as inferior creatures and treated as such, not only by the policjanten and komendanten, but by most of the inmates. Like me, they predominantly spoke Polish, not Yiddish, which increased general contempt for them. When people were needed for work, for example, it became common to say, 'Take two men and three kaëlniks to do the job.'

Some of the more affluent veteran inmates propositioned the female newcomers, asking them if they'd like to be a *kuzynka* or 'cousin'. This euphemism referred to unmarried couples who lived together, despite the fact that sex was forbidden. Most of the girls agreed to this for a tin of soup or slice of bread rather than starve, but for most of the inmates sex was of little interest. Only the *prominente* and those able to sustain their sex drive through sufficient nutrition engaged in this behaviour. One positive aspect of such an arrangement, though, was that it eased the pain of solitude and loneliness.

With the sudden influx of kaëlniks, we reverted to the same overcrowding as before the typhus epidemic. Once again I had to search for a bed. I had once seen a man sleeping in the washroom of the Ekonomia basement and went to investigate. Three or four long double-sided troughs had been installed there and three water pipes ran parallel around the room about half a metre off the ground. One of these carried hot water and offered some warmth. The man was a few years older than me, a refugee from Germany, and didn't speak Polish at all well. He was still sleeping in one corner and I asked if a corner might be free. He said that was fine and then showed me what he was sitting on – a round, wooden barrel lid tightly lodged between two water pipes. He told me where he got it and even where he hid it when he was out at work. I soon found my own barrel lid and made myself comfortable. I was pleased to have found a safe place away from the elements and the stench of the ogolniak. I had no difficulty putting up with the amplified noise of the pipes and constant running water, wooden clogs across wet tiles, or lights burning day and night. Until we were moved into newly erected barracks I slept there, bent forward resting my head on my folded arms.

Although the tension between the kaëlniks and the camp veterans was pronounced, I found myself drawn to them because of our similar backgrounds. Some of them became friends. Adek Frydman, Szymek Mapa, Wilek Pachter and Danek Mackiewicz were assigned to the toolmaking department, together with a dozen women. They were upper middle-class men and well educated, very different from the inmates from the surrounding villages. We got on well and soon cheered each other up, which greatly improved our wellbeing. This had an enormous positive effect on my mental state, relieving loneliness and isolation and increasing my confidence.

*

Once newcomers had registered they were then sent to the only bathhouse of the whole camp – located in Werk A – for showers and delousing. Generally we showered once every three weeks in our shift groups, while inmates from Werks B and C showered once a month.

I longed for shower time, despite the sharp smell of chlorine and carbolic acid. It warmed and soothed me and was a ritual cleansing of my enslavement. I had time to myself, and the water washed away the filth that engulfed me. It was a welcome distraction, a form of escape from the depressing routine of daily life at the camp. I grabbed every opportunity to linger near the bathhouse and often snuck in with other groups – there were always a few hundred inmates waiting their turn – increasing my showers to at least one a week. In the waiting lines I would search for familiar faces and from time to time would see my uncle Felix, who would come over from Werk C.

One day while biding my time for an unscheduled shower, I scrutinised a long queue of women waiting. I realised that the group was from Werk C by their yellow-coloured skin. Suddenly I spotted Lillian Lichtenstein. Was this possible? My heart raced. Nearly four years earlier Lilka and I had picked wild strawberries together in Zakopane. It now seemed like several lifetimes ago. She had not changed much but her beautiful blond plaits had gone and she wore a headscarf to cover her shaved head. She was dressed in rags but her blue-green eyes were still the same.

'Lillian! What are you doing here?' I asked, absurdly. 'Where did you come from?'

She stared at me, uncertain at first. 'Are you Siegmund?' Her eyes lit up. '*Of course* you are Siegmund! Your uncle Felix told me you were here. How good to see you.' Lillian explained she had arrived from Majdanek a couple of weeks earlier.

We reminisced about our last vacation together for some minutes before her group was led into the bathhouse. I saw her a couple more times over the following months and we both enjoyed our chats.

*

The construction of the new and much bigger camp at Werk A neared completion. Some sixty-five barracks, large and small, were erected in straight lines. Four barracks, including an infirmary and hospital, were built outside the camp perimeter. Each barrack consisted of at least two rooms and up to five, depending on its size. There was a square table in the middle of the room, two benches and a sawdust heater. One small 25-watt globe hung from the ceiling. Each pallet was for two inmates to share. No mattresses or blankets were supplied. The conditions were not too bad for those who shared with someone working a different shift, although Sundays were cramped and crowded. I shared a pallet with my friend Mendel Feldman, who worked day shift in the storeroom; however, I alternated each week from day shift to night shift, which meant every second week we squashed together in our narrow space. But we soon got used to it.

CHAPTER 32

THE LATHES DEPARTMENT appointed a new German supervisor called Reinicke from Hasag headquarters in Leipzig. He was a handsome blond in his thirties, of medium height, with blue-grey eyes. He wore a Nazi Party uniform under his white lab coat and was inexperienced in the German treatment of Jews. It was likely the first time he had seen a slave labour camp and he seemed to be overwhelmed. He was delighted that I spoke German and relied on me totally. He asked for my advice and used me as his interpreter. Once he even asked me if I was Jewish. 'Of course I'm Jewish,' I replied.

'But you look normal to me.'

That concluded our conversation that day. His German pride never allowed him to pry into my personal situation, but he bombarded me with hundreds of work-related questions.

A day or two later as we started the night shift, Reinicke received an order from a departmental manager to take special care to finish certain tools urgently needed. The day shift had the machine ready for us to continue the work. I was making my rounds when Reinicke approached me. 'Morgen, machine number eight just finished twenty-four rammers. Check the final product and bring them to the tempering department. They must be ready before the day shift arrives.' He gave me the job order and drawings and pointed to the trolley loaded with the rammers.

I checked the products using a micrometre and realised that all of them were faulty. The machine was incorrectly set and the rammers were two-tenths of a millimetre too small.

'Sir, we have a big problem,' I reported back to Reinicke. 'All the rammers are defective and cannot be repaired. The day shift set the lathe incorrectly. What would you like me to do?'

I saw panic and helplessness in his eyes. 'What can we do?' he asked anxiously.

'We need to make up a new lot of rammers and dispose of the faulty batch. We've still got five hours,' I said, looking up at the big clock on the front wall.

'Where would I get the raw material from? And the correct steel rods? I don't even know what kind of steel I need and where I would find it.'

'Leave it to me,' I said. 'I used to work in the storeroom. I know exactly where to look. The only problem is the keys. You have to get them for me. They're in the office. Go there and send somebody to call me to the office under some pretext.'

He went, and soon I was called to the office. I showed him where to find the keys and returned to my post.

Minutes later Reinicke came with keys and the original job card. We entered the storeroom and, without turning on the lights, I grabbed the rods and together we carried them to the lathe. I volunteered to do the job myself but first the faulty rods had to be disposed of. 'We have to drop them into many recycling bins, no more than two pieces in one bin. Perhaps you can take care of that because you can move around freely. In the meantime I'll get to work.'

Reinicke returned to me some time later and I reassured him that all would be well. 'Sir, we are partners in crime,' I said with a hint of irony. 'What we've done must remain our secret. No-one has noticed anything and no-one here except us speaks German.'

Somewhat strangely the whole affair amused me, especially when I saw how scared Reinicke was. The next day he brought me a small paper bag containing a sausage sandwich. He carefully put it into the drawer of my tool cabinet. This incident restored my sense of worth and had a colossal impact on my confidence.

*

As soon as the siren announced lunch one day, I picked up my dish and rushed outside to get my soup. On the way back to my machine I used both hands to carry my shallow dish, trying not to spill any hot soup. From the other end of the hall, coming towards me, was Koch, the German supervisor who oversaw the revolver lathes department. He was in his late twenties, very skinny and of middling height with a long narrow face and a scalp sparsely covered with thin dark hair. He was well known for his cruelty, and inmates of his department were constantly ill treated. So far I had managed to avoid him.

I moved to one side of the wide passage to make room for him, but he moved as well. I moved to the other side, he did the same, again and again, until we stood there, facing each other. He looked straight at me and began kicking both my shins. I stepped back. My tormentor followed.

The handles of the dish became hotter and hotter, burning my fingers. He kept kicking me, targeting the same spots. He didn't say anything, he didn't shout, he just kicked. I tried to keep calm, but was on the verge of throwing hot soup into his face, regardless of the consequences – if it could have guaranteed his death, I would have too. But it would only have scalded him, which wasn't worth my death. I bit my lips and tasted my salty blood.

Lucky for me, I stumbled and fell backwards, instinctively using my left arm to break my fall. I dropped my dish. Soup splashed on the floor, on my legs and on Koch's polished boots.

He flew into a rage and, with me on the ground, began kicking my chest and gut. Then he ordered me to lick the soup off his boots. I could not move. He gave me another hefty kick and shouted something about cleaning up the floor. I lost consciousness.

I woke up lying on a stretcher in the cloakroom. Two coworkers tended my wounds and cleaned me up. They told me I was lucky that Koch had spared my life. Every few minutes a workmate came to the cloakroom to see how I was doing. I was carried back to the camp on a stretcher and taken to the new infirmary, where, once again, Kanencukier helped me to recover. Three days later I was back at work. The wounds on my shins took a long time to heal and still bothered me months later.

*

A few weeks after the move to the new barracks I noticed that Mendel had begun scratching himself incessantly, especially during the night. A few days later I started to do the same. I went straight to Kanencukier.

'Morgen,' she explained, without a moment's hesitation, 'you have scabies. Unfortunately we've nothing here that can help. You need a special ointment from the outside – it's prescription-free and not terribly expensive.'

'Scabies? What's scabies?'

Kanencukier explained that it was a parasite that penetrates the skin, causing redness, blisters and severe itching. She wrote down the name of the ointment. I rushed to see Mendel and told him of our diagnosis. Neither of us had any money.

Mendel said that he had had scabies when he was a boy. 'More than half of the children in my class had it. I had it between my fingers. The teacher gave us an ointment which we used for three days. My brother-in-law who's here is from Skarżysko-Kamienna and has contact with local Poles. I'll see if he can help.'

I suggested that in the meantime we showered as often as possible, cleaning ourselves thoroughly with industrial soap, which was used on the machines and in plentiful supply. I gave Mendel a small tin box full of it. He would shower every day, sometimes even twice, though I could only shower when I was on day shift – at night the bathhouse was closed.

Two weeks later there was no improvement. On the contrary, the scabies had spread almost to every part of our bodies. I began to experiment with all the chemicals available to me. We tried machine oils, kerosene, petrol, paint solvents, acetone and turpentine but nothing helped, and *nothing* provided relief. The most difficult time was at work, trying to conceal my problem and avoid being caught scratching. If either of us had been discovered it's likely we would have been sentenced to death.

Mendel's brother-in-law said he could help, but needed money to buy the medicine and to pay off his Polish contact for this favour.

We were desperate. The itch was so intense we could not sleep and the warm weather intensified our discomfort. Every second day I used a grinder machine to file back my nails to prevent further infection. Each morning I got up as early as I could and rushed to the washroom to cool down, regardless of what shift I was working. The new facility was much larger than the old one, with timber benches along the walls and hooks above. The concrete floor was covered with wooden slats. One morning, after another sleepless night, I rushed there before sunrise. I splashed cold water onto my arms, chest and back. I repeated the process and headed outside to catch the cooling breeze, but on the way I noticed something green sticking out between the timber slats of the floor. I walked over, bent down to inspect it and carefully pulled out a US fifty-dollar bill. I quickly shoved it into the pocket of my pants, still hanging on the hook.

My heart raced. I was shocked and exhilarated. I had a vision of being rescued from this terrible disease. I peeked at the folded bill, just to make sure I wasn't dreaming. Then, just for a moment, I worried about finding something someone else had lost. But at that instant I recalled my mother's words: 'You must survive. You *will* survive. Someone is watching over you and will protect you.' I did not spend another thought on someone else's misfortune. I did not feel any guilt. Fate had determined that I needed the money more.

I spoke to Mendel later and told him that I had found the money for the ointment.

'This is great news,' he said. 'My brother-in-law has good connections and he'll do this for me.'

I told him to find out how much the ointment would cost, but I was a little unsettled by his remark – '*He'll do this for me.*' Mendel was behaving as if the money was his – as if he would be sharing with me, and not the other way round. We both knew we had to have treatment simultaneously, otherwise we would re-infect each other, but I still wondered if he would try to cheat me. Maybe I was being oversensitive, but I wanted to test him.

The next morning I told him in a woeful voice that I had lost the fifty-dollar note. He lost control and started abusing me in Polish and Yiddish, then punched my face, chest and stomach. 'I'm no fool. You can't trick me. You can't do this to me. I don't care if you lost the money or not. You're responsible for my half and I'll show you how I'll get my share out of you.'

I was astonished by his response. 'Shut up and calm down,' I said, trying to pacify him. 'Everything's OK, I was only joking.' But I knew that I was trapped in this situation and that he could not be trusted. All I could hope for was to get the ointment for the scabies even though it would cost me all the money I had. 'Contact your brother-in-law so we can start our treatment as soon as possible,' I sighed.

'He's not my brother-in-law,' he snapped back. 'A long time

ago he dated my sister – I never liked him then either. Anyway, my sister's dead now.' Mendel burst into tears, crying with as much passion as he had shown while hitting me. Who knows how long this performance would have continued, if not for Majewski, our Polish supervisor, and Mendel's neighbour before the war, who came into the storeroom, interrupting us. 'What's going on?' Majewski said. 'You, Morgen, go back to your work, you have no business to be here at all.' As I was leaving the storeroom, Mendel called out after me, 'Tonight at the camp we'll go to see Joseph.'

The rest of the day I was irritable and impatient. I could hardly concentrate on my work. I accidentally broke a knife on my lathe and reported it to Reinicke at once.

He looked at me not knowing what to do. 'What shall I do?' he asked. 'Is there any special procedure? Are we in trouble?'

'No. Just go to the tools distribution room, show the broken one and ask for a replacement.'

He was so awkward and helpless that I gained great satisfaction from his dependence on me.

Back at the camp, we hastily ate our evening soup and bread and went to see Joseph. We found him sitting at a table in the middle of the barrack with his 'cousin', eating a privately cooked soup and some bread supplied from the outside.

'We'd like a few words with you. Would you step outside for a couple of minutes?' Mendel asked him in Yiddish.

'Not now, I'm busy. Come back in half an hour.'

We turned around and left without another word. We hung around between the barracks to kill time.

'Mendel, I need to know. Please tell me again about when you had scabies before.'

'I told you already. The school supplied the ointment and in a couple of days we were all cured. But at that time only a few spots on my body were affected.'

'Do you think that fifty dollars is enough?' I asked

'What's the rate of exchange for an American dollar?' he asked.

'I don't know the current rates, but maybe you could ask Rabin. He'd know for sure. I don't speak with him now.'

'OK. I'll go see him now and we'll meet in front of Joseph's barrack in twenty minutes.'

'Fine. I'll be there.'

I went to visit Andzia. Sometimes we were rostered on opposite shifts so I wasn't sure if she'd be there. She was. She invited me to sit with her but I refused, not disclosing my reasons. I didn't want to infect her with scabies, or have her find out about it. She looked remarkably well and I told her so. Despite her age, she looked better than many women half her age in the camp. 'For me, looking healthy, clean and fit is a matter of survival,' she replied. 'I'm not the youngest any more. The little bit of make-up I have is a necessity and a lifesaver. Unfortunately, I can't return the compliment. Are you sick? Because you look dreadful.' She eyed me carefully.

I told her that I was just tired after a long day. We chatted for a few more minutes when Mr Zylberfuden entered the room.

'How are you, Mr Zylberfuden? You look well.'

'Thank you. Is there anything I can do for you?'

'Oh no, you've done more than enough for me. However, could I ask you something?'

'Of course.'

I came closer and whispered. 'What do you think the value of the American dollar is in the camp today?'

'That depends. There's a difference between the buying and the selling price. Whatever your intention, maybe I can help.'

'I'm not buying or selling. I'm just curious.'

'The current price is between 480 and 500 zloty each way. Outside, it would be about 100 zloty higher.'

'Thank you very much, Mr Zylberfuden. Please give my regards to your wife.'

I said goodbye to Andzia and went back to Mendel.

'What took you so long?' he said impatiently.

I ignored him. 'Did you see Rabin?'

'No. He wasn't there. Maybe he works night shift. What took you so long?'

'I was talking to somebody about the rate of exchange. I think that I have to exchange the dollars for zloty first and then look for someone to supply the ointment.'

'It's too late!' Mendel said angrily. 'I've spoken with Joseph and he's agreed to take care of everything.'

'How much will he pay for the American money? And how much will the ointment cost?'

'He said that there's enough money for the ointment and maybe a loaf of bread or two.'

'How could you do what you did behind my back?' I said. 'I still have the money in my pocket.'

'Yes,' rushed Mendel, 'give it to me. If I give him the money now we'll have the ointment tomorrow.'

Fifty American dollars converted to zloty was around 5000 zloty. A two-kilogram loaf of bread cost between six and ten zloty on the outside. Inside the camp, the going price for a similar loaf was between eighteen and twenty zloty. A tube of ointment to treat scabies was between fifteen and thirty zloty. Yet we would receive just one tube of ointment and two loaves of bread for the whole fifty dollars. Together, Joseph and his Polish accomplice, and possibly Mendel, were making a minimum profit of 4750 zloty from me.

I was shocked. I realised that I had erred about Mendel. It was a big disappointment and I was seized with sadness. I felt betrayed and deceived by my only friend whom I had trusted. On the other hand, I had mixed feelings. I had actually found the fifty dollars and it was not very honest to keep the money, even though it was impossible to locate the rightful owner. Mostly, despite the social differences between the two of us, I regretted losing a friend more than being deceived.

Disappointment aside, we received the ointment and started treatment. With a slice of bread we bribed the bathhouse komendant to let us shower during the lunchbreak. Then we applied the ointment from our scalps down to our toes, helping each other to rub the hard-to-reach areas. Forty-eight hours later we were as good as new.

A few days later I went to apologise to Andzia for my abrupt departure. At her barrack, a group of inmates surrounded Mrs Zylberfuden's bunk. I asked a woman what was going on and she told me Mrs Zylberfuden had died in her sleep. 'One more victim of typhus.'

I glimpsed Mr Zylberfuden and his children among the growing crowd of people. I didn't want to intrude so decided to postpone my visit for another day. Unfortunately I never spoke to Mr Zylberfuden again, for he died shortly after his wife's passing. He was a true gentleman – a man of great virtue and knowledge. Losing him was more than the loss of a special friend and mentor; it was like losing one's rudder and stability. To this day I remain in his debt.

CHAPTER 33

THE TOOLMAKING DEPARTMENT was never idle. Those of us in the lathes, maintenance and distribution sections worked from seven to seven in two shifts of twelve hours. The grinding and polishing sections and the revolver lathes worked in three shifts of eight hours, while precision instruments, storerooms, milling, planing and steel hardening worked in two ten-hour shifts, from 7 am to 5 pm and from 5 pm to 3 am.

One night shift in early autumn I started as usual, distributing the work for the lathes, tuning up the machines and sharpening knifes. I was in a good mood, finally free of the excruciating itch, and inside my bench drawer I had found a salami sandwich, discreetly deposited by Reinicke. Over time, he had become more relaxed about protocols and that evening made an effort to talk to me.

'Morgen, do you realise that you're the only other person at the plant who speaks fluent German?'

I told him German was my mother tongue and that I also spoke a little French and some English, which I had learned at college with German, Polish and Latin.

'You went to a college?' he asked, surprised.

I explained that my education had been cut off when I was fifteen, at the start of the war, but that I had always been interested in learning.

'What crime did you commit that resulted in your incarceration here?' he asked.

'My only crime is that I was born a Jew.'

'Before I came here,' Reinicke said, 'I was told that the inmates of this camp were criminals – thieves, black marketeers, pimps, prostitutes and fencers.'

'Why *are* you here?' I asked.

'I've only one kidney and some other minor health problems. When I was drafted into the army I was categorised unfit for military duty. So I'm here as part of my military service.'

'Are you married?'

'Yes. I have a wife, a daughter and two sons. The boys are members of the Hitler Youth movement and the girl a member of the German Girls' movement. I'm very proud of them.'

'Your wife must be very happy that you weren't sent to the front.'

'Oh no. She very much regrets that I can't fulfil my duty to the Führer and the Fatherland at the front.'

An inmate needing me to check the set-up of his machine interrupted us. I continued working and soon everyone in my squad had finished his quota although there were more than four hours before my shift finished.

The workers of the ten-hour shift cleaned their machines in readiness to finish and return to the barracks. I saw an opportunity to finish work at 3 am and went to ask Reinicke's permission.

'You may go, providing that everything is under control and all the quotas are fulfilled,' he said.

I assured him that everything was taken care of. 'I'll see you tomorrow,' I said, and headed off.

I joined the group in front of the building. As usual, we were counted and recounted, and then led towards the gate by a deputy komendant. We were waiting for more squads to join us at the gate and for the final rollcall before leaving the plant when the hideous Szlagbaum appeared. He eyed the rows carefully and homed in on three inmates: a kaëlnik whose name I didn't know, Szymek Mapa, and me. He seemed to be looking specifically for us. As we stepped out of the line, Szlagbaum thwacked us on our heads with his rubber truncheon and then escorted us back to the factory. 'I'll teach you not to abandon your workplace without permission,' he told us in Yiddish. 'You, Morgen, don't understand Yiddish. Ha! But I'm going to teach you something you can't fail to understand!'

He led us to the office of the German head supervisor, Erich Dechant. Szlagbaum explained that he had three inmates who had abandoned their posts without his permission. I didn't know what to think. Dechant quickly became infected with Szlagbaum's sense of outrage and shouted that we were saboteurs of the German war effort. 'Szlagbaum, bring in the heavy chair from the next office!'

'Yes, sir.'

Dechant disappeared too and returned seconds later holding a five-tailed whip.

'Fifty lashes for each of you! Who goes first?'

We stood there, unable to move.

'Who's first?' he repeated. He pointed at the kaëlnik next to me. 'You. Come here. Pull down your trousers, bend over, and push your head through the bars on the back of the chair. Szlagbaum, bring a bucket of water. And you two,' he turned to Szymek and me, 'you count the lashes out loud.'

Dechant took off his jacket and rolled up the sleeves of his shirt. He circled the chair a couple of times like a beast circling its prey, then struck with the lash. The poor boy's buttocks were laid open and bleeding. The boy screamed aloud.

'Count!' Dechant commanded.

'One.' The blows fell one after the other and the screams were ear-piercing. 'Seven. Eight. Nine. Ten.'

By twenty the screaming had turned to moaning, then there was silence. Blood pooled around the chair and had spattered Dechant's shirt and trousers. Szlagbaum stood a few paces away with a sardonic smile. We could only hear Dechant's heavy breathing and the sharp thrash of the whip.

'Szlagbaum, pour water on his head.'

The boy started moaning again and Dechant wiped his sweat-covered forehead and continued. We kept counting. At forty, he lost consciousness. At forty-five he stopped breathing. Yet Dechant persisted, giving the full quota of fifty lashes. His victim's lifeless body was carried out on a stretcher.

'You,' he moved towards me, leering. 'You're next.' I could smell alcohol. He was drunk. Now I truly was terrified and thought I was going to soil myself. I had been beaten before but never like this.

Dechant ordered me to pull down my pants and squeeze my head through the same grid of bars on the chair's back. I prayed for a quick end to my suffering and wished that he would strike my head so I could lose consciousness. The chair and the floor around it were wet with blood. Dechant wrinkled his nose. '*Zu viel Schweinerei, bring mir mein Gummiknüppel.*' ('It's too messy. Get my rubber truncheon.')

Szlagbaum returned smiling, carrying a length of hard rubber hose just over a metre long and a couple of centimetres in diameter.

On looking back, maybe I could have got out of this situation by telling them that Reinicke had given me his permission to leave early, but I didn't want to compromise him, and certainly hadn't expected such a severe punishment. I decided not to play hero. If I yelled after the first blow maybe Dechant would show some leniency. He began and Mapa started counting. It was unbelievably painful. I screamed as loud and hard as my lungs would let me. After twenty-five lashes it no longer hurt and I could no longer scream; instead, I whimpered. After ten more lashes I lost consciousness.

I woke in the infirmary. I was on my stomach. My bottom had doubled in size; the swelling was crisscrossed with welts and raw flesh was visible. I could not move. I could not turn over. I was completely immobile. Mapa later told me that Dechant had stopped after forty lashes, and he himself finished up with only twenty because Dechant was too exhausted to continue.

In spite of my condition I was discharged from the infirmary after twenty-four hours, as I was only excused from work for three days. The memory of that pain will stay with me forever. I could not walk; I could not sit. I was only able to lie on my stomach. I didn't want to upset Andzia so I didn't let her know.

I was in a semiconscious state for days, lying motionless, or rather half-kneeling on my pallet. Mendel and another inmate from my barrack helped me from my pallet to the latrine. I've often since thought, why didn't I just die? Strangely, I still had a tremendous will, or need, to survive and this is what I focused on.

On the fourth day, with the aid of two of my comrades, I returned to work. I went to my machine and stood with great difficulty, partly leaning on the bench next to it. Reinicke arrived and noticed my infirmity. 'What's happened to you? Have you been sick? You don't look at all well.' He seemed genuinely concerned, but I also knew he was worried because he depended on me.

'Yes, but I'm better now, except I can't sit and I'm still in pain.'

'Tell me what happened,' he demanded.

'I was beaten. I received forty lashes.'

'Who did this to you and why?'

'Our internal police at the camp,' I lied.

'Why? What did you do?'

'I had an argument with an inmate who accused me of stealing his bread, which I did not do. It was my word against his. Then somebody insisted that he saw me take it. The other inmates are suspicious of educated people and because I don't speak Yiddish I copped a beating. But don't worry, I'm fit to do my job and the work won't be compromised.'

'Which policeman did it to you?' Reinicke persisted.

'There were two, but I don't know them by name. Please, any further trouble could be disastrous for me. Let's forget the whole matter. I'll soon be as good as new.'

'I'm sending you to the empty storeroom next to the grinding department to rest. Make yourself as comfortable as possible. If I need you I know where you are.'

The long narrow room was festooned with cobwebs and a thick coat of dust. Its opaque windows were up very high, almost touching the ceiling. Two rows of half-empty shelves ran alongside opposite walls, where some rusty steel bars had been forgotten. At one end there were empty wooden crates and cardboard boxes in various sizes and shapes.

In the middle of the room three *kaëlankas* sat on low wooden crates holding hands. They were sisters recently transported from Majdanek. The youngest, who looked very ill, was perhaps seventeen years old. She was covered with a rag and shivered and moaned. Her not-much-older sister hugged and tried to console her. Their name was Aszkenazy; they came from a well-known family from Warsaw. The eldest sister, Mrs Pomeranc, was married and had lost her husband and her young son in Majdanek. They were all in a very bad way.

'Why are you here?' I asked.

'Herold, our German supervisor, excused us from work and sent us here to rest. Helena has typhus and we're taking care of her. Herold is an exceptional man.'

'Aren't you afraid of catching typhus?'

'No, we had it many months ago at the Warsaw ghetto.'

I told them how lucky they were to have each other and that I too had recovered from typhus. I also told them about my beating and asked if they could build a kind of stairway from the cardboard boxes. 'I might be able to kneel on one of the boxes and support myself with my elbows in a semi-standing position,' I explained. ' It's the only position that might allow me to rest.'

One of the sisters got up, gathered a number of boxes and erected a three-tier staircase for me in no time.

We talked for a while. They told me how they had survived the uprising in the Warsaw ghetto by hiding in a bunker, how they were nearly burned alive when the Germans set fire to the houses with flamethrowers, how people jumped to their death from burning houses and how they were rounded up and taken to Majdanek. There, their family was killed, with thousands of others.

The siren announced the lunchbreak. The two older sisters went and brought us back some soup. Mrs Pomeranc offered me water to drink and from time to time touched my forehead checking my temperature. She told me that I reminded her of her son. It was very comforting to have someone caring about my wellbeing. I was wondering if I would ever see my mother again. Then I remembered how she hugged me for the last time and assured me that I would survive. With each passing day, I became more pessimistic and was losing faith.

With the help of two of my coworkers, I returned to camp at the end of the shift, carrying a folded cardboard box. After my bread and evening soup, I asked someone to help me to the barber's. Reinicke had told me that I looked untidy.

Sobol did not recognise me. He had erased my name from his list of paying customers a long time ago.

I told Sobol I couldn't sit down for my shave. He called a

policjant into the room. Neither of them believed that I could have survived forty strikes with a rubber hose.

'Who is your komendant?' they asked.

'Szlagbaum.'

'Uh, Szlagbaum.'

'He's a nice man,' I lied.

The policjant grimaced, looked at me and gave Sobol an order. 'Give him a shave, while he stands.'

Sobol called one of his coworkers to do the job. Unfortunately he was shorter than me – I had to lean forward for him to reach my face but still his razor cut my cheeks.

After several weeks – most of it, thanks to Reinicke, spent resting in the storeroom – the pain subsided, but the swelling remained for a long time. Surprisingly, I did not develop any further complications and what was most incredible was that the selections had once again been put on hold. I had been saved again.

CHAPTER 34

In October 1943, Paul Kühnemann, another SS functionary, replaced Anton Ipfling as chief commander of the camp. Kühnemann was anything but representative of the Aryan race: short, swarthy, and with a huge hunchback to match his big abdomen. He resembled a bizarre Quasimodo in his SS uniform and high boots, and his Luger, when holstered, almost reached his thigh. His very large rottweiler called *Jude* was his constant companion – and almost as tall as Kühnemann himself. He would issue commands to the dog – '*Jude! Nim dem Hund!*' (Jew! Take that dog!) – and stand back and enjoy the spectacle. Once he set his dog on someone, the poor victim rarely survived. On assuming command he terrorised the camp by shooting a young inmate in the middle of the Appelplatz after accusing him of stealing. His dog lapped at the puddle of blood that seeped from the dead body. There were rumours that he was not only corrupt but a drunkard as well. We consoled ourselves from time to time that the Red Army was getting closer, but it never seemed close enough.

When I had almost regained full strength, I went to David Nisenbaum's barrack to collect the jam that I had missed for more than a month. I hesitated on the threshold but Nisenbaum spotted me and waved me over. He expressed relief at seeing me and said he'd been to the new hospital to see if I was there.

He had suspected that I'd been killed but hadn't asked too many questions.

I thanked him for his concern and told him what had happened. While we were talking, he filled up my dish with jam and asked me to come the next day to collect some more. I thanked him again and left to sell the jam at once. I even learned to spruik in Yiddish. I sold the lot within an hour and bought half a loaf of bread. One customer was a pleasant-looking young man who asked me for five spoons' worth and then said something in Yiddish that I didn't understand. He saw my embarrassment and instantly changed to Polish. 'You don't speak Yiddish, do you?'

'No,' I said, slightly intimidated. 'But you speak Polish very well, which is rare here. Are you from a village in the area?'

He told me he was from Stopnica, a very small village in the Busko-Zdrój region. 'We spoke Polish at home as well as Yiddish,' he explained. 'I've been here since October 1942, immediately after the main *akcja*. There were one thousand five hundred of us, though one thousand two hundred Jews were sent to Werk C, where only a few have survived. Of the three hundred sent to Werk A, only one-third are still alive.'

I then told him a little about how I came to be there before formally introducing myself.

'I am Moniek Topioł,' he responded, holding out his hand.

'What a coincidence,' I said, excited. 'I know someone else with the same name. He's a fine-looking chap from Busko-Zdrój. I was a guest at his house more than two years ago. His father is the president of the Judenrat in Busko-Zdrój county.'

'Of course!' he exclaimed. 'You met my cousin. He was not only my favourite cousin, but also my best friend. But he did not survive. The family hid in the basement of their own house, which served as headquarters for the local gendarmerie. After the *akcja*, these Germans let them stay under their protection.

This lasted for a few months until somebody denounced them. One day the Gestapo came and executed the whole family on the spot.'

I listened to Moniek tell this story and was almost able to observe myself from a distance. I had become so inured to death occurring, daily, around me; I was unable to show compassion. What had I become?

I changed the subject and asked where Moniek worked. He was at toolmaking department B and operated a planing machine. It was strange that we hadn't seen each other before in the months that I'd been working with the lathes.

We made plans to see each other the very next day, which pleased me enormously. I felt an instant connection to this stranger.

That night I wanted to sleep but could not stop thinking of Moniek. I was so impressed by him but did not know why. I felt a strange mix of curiosity and happiness. He seemed to have the qualities I had missed since being separated from my family. Indeed, he seemed like the brother I never had. He was interesting and genuine. I had never experienced such a connection, such like-mindedness, with anyone else before. I spent most of the night thinking of him. Moniek was a good-looking young man the same age as me, though some centimetres shorter, with a fair complexion and cheeky brown eyes. He had a mischievous smile and a trustworthy face – the sort of face that guaranteed an easier ride through life. The next morning, despite an almost sleepless night, I felt refreshed and invigorated. I could not wait to see him again.

At the plant I finished my chores, then began the routine production. I was restless and looked for a pretext to see Moniek. I felt like a teenager preparing for his first date. Finally, I took a fully loaded trolley of goods intended for the hardening department and detoured via department B.

Moniek spotted me from afar and greeted me with a bright smile. He was very busy and couldn't spare much time but we arranged to meet during lunch. We collected our soup and ate together. He offered me a slice of bread, which I refused. He did not insist. We exchanged a few banalities about the soup and then both tried to work out why we hadn't seen each other before.

'We were probably on opposite shifts,' I suggested. 'And then I was sick for a while with typhus.' Moniek had been sick with typhus too but returned to work after ten days.

We decided there and then that we would have lunch together each day and talk about all sort of things. And we did.

I told him about my life and family before the war. The luxurious lifestyle we led, my time at boarding school and my being a scout fascinated him. He talked about himself and his family too. He had only finished primary school and hadn't had the opportunity to attend college, though he was well read and extremely bright. Instead, he had started work in his father's dry goods business.

After a couple of days he looked at my shabby clothes. 'I'd like to lend you some clothing. I've more than I need and it's getting cold now.'

'I can't do that,' I said. 'It wouldn't be fair.'

'Why not? Honestly, I'd like to lend you some clothes.'

'I'm infected with lice,' I said, red-faced. 'I don't want to give them to you.'

Moniek burst out laughing. 'We *all* have lice. The whole camp is infected. Perhaps if our lice mixed together we could improve their race.' We looked at each other and both laughed hard and long.

Once we had exhausted our personal stories, we talked about politics, economics and social matters, then subjects like the history of Poland and Jewish and European history. Every time we met we spoke about something different. We became almost inseparable. It was marvellous to have someone to talk with, who made me feel good and with whom I felt such kinship.

Every time we went for a walk around the barracks Moniek lent me some of his clothes – a jacket, sometimes a shirt or jumper. I felt that he wanted to give me the clothes, but I always left them on his pallet when we returned to his barrack. Sometimes before our walk he would insist that we eat at his barrack. A homemade soup and bread would be ready for us to eat. He told me that he received regular financial support from outside: Moniek's father had left a large amount of money with a loyal Polish friend to support him. It was best I didn't know much about this and I didn't ask any questions. Many people in the camp had a similar arrangement, though some Poles undertook to support their Jewish associates but never kept their promises. As I had observed, if such arrangements were discovered it meant death for the recipient and severe punishment, if not death, for the helper.

As time passed I began to feel inadequate. 'Moniek, our friendship is the best thing that's happened to me,' I blurted out one day during our walk. 'It gives me the strength to go on and the will to live, but my contribution isn't adequate. I'm embarrassed you're taking care of me – feeding and clothing me – and I'm unable to give anything in return.'

'That's not at all true,' he said. 'You're giving me a great deal more than you think. Firstly, you give me your friendship. Secondly, you give me the pleasure of your conversation. Your stories are so fascinating that I wouldn't give them up for anything in the world. If not for you, I would have lived my life not knowing and experiencing these things.'

'We're both benefiting from our conversations,' I argued.

'Not necessarily,' he went on. 'Mostly you're the lecturer and I'm the student. Take geography. I knew nothing about those different and exotic countries you've spoken of. And I knew nothing of famous historical figures such as Robespierre, Marie Antoinette, Bonaparte. And even in our country, there are Countess Maria Walewska, and Berek Joselewicz, leader of the Jewish cavalry regiment during the Kościuszko Insurrection of 1794. There's so much I'm learning.'

'That makes me very happy,' I said with a shy smile.

He smiled back at me. 'Please, don't mention such nonsense again.'

We continued walking in silence for a few minutes, then Moniek spoke again. 'I want to introduce you to Leopold Laufer. He's komendant of some female barracks on the east side of the camp. He and his wife have two very comfortable rooms. Before you, Leopold and his wife were the only people here who I could have called friends.

'He came from Werk B, where he had a senior role in the camp administration and allegedly mistreated inmates, though the rumours are contradictory. I don't know anything about his past, but since he arrived here I've seen him help many people. Make up your own mind – you be the judge. I've told them about you and we've been invited for dinner tomorrow night.'

The next evening we walked to Leopold Laufer's barrack where he and his wife stood waiting for us. Their quarters were typical of the komendanten, comprising a small room at the end of the barrack divided into two areas, with a doorway but no door. The first room was the living area. In front of the window was a small table with two wooden chairs. In the corner on a wooden crate, next to some kitchen utensils, was a primus burner with a pot bubbling away. A single light globe hung from the ceiling. The other room had a bunk with two pallets, some shelves and two or three wooden crates secured with padlocks. This room had no window. It was the height of luxury.

Leopold was handsome: tall and dark with thick black hair

and brown eyes. His bright smile exuded confidence. He wore dark-grey trousers and a white long-sleeved shirt. There was no sign of komendanten cap, belt or any other insignia. His wife, Iva, was very pretty and no older than twenty. She was as tall as Leopold, with a fair complexion, green-grey eyes and shoulder-length brown hair. She was beautifully groomed and wore a fitted floral dress. 'Welcome, welcome,' she greeted us. 'Please come in.'

Moniek formally introduced me.

'Friends of my friends are potentially my friends,' Iva said with a smile.

At the table I was a little clumsy. I had almost forgotten my table manners and did not know quite how to behave when Iva put a large plate of buttered bread in front of me. The last time I had sat at a table and eaten a meal was at Yankel's 'restaurant' eleven months earlier, although I had come close at Dalski's house. After a couple of mouthfuls of Iva's soup I complimented her cooking, breaking the silence.

I learned that Leopold and Iva had only been in Werk A for two months. Before long it was clear that Iva was much better educated than her husband, though both seemed intelligent and bright. They both came from Skarżysko-Kamienna, and Iva from a prominent Jewish family there.

'How was life here in Skarżysko-Kamienna before the war?' I asked.

'Probably like any other town in the area with a large Jewish population, although the Jews didn't work in the munitions industry,' she explained. 'Poles were better off, especially in managerial positions.'

I told them that I had lived in Starachowice-Wierzbnik at the beginning of the war.

'I'm aware that you and Moniek are good friends and you spend a lot of time together,' said Iva. 'Moniek tells us that he can't get enough of your stories. What do you talk about?'

'Actually, we talk about everything.'

'Like what? I'm curious.'

I told her that we talked about books, and she told me she loved to read too. I was impressed to find out she had read many of my favourite titles.

We finished the meal and were treated to plain biscuits and coffee brewed from roasted malt. We stayed for another half an hour, then thanked them for their hospitality and rose to leave. Iva said she'd invite us again soon.

CHAPTER 35

THE NEXT MORNING Kühnemann ordered an unexpected rollcall. An inmate in handcuffs, escorted by two Werkschutz, was brought into the Appelplatz.

Kühnemann, his rottweiler by his side, wasted no time on pleasantries. '*Der Schweinehund hat ein Brot gestohlen, er wird mit dem Tode bestraft.*' ('This filthy swine stole a loaf of bread and will be shot.') He unfastened his pistol, looked into the man's eyes and shot him, point blank, in the middle of his forehead. The man was dead before he hit the ground and the whole spectacle lasted no more than a few seconds. Szymek Mapa, who stood next to me, shrugged his shoulders and mumbled, 'Lucky guy. He's finally free.'

For some reason Moniek wasn't at this rollcall. Later he said to me, 'He was neither the first nor the last. God only knows how many more will follow.' We both fell silent.

We did not see each other for the next two days and I found myself missing him. On the third day I went to his barrack.

'I'm glad you came.' He greeted me with his usual bright smile. 'I've missed you and have been meaning to talk to you. I felt very low after hearing of Kühnemann's killing, despite making such an insensitive remark. It affected me deeply, even though I wasn't there.'

'Cheer up, Moniek. It's OK. Let's get back to our dream

world of films and books. Dwelling too much on our situation is dangerous and destructive.'

'You're right,' he sighed deeply.

We went outside to escape the noise and stuffiness and soon started discussing *All Quiet on the Western Front*, a book we were both impressed with and that seemed relevant to us now.

'I wonder what Remarque thinks about the current war?' I pondered. 'I'm sure he would never have believed there could have been another war, let alone one more savage than the one he described. Now we have an all-consuming war, not just for the armed forces, but one that violates innocent civilians.'

'I agree,' Moniek said. 'The film, too, made a colossal impression on me. I thought that after the book and the film, no-one would wage war again. How naive of me.'

Moniek had told me that his town had no cinema, but once a week a film screened at the fire brigade hall, mostly old Polish movies, though Jews did not usually attend. *All Quiet on the Western Front* was the only film Moniek had seen.

Film, however, was a passion of mine and we had seen several films a week at boarding school.

'Tell me more about the films you've seen,' Moniek asked.

I told him about the first film I had seen. It was on my fifth birthday. Dodzik, my second cousin, was about eleven years older than me and a passionate movie-goer. He came to my party late with a present but could not stay long because he was going to see an important movie called *The Kid*, with Charlie Chaplin and Jackie Coogan. I asked him to take me with him. He was reluctant to do so, but my parents, who had seen it, persuaded him. I ran to find my coat, quickly apologised to my few remaining guests and went to the cinema.

The experience didn't turn out as I had hoped. As a five-year-old I could not do without the toilet for two hours. I pleaded with Dodzik to show me where it was, but he didn't want to miss any of the film, which had no intermission. I wet myself and burst into tears.

Back home my mother saw my red eyes. 'Why have you been crying? Didn't you like the film? Did it scare you?'

I told her that I had wet myself and how embarrassed I was because of it.

She hugged and kissed me. 'I promise, nobody will ever know.'

I felt no shame in telling Moniek this story.

From that time on I had seen films every week. There were cowboy movies with Tom Mix or Ken Maynard. All of them were silent and flickered in black and white with a piano accompaniment – the pianist playing loud and fast in the dramatic scenes.

I told him about Al Jolson's *The Jazz Singer*, the first film with sound. It arrived in Poland in 1930, three years after its American release. I told him about *A Midsummer Night's Dream*, starring James Cagney, Olivia de Havilland and Mickey Rooney, describing every scene as accurately as I could. This fascinated Moniek as he was a great admirer of Shakespeare's plays, especially the tragedies. Then there was *The Story of Louis Pasteur* with the Jewish actor Paul Muni, who also starred in *The Life of Emile Zola*, which centred on Zola's fight to exonerate army captain Alfred Dreyfus, and *The Hunchback of Notre Dame*, featuring Charles Laughton and Maureen O'Hara. I told Moniek that Kühnemann was a dead ringer for Quasimodo and we laughed and laughed.

Our conversations kept us sane and gave us something to look forward to each day. Although I was still physically run down, my attitude had lightened considerably. Moniek's presence was a blessing.

*

The days became shorter and heavy rains and cold winds arrived. Hoarfrost settled on roofs and on the windowpanes of the barracks. The mud became deeper and heavier. Winter came early. In November it snowed for days and the temperature at night dropped to minus ten degrees Celsius. But despite the cold, the mud never froze, trampled constantly by thousands of feet.

From the time Moniek and I became firm friends I paid less attention to the goings-on of the camp. In that period at Werk A, more than 500 inmates had lost their lives – some from starvation and illness, but most had been categorised as muselmen and selected to die.

*

In the middle of November, 2500 new prisoners arrived from camps at Kraków-Jerozolimska and Płaszów. They were immediately allocated to the barracks and within days to the work commandos; 500 were sent to Werk C. Coming from Kraków, they were predominantly middle class and had brought some personal belongings with them, which pleased the guards and policjanten very much. They included some intelligentsia. Among them were former schoolfriends of mine: two brothers from Katowice, Benek and Ignac Genendelman, and Moniek Rechnic. Although this new group spoke only Polish, there were so many of them that they escaped the humiliation that I had endured from the Yiddish speakers.

That winter, without warning, I fell ill with pneumonia and meningitis. Moniek took me to the new, luxurious hospital where there were about 100 beds, straw paillasses, bed linen, pillows and blankets and no more than a dozen patients. Almost all of them were victims of beatings and work-related accidents. Some were inmates at the revolver lathes department. I was there for ten days and Iva brought me homemade soup and a slice of buttered bread every day. Moniek and Mrs Kanencukier also visited me daily. What an astonishing difference from my last hospital visit! Four days after leaving the hospital I was back at work.

Iva and Leopold invited us to dinner again. Although I was still a little weak I was eager to go, both for the nourishing conversation and food. That evening the conversation turned to one of faith. Some of us wondered aloud how God allowed the madness of this war to happen.

'Yet God performs miracles!' protested Leopold. 'Look at us – we are still here!'

'Well, at least for tonight,' quipped Iva.

Moniek glanced at each of us. 'Maybe there aren't even the thirty-six righteous people left in this generation for God to be bothered saving humanity,' he said pensively.

Leopold sat upright and asked Moniek what he was talking about. I looked at Moniek with particular interest as this was one conversation we had not had before.

'The thirty-six righteous – the Lamed Vav,' Moniek began to explain to Leopold. He told him about the kabbalah origins of the thirty-six and that they were also called *Tzadikim Nistarim* or the Hidden Righteous, and that were it not for them, *all* of them, if even one of them was missing, the world would end.

'I had heard,' said Iva, 'that they are usually poor and unknown – that no-one can identify them. I also heard that they appear, by mystic powers that only they possess, to help people in times of great peril. It is because of them that God does not destroy the world even when sin engulfs us all.' She paused for a moment deep in thought. 'But I believe that when one Lamed Vav dies another immediately takes his place.'

'But the *Tzadik Nistar* does not even know he is chosen for the task,' Moniek said in a hushed voice.

I wasn't sure I shared Moniek and Iva's belief in the thirty-six but felt I had to say something. 'Since the war began, five years ago, I've cheated death on many occasions. At times it's been because someone helped me; at other times it seems to have been dumb luck. I don't know what it is – whether this is a question of faith or not – but I feel as if someone, or something, has been looking out for me. Maybe it's divine intervention or a series of miracles, I don't know.' I smiled and shrugged. 'My mother believes in the Lamed Vav,' I said quietly. 'Maybe. I don't know. Maybe some things just can't be explained.'

That night I dreamt about my mother, probably because I always associated talk of the thirty-six with her. And once again she reassured me that I was destined to survive.

*

The winter of 1943–44 was exceptionally severe. Snow, frost and strong winds took their toll but the hardest thing to bear was the daily rollcalls. Sometimes we stood for hours in the biting frost. We stamped our feet to keep warm and rubbed each other's backs. Many inmates suffered frostbite on their noses, ears, fingers and toes. I still wore the patched-up overalls that Biernacki had given me, held together by a few threads. I bound old rags around my feet, which I then pushed into clogs.

Still, I was lucky enough to work inside a well-heated department while many hundreds had to work outside. Although they worked physically hard, they couldn't warm up properly, because of their low calorie intake. Many did not survive.

As we returned to the camp one morning after a twelve-hour shift, we saw a long queue in front of the apparel storeroom. A large quantity of clothing and shoes had recently arrived, after the extermination of prisoners elsewhere. Mendel Wajntraub stopped the squad and announced that anyone who wanted clothes had to line up in front of the storeroom in an hour. Some of us lined up at once, not wanting to miss out. An hour later more than 200 of our group were waiting patiently. I stood next to Mendel Feldman, who was much better dressed than me, while Wajntraub checked to make sure everyone in line was from our squad. As he neared me he yelled, 'Morgen, get out of the queue.'

'Why? Look how much I need something to wear. Look at my rags – they're holes being kept together by a few threads. I honestly need some clothes.'

'What about those garments you parade about in on Sundays when you go for walks?' he shouted.

'They're not mine! I just borrowed them.'

'Get out of here, quick! You *shminteligent*.' He hit my head and shoulders with his truncheon.

I never received any new clothes and remained in my ragged overalls for another seven months.

At the beginning of spring another transport arrived from the Łódź ghetto and the Płaszów concentration camp where the Krakovites were imprisoned. None of them brought any belongings, which angered the Werkschutz and the policjanten. The newcomers replaced those who had perished during the winter months.

CHAPTER 36

ONE SUNNY CLOUDLESS DAY I went to Moniek's barrack. I hadn't seen him at work and he hadn't appeared at lunch that day. I was told that he had not returned yet from the plant. I went back a little later and he still hadn't appeared. On leaving the barrack I turned to the main road and saw a policjant walking with two men who carried a stretcher. On it was a body covered with a cloth.

I rushed forward, my heart in my stomach. 'Who is it? Was it an accident? Is he injured?'

'No. He's dead. We collected him from a cell at the Werkschutz watch-house. He was clubbed to death and left in a pool of blood on the concrete floor.'

'Why? What did he do?'

'We don't know,' one of the men answered.

'He's not the first,' said the other. 'In the past few days we've collected six men and two women. Lately, the Germans have become nervous. It must be because of the news from the eastern front.'

'Who is he? What's his name?' I asked, pointing at the stretcher.

'The Werkschutz told us his number and his name. Popioł or Topioł – something like that. Ask the policjant, he'll know.'

Everything stopped for a moment. I could not breathe.

311

I ran after them, gasping for air. They were by the small barrack where dead bodies were stored for cremation at Werk C.

'Please. Can I see him?' I pleaded with the policjant.

He shrugged his shoulders. 'Help yourself.'

With trembling hands I lifted the blood-soaked cloth and froze in horror. I recognised the trousers and shoes.

Moniek. My best friend in the whole world. Moniek. My only friend in this godforsaken place.

But the bloodied mess on the stretcher did not resemble any human shape: his torso and head had been completely crushed. I saw his bloody hands and noticed that his fingernails had been torn out.

The two men impatiently carried the body inside the barrack and left after locking up the 'morgue'. I stood there, leaning on the closed door unable to leave. I wanted to say a prayer, but nothing came to my mind. I sobbed. I wailed. I stood there crying for at least half an hour, then went to Leopold's barrack. I told Iva the news.

'What? Who? How do you know?' She swooned and nearly fainted. Tears ran down her cheeks.

I told her what I'd learned and she said she'd check with Leopold at once. I followed her, too stricken to know what to do next. Iva took a detour from the path to the administration barracks and headed towards the morgue. I sensed her intention. 'Don't you dare go inside. I will not allow you to see him. It's too gruesome.'

'No,' she sobbed. 'I won't go in. I just want to pay my respects for a few minutes. He was a good man and a true friend. I can't believe that he's dead.'

We stood there together crying. I imagined how he suffered, how terrified he must have been when the butchers worked him over. I felt something collapse in my heart. Moniek's death upset me more than any other I had witnessed or learned of throughout the war.

We reluctantly left our posts and went to see Leopold, who rushed to policjanten headquarters at once to find out what he could and soon returned. 'The policjant who escorted Moniek's body said that there was a call from the watch-house requesting them to pick up a body. He took two men from the death commando and had him carried to the morgue. He was only given Moniek's number and name for the register. He was not told why he had been killed or who had done it.'

We went back to their barrack, each of us absorbed in our own thoughts. 'I'll go and see Komendant Albirt or Teperman, the chief of police,' Leopold spoke up. 'I might learn something more concrete. I won't be long.'

Iva started to prepare the dinner and asked me to stay. We started to speculate about the reason for Moniek's death. I thought he must have been searched and found to have had a large amount of money. As he did not want to divulge any names, he suffered the consequences and paid with his life.

Leopold returned without anything definite, although Teperman's explanation was similar to mine. We ate and talked about Moniek. We talked about his values, good character, his integrity, decency and thoughtfulness. I mentioned, after deep consideration, that he had sacrificed his life to protect his benefactor. And I was sure that Moniek also knew that even if he had disclosed the people involved he would have been unable to save his own life.

We talked about him until the approaching curfew compelled me to return to my barrack. Mendel was already asleep. I, however, lay on my back with my eyes wide open all night.

In the morning he turned over. 'Are you angry with me? You don't talk to me any more; you don't pay any attention to me. Have I offended you?

'You talk like a jealous lover,' I sneered at him. 'I don't remember promising you my friendship. We worked together and accidentally became partners. We share the same pallet and shared the same illness, but that doesn't mean that you're a part of my very limited private life – the bit that the Germans allow me.' I still hadn't forgiven him for the scabies ointment incident.

'But you neglect me!'

'What? Don't be stupid. I didn't promise you anything.'

'But you used to be such a good friend,' he whined.

'A shame I can't say the same about you,' I said, no longer caring.

I arrived at work angry and exhausted. I was miserable and spent the whole day thinking only of Moniek. On the way back to the camp a policjant hit me several times with his truncheon. He had lost count of us, exactly at the moment I was passing through the gate. It hurt, but I wanted to suffer. I wanted to feel the pain and to mourn Moniek. He had suffered much, much more before he died.

I have missed Moniek every day of my life.

CHAPTER 37

A FEW DAYS LATER I was sitting at my machine during the lunchbreak missing my friend when two policjanten approached Szlagbaum asking for me. He ordered me to go with them.

'Where are you taking me?' I asked.

'You've been summoned by the chief commander of the Werkschutz.'

'What's happened? Why does he want to see me?'

'You'll find out soon enough.'

I knew that very few inmates returned alive from the watch-house. My mouth was so dry I could barely swallow. This had something to do with Moniek. The policjanten escorted me to the front porch of the watch-house and handed me to a Werkschutz who then escorted me to a room at the end of a corridor. My feet felt like lead. I knew that I had to stay calm to survive; I had to keep my wits about me.

All my close brushes with death since leaving Katowice flashed before my eyes: the 'execution' in Będzin; the Werkschutz with Mala; coming face to face with the guards at the barber shop after escaping from Werk C; my night's journey from Skarżysko-Kamienna to Staszów; my encounter with Wacek; travelling without documents or tickets; the ambush in Wolbrom; Goldberg and Dechant and Koch. All these events ran through my head like a movie reel.

The door stood wide open. The room was a windowless interrogation cell containing a small desk and a chair. Truncheons, batons, clubs, sticks, canes and other beating instruments hung from the wall. Two German Werkschutz were waiting, their legs wide apart in long shiny boots.

The higher-ranking officer barked at me in Polish. 'Your name and number.'

'Zygmunt Morgen, number eighty eighty-seven.'

'Do you know why you are here?'

'No, I don't.'

'Empty your pockets.'

I took out two little tin boxes and a few pieces of an old newspaper, neatly folded.

'What's in the boxes? Open them up!'

I opened the first box, containing grey soap.

'Open the other box. What's in there?'

'Cigarettes stubs, collected from the ashtrays at the plant's offices.'

'How did you get the newspaper?' he asked, pointing at the scraps on the desk. 'You know it's forbidden.'

'Yes, I know. I collect any paper that I can use in the latrine out of the waste bins.'

'Where is your money?'

'I don't have any money.'

'Don't lie to me!' he screamed. 'Undress. Quick!'

I took off my clothes and stood there in my dirty underpants. The other officer began to search my overall, swearing in German. 'The bloody Jew is lice-infested. Search him yourself. I don't want to get sick. The only thing this one has is lice – there's no money.'

'I'll take care of him. I'll find out what he knows,' said the senior officer, who pointed at me, indicating that I should dress myself.

'Do you know Topioł ?' he asked.

'Yes, I do.'

'Do you know where he is?'

'No, I don't.'

From the adjoining cell came a terrifying scream, followed by indistinct shouts. Someone was being tortured. The junior officer asked in German, 'Should I close the door?'

'Better let him hear it,' was the reply. 'It'll soften him up.' He turned back to me. 'What's your connection with Topioł ?'

'We met a few times for lunch at the plant and in the camp.'

'What did you talk about?'

'Nothing specific. We talked about our families.' While I answered these questions, the junior officer walked around the room and had stopped behind me.

'You're lying!' the interrogator yelled.

At that very moment, the one standing behind me punched me in the back of the head. Losing my balance, I fell forward.

'I'm not lying. We also talked about books.' I could hardly talk and hardly see.

'What kind of books?'

'Books we read at home before the war.'

'Where are you from?'

'From Sandomierz.'

'Aha, from Sandomierz,' the senior officer repeated. He turned to his comrade. 'I believe he knows more than he admits. We have to get it out of him. He must know the contact.'

'Shall we start?'

'No. I have a better idea. You know I detest violence and the mess it makes. Call in the dental technician.'

'Yes, sir. Straightaway, sir.'

'You'll tell me what I want to know when the dentist takes care of you,' the senior officer smiled.

The Werkschutz returned with a German officer wearing a

white coat over his uniform. He looked at me and nodded his head. 'Let's go.'

They grabbed me under my arms and led me out of the cell to the end of the corridor and into the adjoining building. We entered a primitive dental surgery that serviced the staff. I was placed in a dentist or barber's chair in the middle of the room. I was so frightened I couldn't fight any more. I still had no idea what was about to happen but I had given up. I had given myself up to my fate.

A pedal-activated dental drill, which looked more like a spinning wheel, was wheeled towards the chair. The two officers strapped my arms to the armrests and, from behind, held my head firmly against the headrest.

'Open your mouth. Let me see your teeth,' shouted the dentist.

I obeyed and he jammed something into my open mouth, preventing me from closing it. He started pedalling the wheel, activating the drill. He held it against my right upper incisor. The drill heated up and, as he did not bother to spray any water to cool down my tooth, the pain was unbearable. It was agony. He drilled until he had penetrated the enamel and hit the tooth's nerve. I almost jumped out of my chair but the officers held me down.

The dentist stopped drilling and picked up a dental hook. He used this to prod the tooth's exposed nerve. I thought my brain was going to explode inside my head.

'Who is the man who supplied Topioł with money and letters? What is his name?' someone screamed at me.

I tried to answer, 'I don't know!', but all I managed was a guttural sound, as my mouth was still clamped open. The dentist jerked at my head.

'Just tell me his name and you can go.'

'You must know something – after all, you're such good

friends. We won't stop working on you until you tell us the name of that person.'

The dentist removed the clamp.

'I swear I don't know anything. I can't bear the pain any longer,' I pleaded. 'I *am* telling you the truth. Kill me or let me go.'

The senior officer spoke in German. 'He knows nothing and they were not from the same village. There's no connection. Let him go.'

The Germans then ordered me to stand. I was dizzy, weak at the knees, and trembled all over. The officer summoned a guard. 'Escort the Jew back to his department.'

Much to my surprise I was still alive. I thought of my mother's conviction that I would survive, and once more I believed it. I was, however, in terrible pain. With every breath, the air aggravated the exposed nerve. In time I learned to plug the hole with putty made from bread.

Within a week of this incident a policjant, Hayim Wajntraub, Mendel Wajntraub's younger brother, was clubbed to death by at least five German supervisors from our department. It became evident that he was an informer, extortionist and blackmailer. As long as he spied on inmates and Poles he was successful and rewarded by the German internal security. It seemed, though, that he became overconfident; he began to inform on German supervisors too, which was his undoing.

Informants were the most feared inmates in the camp. They cooperated with the Germans against their own people. None of the inmates felt sorry about Wajntraub's sticky end. No-one mourned *his* passing.

PART VI

MAY 1944 – JANUARY 1945

CHAPTER 38

IN THE SPRING OF 1944, rumours intensified that the Red Army was advancing, having already liberated the far eastern Polish territory. Over the years we had heard many such stories, only to be disappointed when nothing happened. On one occasion we heard a distant rumbling and assumed that it was a spring thunderstorm. It lasted for a few days and then simply stopped. We learnt later that it was heavy artillery shelling, about 300 kilometres away, near the Wisła River.

Around the end of May, Reinicke called me to his office to tell me that the entire department and staff would soon be relocated. 'We'll start to dismantle the machines soon and maybe start transferring them as early as next week. But don't tell anyone else about this yet.'

On returning to camp, I went straight to Leopold and asked him he knew anything about the move.

'No, and I don't understand why they'd want to relocate,' he said. 'They've got a perfect location here, well equipped and, right in the middle of a dense forest, well camouflaged. And they're still able to find a steady supply of Jewish labour.'

His words made sense. I headed on to David's barrack for my jam and asked him if he had heard any plans about relocating. He too had heard nothing.

A few days later Reinicke ordered us to finish the jobs we

were working on but not to start any new orders for a week. We were to clean each machine thoroughly, secure all the oil or store it in special containers. As soon as a machine was cleaned it was stripped, and all removable parts and tools were packed in wooden crates ready for shipment. As no address or destination was marked on the crates, talk spread that we would be moved to Leipzig, Germany, the headquarters of Hasag Werke.

The plant's vast network of rail lines accessed every department, and goods carriages delivered raw materials and took away the finished products. The entire staff helped load the wooden crates into empty carriages placed at the loading ramps, a task that lasted for days, though the crates weighed no more than 200 kilograms. The machinery, however, was quite a different proposition and some pieces weighed up to 3000 kilograms! No-one knew quite how to manage this. We tried pushing, with six people and then ten, but the machines would not budge. We hemmed and hawed, wondering what to do next, when I remembered once seeing workers move long and heavy objects in an unusual fashion, either at the railway terminal in Staszów or with my father in Starachowice-Wierzbnik. I told Reinicke that we needed some crowbars, a few wooden blocks and at least three water or gas pipes around eight centimetres in diameter and longer than the width of the machines. We also needed many groups of six. Reinicke wasted no time in writing out the necessary orders.

An hour later we had all the equipment required and I explained the procedure. By lifting the machines with the crowbars, we were able to insert the pipes under them, and this enabled us to roll the heavy load as if on wheels. Bit by bit, by moving the pipe from the back to the front of the machine, we rolled the contraptions up the ramp and straight into the train carriage. We executed this task well, although a number of inmates were killed over the many days it took to complete it, mostly from being crushed. In the meantime, the women packed wooden crates and cardboard boxes.

Once everything was loaded Reinicke announced that our department and those producing infantry ammunition were moving to Częstochowa, while other departments were relocating to Germany. It seemed plain now that the reason for the move was the advancing Red Army that had, in the summer of 1944, reached the Wisła River.

Rumours quickly began to spread that we would be sent to extermination camps or executed at Werk C. It made no sense that the Germans would let us live when millions of Jews had already been exterminated. Some inmates began talking about a mass escape or uprising before realising no-one was physically or emotionally ready for such an undertaking.

I asked Reinicke outright if we really were going to Częstochowa and not to Leipzig and he assured me that the two infantry munitions departments and relevant toolmaking departments were bound for Hasag Częstochowa. He also explained that because Częstochowa had more than enough supervisors, he was headed for Leipzig, although he would have preferred to stay with his department. With a shrug he said, '*Befehl ist Befehl.*' ('Orders are orders.')

That was the last time I saw him. Reinicke was a simple man, but was one of very few Germans I met during the war who retained a sense of decency.

*

The last days of July 1944 were sunny and warm. I took a stroll between the barracks, remembering Moniek and our precious conversations, when a policjant stopped me. 'Come with me.'

'Where to?'

'Camp Commander Kühnemann wants help packing his belongings.' He led me to the commander's quarters, picking up two more inmates on the way. Kühnemann ordered us to nail up some wooden crates, then asked which of us spoke German.

I raised my arm. 'I do.'

He gave me a written note. 'Read it out aloud.'

'Frau Marta Kühnemann, Annaberg O/S,' – I read *O/S* as *Oberschlesien* – 'Kaiser Wilhelm Strasse 66. Deutsches Reich.'

'How do you know what the letters *O/S* stand for?' he asked in surprise.

I told him that, like him, I was also from Oberschlesien, or Upper Silesia. The Polish name for the region was Górny Śląsk, and I suppose Kühnemann had not expected me to know its German name.

He gave me a piece of cardboard, a pair of scissors and a marker pen. 'Write the address on both sides of each crate and box. Cut out cardboard tags, write the address on each one and attach one to each suitcase. Everything must be ready in half an hour. Then take a trolley and load the luggage onto the waiting truck.' We did as we were asked and I memorised Kühnemann's address, just in case.

Andzia was also headed for Częstochowa – the town also happened to be her birthplace. We wished each other a safe trip and reassured each other that we would meet up in our new location in a day or so.

The next morning we lined up early for a very long rollcall. We were counted, our names checked and numbers compared and matched against a list by the four komendanten from our department. Inmates who worked in our department but not in production, such as cleaners or storemen, were taken away and never seen again. Only electricians and mechanics joined our work commandos. We were given half a loaf of bread for the journey, a distance of close to 200 kilometres, though nothing to drink.

Just outside the barbed-wire fence a long train of some fifty open goods carriages waited to accommodate over 3000 people. Men and women were separated and at least sixty persons were allotted to each dirty wagon, previously used to transport coal. Within an hour we were ready to leave. Armed SS guardsmen took up positions on the back platform of every second carriage to escort us during the journey – apparently the Werkschutz were not reliable enough for the task. We pulled out of Skarżysko-Kamienna around 7 am on Saturday 1 July 1944.

As the train increased its speed, some inmates became anxious – Jews on a goods train guarded by the SS was a dangerous combination. I was a little more at ease because of Reinicke's reassurance. Nevertheless we all felt a sense of freedom and enjoyed the changing scenery: we saw forest vistas, peasants working in fields, shepherds guarding their flocks. Everything seemed as it was before the war.

We were ordered to sit down as the train passed stations so passengers on the platforms would not see that prisoners were being transported. If we did not obey this order we were to be shot on the spot. The Germans were very secretive about their activities. At most stations our train was shifted to a sidetrack, to let a military or passenger train pass. Through slits in the carriage wall we saw long hospital trains full of wounded soldiers heading westwards.

The billowing smoke deposited black soot in our lungs and we soon looked like coal miners fresh from underground. Only once were we were allowed to leave the train, five carriages at a time, as a latrine stop. We were grateful to use foliage from nearby shrubs as toilet paper, yet this process took more than two hours.

At midday, there was no escaping from the sweltering sun. It was a scorcher. Everyone was unbearably thirsty. My throat dried out and my lips had split. The bread had been eaten a long time earlier and my stomach rumbled unhappily. Ironically, one positive aspect was that we were so dehydrated we had no further need to urinate.

After ten gruelling hours, we reached our destination. The train moved right into the factory area, though not all of it could fit inside at once. On the camp's tallest building, in oversized lettering, were the German words: HASAG – WARTAWERK – TSCHENSTOCHAU.

CHAPTER 39

HASAG WARTA WAS A FACTORY AND CAMP on the Warta River in Częstochowa. It produced ammunition for rifles and machine guns, the same as Hasag Skarżysko-Kamienna. The Warta Werk camp was much smaller than what we had been used to – Werk A alone was about four times its size – and they weren't prepared for such a huge influx of workers. There were only a couple of hundred veteran inmates, but their numbers had recently been boosted when 250 prisoners had been transferred from Kraków.

We lined up in two groups in the assembly yard. The policjanten here were called OD-men – *Ordnungsdienst* or 'order duty' men. Although they all had truncheons, only a few used them. They explained that here, unlike Skarżysko–Kamienna, they were splitting the infantry shell department into two, and that 1000 inmates would be sent about three or four kilometres away to another Hasag camp at Pelcery, a suburb of Częstochowa. Most inmates did not know which group to join. They ran back and forth trying to decide where was better, where was safer. I had decided never to volunteer for anything ever again after being told I was going to Starachowice and ending up in the hellhole of Werk C: I was only ever going to act on instinct again. I wanted to stay put.

The inmates for Pelcery were selected and marched away, while the rest of us awaited further orders. In the meantime we received a fresh coat of paint: a large white letter *H* for *Häftling* (prisoner) was painted on the back of our shirts, joining the existing red stripes.

A group of OD-men, including some well-dressed civilians, appeared. They were the top administrative functionaries of the camp. Komendant Frenkel introduced himself as the head of the OD. He then introduced a German Jew called Joles as the camp's chief komendant. Joles gave a short speech in German, containing a few promises and some warnings, then finished with an abrupt '*Weitermachen!*' (carry on) and left with his colleagues.

The OD-men selected twenty inmates, including myself, to report to a storeroom on the other side of the Appelplatz. We had to carry nearly 600 new paillasses, still to be filled with straw, to sleeping quarters all over the camp. Two inmates loaded fifty kilograms of these folded paillasses onto our backs. I collapsed before I could even move. This work was far beyond my physical ability: after nearly two years spent in camps I was emaciated and malnourished and weighed just over forty kilograms. Somehow the task was completed, without my help, and the straw arrived a fortnight later.

Warta Camp did not have barracks like Skarżysko-Kamienna; old dilapidated industrial buildings under renovation by the builders' and painters' commandos had been converted into sleeping quarters. The camp was located in a huge area inside the grounds of the factory. There were no trees or shrubs and the sun rarely shone there. Two Jewish industrialists, Grossman and Markusfeld, had founded the factory in 1896 as a jute mill to manufacture potato sacks. It went on the market in the 1930s, though remained empty until the Germans invaded and then established a fully equipped plant to produce ammunition.

The factory was surrounded on three sides by a very high brick wall with watchtowers equipped with machine guns and huge spotlights, manned by Ukrainian Werkschutz guards. The boundary of the fourth side was the river Warta. It was impossible to escape by swimming the river, though, as the opposite bank was also part of the camp. There was only one point of entry for the goods trains, and the rail sidetrack was constantly guarded. The main entrance for other vehicles was via a bridge over the river. From the main road and the bridge, there was a side road with a boom gate and guard post. On both sides of the road were administration buildings, storerooms and Werkschutz quarters, and just before the bridge, another boom gate and the main watch-house – once again the most feared building in the camp.

The good news, though, was the food. Our soup that first evening contained potato, barley, parsnip and even traces of meat. It was truly marvellous.

At dusk we were sent to the bathhouse, which was much smaller than Skarżysko-Kamienna's, and learned we were to shower weekly. We undressed, put our clothes on hangers and deposited them in the delousing chamber, collecting them after we had washed.

Inmates had queued by the door of another adjoining room so I joined them. Inside was a table and, behind it, shelves filled with laundered underwear. In front of the table was a huge basket. One by one, the inmates approached the table and showed their dirty underwear to the supervisor before dropping it into the basket. The Jewish supervisor was a doctor from Moravská Ostrava in Czechoslovakia. I don't know how he came to be there, the lone Czech in the camp, and he spoke only Czech and German. I was embarrassed to show him my now charcoal-coloured threadbare underpants that I had worn for more than a year, but was absolutely *thrilled* to receive a clean pair! Unfortunately this changeover occurred only once more, a week later – there were simply too many of us in the camp now to keep this system going.

I was allocated to a second-floor room in a three-storey building. About sixty of us placed our paillasses in three rows on the timber floor and slept at once. In the morning we had 'coffee' brewed from malt or some similar grain and received our first bread, which tasted like the real thing.

Yumek Kielman and Szymek Mapa joined me for a walk around the camp. Kielman had been in the workgroup I supervised at Skarżysko-Kamienna, and Mapa was the kaëlnik with whom I had received a flogging from Dechant. By now I knew both men quite well. Together we started talking to some veteran inmates, telling them that we had come from Skarżysko-Kamienna.

'That's interesting,' someone said. 'A few days ago, about two hundred men and women arrived here from Skarżysko, but they were totally yellow, even their hair. We thought they were Mongols, or some unknown race. They spoke Yiddish. They were very apathetic and listless with their sad yellow eyes. Who are they?'

'They are the unfortunate inmates of Skarżysko-Kamienna Werk C,' we explained. 'They worked with picric acid, filling artillery shells with explosives, and this made them yellow. They suffered horribly and most only survived a few weeks. Where are they now?'

'We don't know,' they replied. 'They were only here for two days when the SS-men came, loaded them on trucks and took them away. There were rumours that they were taken to the local cemetery, shot and buried in a mass grave. In these evil times, rumours turn out to be true.'

These inmates had arrived three months earlier from Płaszów concentration camp and belonged to the painters' commando.

'Who is the camp commander?' I asked.

'SS-Sturmführer Fritz Bartenschlager,' two of them answered simultaneously.

We looked at each other and I felt my skin crawl. 'Oh no!'

'What's wrong?' Mapa asked.

'We must warn the girls. He was the head of the Werkschutz in Skarżysko-Kamienna. He raped and murdered many inmates, mostly pretty young girls.'

Fortunately, Bartenschlager was transferred to yet another camp soon after we arrived.

It took a fortnight to prepare the plant and all its departments for full-scale production. Scores of electricians were engaged in this task, while other workers unloaded train carriages and shifted machines into position, and still others unpacked the wooden crates. Many departments were housed in one huge building, the largest being that of the semiautomatic revolver lathes. There were also a tempering department, rows of grinding machines, milling machines, a storage and distribution room and a quality control department.

The supervisor's office was located on the mezzanine floor, which had windows running the building's full length, providing an uninterrupted view of the whole plant. On our first workday the new German supervisor, a tall young Aryan man in a grey dustcoat over civilian clothing, approached our group. He introduced himself as Kirsch and then asked for me by name.

'I am Morgen, sir,' I said, stepping forward with some apprehension.

'You speak German and you were the foreman in Skarżysko-Kamienna.' This was a statement rather than a question.

'Yes sir, that's correct.'

'Nominate two men as your deputies.'

'Yes, sir,' I said, and Kirsch left us.

I decided on Yumek Kielman, who was the most experienced turner, and asked him who our second deputy should be.

'Perhaps Szafran,' Kielman proposed. Szafran was a former cleaner and soup carrier who had posed as a production worker in our department when he realised it was the only way he could be relocated to Częstochowa.

'But he hasn't got the faintest idea how to operate the machines. It would be too dangerous for him, and for us.'

'We'd have to cover for him,' Kielman admitted.

I knew that Szafran had no chance if discovered and agreed to Kielman's suggestion, thinking that maybe he was repaying a past favour. The three of us became responsible for running the lathes department.

Kirsch knew even less than Reinicke had, but he was a keen listener and avid student. He trusted me and we developed an unexpectedly civilised relationship. In time he made an effort to ease our hardships. He treated me to cigarettes and daily sandwiches, but most importantly he instituted a double ration of bread for all workers in his department and he never hit anyone.

We were lucky, in a way, to have Kirsch as our overseer. Richard Pawlowski, the supervisor of the revolver lathes department, mercilessly tortured and even killed his workers for the most negligible reasons. His wife, Dora Pawlowski, a supervisor in the polishing department, was not any more humane in her treatment of her female workers. Several of the supervisors treated us with brutality, viciousness and contempt, despite the fact that they needed us slaves, as we were the only workforce in this camp.

We continued working in two separate twelve-hour shifts, as we had at Skarżysko-Kamienna, and got used to this routine.

I had heard that my uncle Abraham and aunt Rozia had been living in the Częstochowa ghetto for some time, but they weren't at Warta. I asked many inmates if they knew or had heard anything about them without success. One even became abusive when unwittingly I approached him a second time with the same questions. At that moment an OD-man appeared and defused the situation. 'Who you are looking for? Who are your relatives?' he asked.

'Abraham and Rozia Aronowicz, my uncle and aunt. They have two children, a daughter Paula and a son Bolek.'

'I know Bolek very well. The four of them are at the Apparatebau Pelcery camp nearby.'

'Really? You know Bolek?'

'Yes. I often see him when I go to Pelcery. As a matter of fact I'll be taking a group of inmates to Pelcery tomorrow.'

'Would it be possible to take me with you?'

'It can be done. I'll put you on the list. What's your name and work commando?'

'Zygmunt Morgen. Kommando Werkzeugbau.'

I followed him to the administration building, where he confirmed that we would leave at 7.30 am the next morning. I asked his name; it was Edward Holzer.

'Be prepared to push a trolley loaded with all kinds of wares,' Holzer told me. 'Some Werkschutz guards will escort us.'

CHAPTER 40

I HAD NO PROBLEM CHANGING MY SHIFT and the next morning a convoy of three carts and a dozen inmates left the camp. As we walked along the tree-lined street I realised how important nature's beauty is to our wellbeing. I breathed the fresh air deep into my lungs.

The street was full of people on their way to work and children on their way to school. Most of them tried not to notice us, though it was clear they were astonished – with mouths agape – to see such a motley group and its guards. As we neared Pelcery, I saw that the secondary road to the plant was paved with gravestones taken from a Jewish cemetery. The loving inscriptions to the dead were clearly visible. The rounded shape of some of the headstones could still be seen, while others had been cut – and we were walking on them. The baseness of the Germans seemed boundless – not only were they targeting living Jews for extermination, they were killing the dead a second time.

We arrived at the gate at around 8.30 and were counted and registered. Our Werkschutz escort left us and local guards led us to the storerooms to unload the goods we had brought. That took an hour and then we were free to stroll about the camp and meet at the guardhouse near the gate no later than 4 pm sharp.

I asked Holzer if he could help me find my relatives. First we asked at the administration barrack. While there I recognised my fourteen-year-old second cousin, whose house we had sheltered at on our way to Starachowice-Wierzbnik a few years earlier.

'Mark Faktor?'

'Yes, that's me.'

'I'm so glad to find you here,' I said.

He looked at me dumbfounded. 'Who are you?'

'I'm Siegmund, your second cousin. I last saw you in August 1940. My mother and I stayed with you for about four weeks until your whole apartment block was evicted by the Gestapo.'

'Oh yes. Yes, I vaguely remember. So many things have happened since. What are you doing here?'

'I'm from the Warta camp and am here to find my aunt and uncle Aronowicz. What's your job here?'

'My job's maybe the best in the camp. I'm the *Läufer*, the camp's messenger.'

Mark knew where my relatives were and promised to take me to them after he had completed a few more errands. Holzer left me with a reminder to meet at 4 pm. I waited patiently for Mark's return, observing the marked differences between the old inmates in the camp and the Skarżysko-Kamienna newcomers. The Częstochovites were much better dressed and looked healthy.

'I'll take you to your cousin Bolek,' Mark said when he reappeared. 'He works as a draughtsman at the main toolmaking department. I'll call him first.' He disappeared inside a small two-storey building for ten minutes. 'He can't come right now but will see you soon after finishing some important drawings. In the meantime I'll take you to your uncle Abraham.'

We walked to the end of the huge camp where rows of wooden barracks painted in camouflage colours were packed together. I couldn't wait to see some family members.

'The last barrack, just before the barbed-wire fence. You can see it from here,' Mark pointed.

'Yes, I can see. Let's hurry.'

Mark knocked at the door. I stood behind him. The door opened.

'Hello, Mark,' said a young woman. 'What brings you here?'

'Paula, I brought you a visitor from Warta.'

'That's strange. We don't have anyone at Warta.'

'It's me,' I said, 'your cousin Siegmund from Katowice!'

'Siegmund from Katowice? Here? Oh God! Daddy, come quickly. Siegmund, Uncle David's son, is here. Quick!'

Paula pulled me inside and hugged me.

'I don't believe it. Andzia just arrived here too! I'm so happy to see you, but you look like a beggar. You, Auntie Eva's most pampered child.'

'Are you kidding? I thought I looked wonderful,' I said jokingly.

Uncle Abraham also hugged me and I asked where everyone else was.

'Rozia's at work right now,' he explained. 'I'm on the night shift. Bolek is also working and Paula is on sick leave – she's had diarrhoea.'

Here was a family still intact: a father, mother and their two children. They occupied a family barrack, which was two rooms fitted with bunks, chairs, a table and cooking facilities. Pelcery must have been the most humane camp in the whole of the occupied territory.

Paula brought me some soup and Uncle Abraham and I exchanged stories. He told me that when they first arrived at the camp, they hadn't been searched and nothing had been confiscated – they still had many of their belongings.

I mentioned that I had seen his brother Hamek at the Skarżysko-Kamienna camp some months earlier.

'You saw Hamek?'

'Yes. He came from Radomsko with a group of some two hundred men.'

'Do you know where he is now?'

'No. He was still in Skarżysko-Kamienna when I was relocated to Warta. The camp was liquidated and I don't know what happened to him.'

I talked some more about life in the camp and he did not ask any more questions. He sat still, lost in thought. But when I spoke about being tortured with a dentist's drill, Uncle Abraham came back to the present. He knew a dentist nearby and left at once to get him. Within minutes he returned with a man around his own age, perhaps in his early fifties, who carried an old doctor's bag.

The dentist looked into my mouth and initially diagnosed a severe case of scurvy: the only thing to help that was to eat fresh fruit and vegetables. He then prodded my damaged tooth, removing the bread putty I had packed into the hole. He touched the nerve with his metal instrument and I jumped in my chair.

'I'll pack the tooth with something in order to kill the nerve, then cover the cavity with gypsum. By the time the gypsum dissolves, the nerve will be dead and you'll be fine. This is the best I can do. The other option is to extract the tooth. Bearing in mind that this is an incisor and I don't have any anaesthetic, I definitely wouldn't recommend this option.'

The whole procedure lasted less than twenty minutes. In between moans I thanked the dentist and Uncle Abraham.

Mark knocked on the door again to take me to see Bolek.

'Don't go yet,' cried Paula from the next room. 'I haven't finished yet.' She appeared in the doorway holding a brown woollen cloth. 'I'm sewing a jacket for you. It'll be ready in half an hour. Please wait.'

'Don't worry, he'll be back,' said Mark, and off we went.

Outside the building where Bolek worked was a tall, elegantly dressed man in a business suit, white shirt and tie. A high-ranking German official, I thought. We got closer. It was Bolek. Not even camp functionaries wore suits; at best they had outdated Polish military uniforms. It was so bizarre to see such a beautifully turned-out man in a camp where 90 per cent of inmates were covered in rags. Indeed, the last time I had seen men dressed like this was August 1939.

Bolek hugged me and, teary-eyed, told me I was a bag of bones. I told him that I had already gained a kilogram or two since arriving in Warta.

'Don't worry any more. We will take care of you,' he said. 'Now let's hurry home for some lunch.'

I could not believe my ears. I had found family and was no longer alone in the world. I had relatives who cared about me. I belonged!

Bolek asked me about my work and I told him I had been foreman of the lathes machines in the toolmaking department and that I had the same job at Warta, but with two assistants.

'Excellent!' Bolek exclaimed. 'I'm the head draughtsman of the toolmaking department here at Pelcery and have a very good relationship with my supervisor, Mr Fritsche, who is a top executive at Hasag. I spoke with him today and he's promised to transfer you to our camp, providing that you can do the work. He's going to interview you this afternoon at 3 pm.'

This was wonderful news. Immediately I told Bolek about my assumed surname and why it was necessary, but he assured me that wouldn't be a problem.

Auntie Rozia arrived for lunch and we hugged each other. Paula had finished the brown woollen jacket and held it out to me with her bright smile. It fit like a glove and I gave her a big kiss on her cheek. Rozia, who was my father's eldest sister, stole glances at me through the meal, sobbing quietly. She insisted that Bolek find a way for me to stay with them.

I was so happy. I felt such warmth and concern from all of them. I could not help but wish for this radical change in my life to be realised. How much more civilised life would be once again. We ate our soup and bread at the table, eating from plates with real cutlery.

Fritsche was a handsome, fair-haired man and softly spoken, a contrast to most raucous German supervisors. He sat behind a desk littered with technical drawings. I stood in front of him. Bolek, standing behind, introduced me. Fritsche asked me a lot of questions and then a final one: 'Would you like to move to my department?'

'Yes sir, very much, sir,' I said.

'I know your supervisor Kirsch very well. I'll speak to him and am sure you can be here with us within a few days.'

I thanked him for his time and for his efforts, but in spite of this wonderful news I remembered it was getting late. I asked Fritsche outright what time it was.

'Twenty minutes past four.'

'I'm in real trouble,' I gasped. 'I had to be at the gate no later than four o'clock. My group will have left and I'll be severely punished.'

'I'll order a Werkschutz to escort you back to Warta.'

'I'll get twenty-five lashes for missing the group.'

'If you get into trouble, tell the Werkschutz officer to call me and I'll confirm that I kept you here for an interview.'

Bolek and I ran to the gate. Indeed, the group had left, even though Holzer knew that I was still in the camp.

'Who is Morgen?' shouted a Werkschutz from the doorway of the watch-house.

I raised my arm.

'I have an order to escort you to Warta. Let's go.'

Bolek and I embraced each other. 'So long, brother,' he said, 'and don't worry. In a day or two you'll be back here with us.'

They were waiting for me at Warta. A guard took me directly into the watch-house, to a windowless room where whips, sticks, clubs, rubber hoses, ropes and truncheons hung from the wall. 'You can choose,' he indicated with a sweep of his hand.

'I was at Mr Fritsche's office where I had a long interview,' I stammered. 'Please, call his office. Please. I'm telling the truth.' He hesitated, then left the room, returning a few minutes later.

'Piss off,' he yelled and kicked me.

With a deep sigh of relief I ran from there as fast as I could. I had escaped this punishment and would soon begin a new life in Pelcery. I was in such high spirits. That day had a huge effect on my mood, self-esteem and my will to survive. My toothache had eased, I had a new jacket and soon I would be with family again.

CHAPTER 41

I WALKED PAST A WORKTABLE the next day where a girl was struggling to unroll a length of thick brown paper. She was a quality controller in Richard Pawlowski's department and had to keep her table very tidy. She held the paper with one hand, and with the other tried to remove stencils from the table. I stopped to help her.

She was strikingly beautiful – with the biggest brown eyes I had ever seen and full red lips. She thanked me and rewarded me with a dazzling smile. For the first time since being an inmate I was interested in a girl. In fact, I was smitten.

Kirsch called me to his office and asked how everything was progressing. 'Is everything going smoothly? No interruptions with production?' He asked more questions, which was strange, as he was usually indifferent to what went on. I suspected something and he told me he had received a phone call from Fritsche. 'He wants you to work for him and was very persistent, but I categorically rejected his request. I cannot let you go. Why is it that he wants you and not anyone else?'

'My cousin works for him. He's a highly qualified draughtsman and wants me there. Please let me go.'

'I can't,' he said, firmly. 'You're my best worker and I rely on you. Without you, I would be lost. I can give him two other Jews, even three, but not you.'

I tried to think fast. I wanted to be with my family so much. 'Maybe if I trained someone to replace me, you'd let me go,' I suggested.

'Maybe. But for now you're staying here so you'd better get back to work.'

I was very disappointed to be denied the transfer and was cranky for the rest of the day. Once again I had to survive with what little I had. Weeks later I tried to visit my cousins again but was only able to send a message through another inmate. I received word back that Kirsch simply refused to release me. All they could do for me right now was to send a few slices of bread.

I did not realise then that Kirsch's refusal to transfer me almost certainly saved my life. Paula was to be the sole survivor of her family. Rozia and Abraham Aronowicz did not survive their camp's transfer to Germany in January 1945. While being transported by train they froze to death, together with hundreds of other prisoners in the cramped open carriages. Bolek starved to death during one of the 'death marches', from Buchenwald, in April 1945. An eyewitness saw him chewing grass minutes before he died.

*

Without warning discipline was tightened. The Werkschutz took to beating and abusing us without provocation. At the plant, and especially in the revolver lathes department, the situation became impossible. Pawlowski had previously punished slow workers by taking them to a room where he clubbed them, often to death. Now he did it openly, and without reservation. Inmates and supervisors were both witnesses to his brutality. Bloodied lumps of torn flesh were removed on stretchers. We tasted the hate and fear in the air. This went on, day after day, after day. There had to be something we could do to help these poor men.

On my next night shift, when Pawlowski was not working, I went to his department. I studied the revolver lathes production process carefully, then spent two nights experimenting with new, more efficient ways to produce the rammers.

I approached Kirsch, who was well aware of the problems in Pawlowski's department. He told me that Pawlowski was convinced that inmates were sabotaging the manufacture of the rammers.

'And that's why he beats them?' I asked. 'The work they do is delicate and must be done with extreme care. The problem is that terrorised people can't take that care. Using too much force easily damages the tools.'

I said that I might have a solution to this problem and explained that the rammers were manufactured on unsuitable machines, using fragile, expensive and incorrect tools.

Kirsch took me into his office to hear more. He showed me to a chair. This was the first time I had been asked to take a seat in a supervisor's office. 'Continue,' he said.

'New production techniques will mean radical changes to this product. I've done some successful preliminary tests but will need several things to continue. I'll need your approval and support. I'll also need a small, high-speed, precision lathe; access to the tool depot; widia (a high-speed steel used to make profile knives for turning); and sufficient steel to experiment with.'

'This all can be done, but under one condition,' Kirsch said, and smiled. 'You won't neglect your normal workload.'

He sighed. 'Between you and me I'm fed up with the war, with the killing, the suffering, the misery. Nations are killing each other and what for? For a better tomorrow? Dead people don't have a tomorrow.'

His words surprised me and I admired his courage. By saying what he did, he committed high treason. Theoretically, he had put his life in my hands.

He got up and headed for the door. 'I'm going to tell Pawlowski the good news.'

'Don't rush, sir. This might not work. Don't tell him anything until we have a ready-made product. Also, don't make it too easy for him. You should take the credit for this and be rewarded.'

Kirsch made no comment, but dismissed me. 'Go and start working.'

Within an hour I had a high-speed precision lathe. The machine was small enough to fit on a simple workbench. I worked on the profile knife and by the end of my shift everything was ready to be trialled.

That night I did not sleep. My first priority was to help the poor inmates, to save them from the beatings and torture. But did I really want to aid my enemies? Was I helping cause the deaths of many others? I tried to reassure myself that my decision was the right one.

The next morning I checked my new machine, the tools and materials and, after a silent prayer, I manufactured the first rammer. I inspected the quality and checked the measurements. It seemed to have worked. I made about half-a-dozen more pieces, checked their accuracy, then took them to the tempering department, where the inmates helped me to process them. I then took them for grinding and polishing, followed by quality control. The results were satisfactory.

Kirsch stopped by only once during that long day and asked if it was going well.

'Yes sir,' I replied, though I kept the results to myself. I didn't tell anybody what I was doing, not even Kielman and Szafran, who were a little puzzled by my activity.

On the third day of testing I told Kirsch that we were ready to notify Pawlowski. The new method was surprisingly quickly accepted and introduced. From the factory floor we could see, up through the office window, Kirsch and Pawlowski celebrating with a few drinks and patting each other on their backs. Most importantly, the vicious beatings stopped.

I had expected to feel a great sense of satisfaction in helping my fellow inmates and yet I had this dreadful nagging pain in my gut. I had aided the enemy. I felt like a traitor and a collaborator. What had I done?

My conscience refused to let me sleep and I tossed and turned thinking of what to do next. I decided that the only way I could compensate was to slow down production or sabotage it in such a way that nobody would be in danger. Suddenly, I knew exactly what needed to be done and how to go about it. I could sabotage the products we were manufacturing while the workers still produced their required quota on time.

The plan was quite simple: I would alter the bullets we were producing, making them narrower in diameter than their original calibre of 7.62 millimetres. I would change them by only two hundredths of a millimetre – the difference would be hardly noticeable, yet the fired bullet would no longer have the twist it required and would lose accuracy, propulsion and range. When the bullets were fired, they wouldn't penetrate their targets. I knew this because I had learnt about rifles and guns and ammunition and how they worked in cadet-training, while I was still at college.

To change the current set-up was difficult and dangerous, but not impossible. From that moment on, I concentrated all my efforts and energy on this task. I spoke to Kielman and Szafran and told them that from now on I only wanted to work night shifts.

'With pleasure!' both of them exclaimed.

'Have you found yourself a *kuzynka* or are you suffering from insomnia?' Szafran asked teasingly.

'Actually, both,' I smiled – only lying about the girlfriend.

'Don't take any notice of him,' said Kielman, slapping Szafran on the back of his head. 'He's just jealous.'

I contemplated sharing my secret with Kielman. It was a risky move but worth considering, as I wasn't sure if I could carry out my plan on my own. For the time being, though, I decided to go it alone.

The machine operators never measured the products or checked them against any of the technical drawings – these weren't made available to them, nor did they have the skill to understand them. Everything that was checked manually was done using testers and templates. I concluded that only the templates and testers needed to be replaced, in one changeover and in total secrecy. I needed to create about 150 new templates and testers – some had to be increased in size while others decreased. At the same time, the relevant automatic and semiautomatic machines had to be reset to coincide with these new measurements.

I made a coded list of all articles to be replaced and another for those items that had to be increased in size, as well as those to be reduced, like turned or planed items. I worked out the quantity of spare units kept in the storeroom that also had to be replaced. This preparatory work, which included finding a secure hiding place to store the goods, took three nerve-racking nights.

At the same time I began to steal both the testers I needed to change and the raw material to make the replacement testers and templates. I completed this task in about three weeks, working alone, but as the time for the changeover neared, I knew I would need help to carry out the final part of the plan. Whatever the danger, I had to speak to Yumek Kielman.

'I have a big favour to ask of you,' I said to him at the end of a shift one morning.

'What? Do you want to switch back to alternate shifts?' he asked, raising his eyebrows.

'No, I need your help.' I took a deep breath. 'I had a small mishap and need to replace some testers but I can't manage the job by myself.' I looked him straight in the eye.

'No problem,' he said, and returned a special look of acknowledgement. We had an understanding. 'Just tell me, what, when and where, and I'll be there.'

'This is confidential – I would say top secret. No-one can find out, especially the Germans.'

'You can count on me.'

'Are you sure? It could be very dangerous.'

'I'm positive.'

'Thanks,' I said and squeezed his shoulder. 'And this can only be done at night.'

'I understand. I can start on the night shift tomorrow.'

'OK. Tomorrow then.'

As we entered the plant the next day Kielman whispered, 'Is everything still going ahead? No changes?'

'No. Everything's fine. We'll start in about half an hour. I'll explain the procedure to you then.'

Most of the Germans left the premises during the night shift leaving only a skeleton staff behind. We waited until everyone settled down and was concentrating on their work. Only one supervisor began his rounds, stopping briefly at some machines just to assert his presence. We knew that afterwards he would go to his office to have his coffee and would not reappear before midnight. As soon as he had closed the office door behind him, we sprang into action.

I led Kielman to the end of a narrow passage between two rows of machines and asked him to help me lift up a heavy floorboard, beneath which all the stuff was hidden. We quickly transferred everything to the nearest workbench. Kielman was astonished by the quantity of testers and templates. Shaking his head, he whispered, 'You must have had more than one little mishap!'

'I'll explain later,' I said. 'We must hurry. We need to replace all the testers and templates and, most importantly, dispose of the original ones safely. They have to disappear from the face of the earth.'

We worked through the whole night, on guard at all times. We completed the changeover before the day shift arrived and had put all the obsolete items into my hiding place under the floorboard. The disposal of these pieces was spread over several nights to avoid being exposed. We were utterly exhausted and could barely stay on our feet, but the job had been done. I felt tremendous, having done something that restored my self-respect. Kielman proved to be a tactful and true friend. He never once asked me for an explanation, though I believe he understood the situation perfectly.

CHAPTER 42

WEEKS PASSED and the sabotage remained undetected. Kirsch initiated conversations with me more frequently now, though in reality they were monologues. He only spoke to others about work-related matters, and even then he invariably used me as translator – he spoke no Polish and the inmates didn't speak German. Maybe he forgot himself because he spoke to me in his mother tongue. At any rate he was careless at times and expressed his contempt for Hitler – a sign of disrespect that could have meant his death.

I never commented on what he said. And even though he treated me well, I felt intimidated. One day he told me that the German army was faltering and had begun to retreat. Another time he said that I would soon be free and that *he* would be incarcerated in a camp. At Warta we had far less information coming into the camp than at Skarżysko-Kamienna, where we had worked with local Poles, so in some ways I was grateful to Kirsch for any information.

One evening when I arrived at work, Merring, the general manager of Hasag Częstochowa, confronted me. He was a short, swarthy man, slightly overweight, and wore the uniform of the National Socialist Motor Corps, a low-ranking Nazi Party auxiliary unit. He stopped, spread his legs and looked at me. 'You! Come here. Quick!'

'Yes sir,' I responded immediately.

Merring did not speak and instead raised a fist and slammed it in my face with such force that I fell backwards onto the floor and lost consciousness. I woke up on a stretcher minutes later, surrounded by coworkers and Kirsch. They asked who had hit me.

'I don't really know,' I mumbled. 'Maybe I fell and hurt myself.'

'It doesn't look like a fall,' said one workmate. 'It looks more like a professional boxer's blow.'

Somebody brought me a wet cloth, to stop my jaw swelling and ease my pain.

'Men, back to your machines. He'll be all right,' said Kirsch. After the men had gone, Kirsch asked who had hit me and I told him.

'Oh, that clown,' he scoffed. 'He's a member of an insignificant organisation, parading around in his fancy uniform, obsessed with power. But he is unpredictable and can be dangerous.'

'I think he broke my jaw.'

'Get one of your men to help you to the infirmary and remain in the barrack until you recover.'

I was back at work two days later. Just a few days after that I stood watching the beautiful girl whose table I had helped organise. She was reading a letter. Somebody must have alerted her that a supervisor was coming. I watched her tear the paper into pieces and put them in her mouth to swallow. Unfortunately, Merring approached from the opposite direction. 'What are you stuffing in your mouth?' he bellowed – so loudly that his voice overpowered the din of the machines.

The poor girl choked and trembled.

'Why are you eating during your work shift?' Merring demanded, his face now beet red. Almost without breaking stride he slapped her face hard and kept walking. She flew to the floor.

I felt for her, but knew that if Merring had known what she was really chewing her pain would have been so much worse.

In spite of the success I'd had in reducing Pawlowski's beatings, conditions in Hasag Warta became increasingly violent. Everyone had become anxious; it seemed as if we were all waiting for something to happen. The Werkschutz became restless and twitchy, the German supervisors now dressed in uniform rather than civilian clothes and the OD-men became aggressive. We all felt the tension, but couldn't pinpoint the reason.

So it came as a great surprise that on New Year's Eve 1944, the Germans and camp administration allowed the men to visit the female barracks and vice versa. I went along to the women's barracks to satisfy my curiosity. A few very lucky husbands hugged their wives; sisters and brothers sat together and others visited relatives. At the far end a small group of friends was remembering the good times before the war. Impulsively, someone started to sing and the group joined in. I knew some of the men, so I joined in as well. Heads stuck over the edge of the bunks, watching us.

As I scanned the top row of bunks, a pair of sparkling dark brown eyes drew my attention. It was the girl whose table I helped rearrange, the girl who Merring had hit. My head began to spin; the sight of her took my breath away. This beautiful girl looked back at me. I heard bells ringing in my ears, blood rushed in my veins. The whole world was spinning. A bright angelic smile exposed a row of white teeth. She was the most beautiful girl I had ever seen. I asked her permission to sit and talk with her. She smiled and agreed and I climbed up the three tiers to the top where she sat.

'Hi, my name's Zygmunt.'

'Nice to meet you. I'm Hanka Tuchmaier and this,' she pointed to the fresh-faced young girl next to her, 'is my sister Stefa.'

'Hello, Stefa,' I said.

She turned her head away without saying a word. Hanka was a little embarrassed and tried to apologise. 'She's . . .'

'Don't worry,' I interrupted. 'It's quite normal for her to be apprehensive.' I turned to Stefa. 'Don't be afraid, I won't take your sister away from you.'

Stefa smiled. It was her turn to be embarrassed with me having read her mind. She climbed down from the bunk leaving Hanka and I together. I felt very comfortable, which seemed strange in itself. I took her hand and looked into her eyes. We didn't talk much yet I felt such happiness. This was love. I knew that my whole life was about to change.

Hanka walked me out of the barrack when it was time to leave. She leaned against the outside wall. I looked at her, holding both her hands. We stood there for a while and then I kissed her goodnight on the cheek. Hanka did not object. She covered her cheek with her hand and trembled slightly.

That night I could not get to sleep. I was a bag of bones – lice-infested, underweight, ragged, hungry, exhausted, possessed by panic and resignation and I had fallen in love! But how were we to have a future together? Did she feel the same as I did? Then I started worrying about my inability to concentrate on work when all I wanted to do was daydream about Hanka.

I must have fallen asleep eventually because I remember the dream I had. I was in the middle of a dense forest, resting in a small clearing on very soft green moss. It was a similar place to one I knew near Starachowice-Wierzbnik. My mother walked out of the forest towards me dressed in a long broadtail coat.

'Why are you wearing a fur coat? It's so warm here,' I said.

'I had a very long way to come, over snow-covered land, and did not have time to change.'

'Your face is so fresh and relaxed. You look very happy,' I said, admiring my mother's beauty.

'That's because I saw the girl you met. She's a very good

person. Do not let her go and do not leave her. Take her with you through your long life. You will be very happy together.'

I told my mother I would do this, as I had fallen in love with Hanka. She smiled at me.

'Now, my darling, I have to go. I've a very long journey ahead of me. I have to visit Halinka and Don. Halinka is expecting to give birth to her first son.'

Although I slept only three hours, I woke rested and refreshed. I remembered my dream in detail, though was not sure what to make of it. But I *did* know that I could not wait to see Hanka again.

I saw her arrive at the plant. Her loosely combed dark hair surrounded her fair face, her eyes flashed in all directions. Later she told me that her most precious possession was a three-pronged comb. She left the hall for the neighbouring department. I stretched my neck to see her leave; I could hardly bear to let her out of my sight. I watched the door for her to return. Finally, she appeared. My heart raced. I walked over to her and for a moment we simply stood together, enjoying our closeness without the need for words. Then I noticed that Pawlowski was looking in our direction, trying to find someone to pick on. 'Be careful, Pawlowski is watching us,' I warned.

'I'll meet you during the lunchbreak,' Hanka said, and I returned to my work. Kirsch was waiting for me.

'Your improvement in production of rammers was a big success – it solved a lot of problems.'

'I know. Do you think that I did the right thing?'

'Definitely. I understand your predicament, but it won't make any difference any more. The war is lost all the same.'

'Is it really that bad?'

'Hopeless,' he said, and walked away. It was not the first time he had made comments like this, so I didn't pay any attention.

Finally, the siren signalled the awaited lunchbreak. I collected my soup and went to Hanka's table. She had a chair while I sat on a wooden crate, resting my soup on my knees. 'I kept waiting for our break,' I told her, 'but the hands on the big clock were so slow, I swear it was playing games with me, sneering at me.'

'I thought the same thing,' said Hanka.

'Still, today's the best day I've had for a long time and it's because you're in it. If we survive I'll marry you!' Strangely, this seemed the most natural thing in the world to say.

'Of course we'll survive. We have to.' Hanka had no room for negative thoughts and I liked that.

'I dreamed of my mother last night. She likes you and told me to marry you and take care of you forever.' Hanka blushed. 'After the war, I'll take you to Katowice, to meet my family.'

'Before we go to Katowice, we'll have to stop in Suchedniów so I can introduce you to my parents.'

'It's a deal,' I said, with a bright smile.

As we spoke, I studied Hanka's graceful manner and luminous face.

After my evening meal, I visited Hanka's barrack and asked one of the girls going in to tell her I was waiting. She came out flushed and slightly trembling. She averted her eyes as she smiled.

'Are you cold?' I asked.

'No, not at all. I'm warm.'

'It must be at least ten below zero out here.' I put my arm around her shoulder. She *was* warm. We started walking.

'I have woollen clothes on and don't feel the cold.'

She was lucky, because I was freezing, in spite of Paula's jacket. Unfortunately there was nowhere inside where we could be together. It was forbidden for men and women to meet in the barracks and in the washrooms.

'Why don't you take me back and we'll see each other tomorrow during the break,' Hanka suggested, well aware of how cold I was. I kissed her on her forehead. What a lovely girl.

The next day we talked and talked. Hanka told me her family, together with all the Jewish population of Suchedniów, was 'deported' on Yom Kippur 1942. Her older sister Hela had escaped to the USSR with her fiancé, where they married and had a child. It seemed an omen that our families shared these similar fates.

Hanka also told me that her ten-year-old brother Moishele had been arrested in 1941 for not wearing a Star of David armband, although it was only compulsory to wear one from the age of twelve. He was transferred to Kielce, the regional capital, and the family lost all trace of him.

'I witnessed a similar case when I was living with my parents in Starachowice-Wierzbnik, some four years ago,' I told her. 'It was terrible.'

That evening we briefly met again, though we were both exhausted. After I kissed her cheek goodnight she kissed me back on my left cheek. We parted and I returned to my barrack and lay down on my pallet. Again I couldn't fall asleep, contemplating and searching for some sense and logic to my present situation. During the two and bit years of my incarceration, I had never shown any interest in the opposite sex. Why was I now falling in love? There must be some reason for this. Was this my last chance to experience love before my demise, or did it herald something? Was Hanka a part of my mother's prophecy?

In those days after our first meeting, we grabbed any opportunity to meet and exchange a few words and if not words then at least a quick glance. I tried to visit her every day, but for obvious reasons our meetings were sporadic and brisk. We never spoke in detail about our past or even the present – it was too painful. Instead we dreamed about our future – we wanted to believe that we had one.

One day after work I went again to meet Hanka and again I had to ask someone to call her out. I had been waiting for a while outside her barrack when Stefa appeared at the door, conveying a message.

'My sister is not ready to see you yet. It will be at least another ten or fifteen minutes before she can come out.'

'What has happened? Is she all right?'

'Yes, she is all right, but she is very busy. She is asking you to wait.'

I went away a little puzzled, not knowing why Hanka couldn't see me. When I returned after a while, she was standing in front of the barrack, holding a bundle under her arm, waiting for me. Her bright smile compensated me for my doubts.

'I have something for you that I made all by myself,' she exclaimed. She unfolded the bundle and it was a Russian-style shirt, made out of her grey blanket. 'It will keep you warm. I saw you the other day shivering from cold.'

'It is not that bad. In the barrack, it is not very cold and at the plant, it is warm – and the few minutes' walk from the barrack to the plant is bearable. You need the shirt more than I do. Please keep it for yourself.'

'Absolutely not! I made it with love. I sewed it by hand with a borrowed needle using threads ripped from the edge of the blanket and I implore you to accept it. I made it myself and you will be hurting me by refusing.'

Her eyes filled with tears and she began to cry, with the intensity of a little child deprived of its favourite toy. I gave up. Standing there, I took off my jacket and put on the shirt. Hanka radiated with happiness. The shirt carried the warmth of her body and so I was warmer still.

CHAPTER 43

IN JANUARY the rumours began to multiply: the Red Army had rapidly advanced into Poland, we were going to be sent to Germany to be shot, the entire factory was going to be blown up with all the inmates inside. The truth was nobody knew anything.

There were voices of dissent, but we had no weapons and our will to resist had been spent a long time ago. We were broken creatures. Our only hope was that the Russian offensive would be quick and decisive, and that the Germans would be more preoccupied with escaping than killing us.

Kirsch asked Kielman, Szafran and me to prepare a list of all department inmates and to put a cross next to the best workers' names, circle those of the second-best workers and ascribe the letter S to the worst. We were afraid that we might condemn some of our fellow workers to deportation, or worse to extermination, and marked the entire list with crosses.

Kirsch looked at it and shook his head. 'I understand. *All* our workers are good.'

'The best, sir, the very best,' we chorused.

The next day was 13 January. At rollcall about 1000 names were called out and those inmates ordered to line up within the hour with their belongings. The rest were sent to their working commandos and the night shift workers back to their barracks.

Those selected were marched to the rail carriages and sent to Germany. No inmate belonging to our department was selected.

I went back to my barrack to sleep but was woken by somebody shaking me roughly. Kielman was leaning over me. 'Do not go to the plant tonight! Three Germans in Gestapo rubber coats have been looking for you. Kirsch sent them to me. I told them that you're working nights and they sent me to call you.'

I had such a fright that I could not breathe. I started sweating and my heartbeat accelerated severely. My mouth dried out and what remained was a bitter taste. I tried to keep my self-control, but I started shaking. I was not sure if Kielman noticed. I sat up on my pallet. 'Did they say what they want from me? Did they say anything?'

'Not a word.'

'Were they looking for anyone else?'

'No. They only asked about you.'

'Did they look for any tools or inspect any machines?'

'I didn't see.'

'Did they look into the grinding or polishing departments?'

'I don't know.'

'Did Kirsch accompany them?'

'Only when he told me that the men wish to talk to you. Then he went back to his office . . . But I felt his uneasiness.'

'Were they rough or did they try to be polite?'

'I can't say. They spoke normally. Look,' said Kielman with a sigh, 'I have to go back now and tell them I couldn't find you. You need to go into hiding.'

'Good God, where am I going to find a place to hide?'

'I don't know, but you have to find somewhere fast. Good luck.' And with that Kielman was gone.

I started to panic and lost my head. I was sure I had been identified as the saboteur. I am finished, I thought, after so much suffering, fighting and struggling. And now, when for just two short weeks I had been madly in love and had something to live for. Maybe I was paying the price for my rare moment of happiness, for loving Hanka. I was always afraid of feeling good . . . My knees buckled under me. I felt trapped. But the worst thing was that this was happening now, when there was actually someone who cared for me. Someone would suffer losing me. Why couldn't they have caught me before I met Hanka? Why should she have to pay for my actions? Then I stopped myself from going round in circles. Maybe going into hiding wasn't such a bad idea, after all.

To make good use of time I went in search of a hiding spot while waiting for Hanka to return from work. Where could I survive temperatures between minus ten and minus fifteen degrees Celsius? Where could I get food and water? As I headed back to Hanka's barrack, I took a short cut through an abandoned construction site. Building had started on a new latrine and bathhouse block some months earlier but was stopped because of bad weather. The long, narrow building had a rough concrete floor and was almost at lock-up stage. The windows were glazed though doors were still to be installed. A double-sided concrete trough in the middle ran the length of the building. Above the trough was a simple water pipe with taps attached, though the water was not yet connected. I crawled under the trough and discovered a gap between its two parts. The space was only just big enough to crawl in, lie down and turn from side to side, but if I lay there, no-one could see me. My sanctuary. The site was not illuminated, which was good for me, and it was at the end of a dead end road, where no-one would walk past. Bricks, planks, building blocks and rubble, all covered with snow, impeded access.

I rushed to see Hanka and briefly explained my situation. She gave me the other half of her blanket at once. I didn't dare return to my barrack to get my belongings, but I had some bread in my pocket from my previous ration and it would have to do. I asked Hanka to walk with me to my hiding place, as she was the only person I could trust my life with and with whom I could share this secret. She was sobbing as I hugged her and pushed her meagre daily portion of bread into my hand. I was too tense and too distressed to cry. I showed her the spot where I would conceal myself, then asked her to leave.

I stood in that empty building trying to assess the situation. It was too early to prepare my makeshift bed – somewhere between six and seven pm. For a while I marched briskly up and down the room, throwing my arms around my body to warm myself. Then I looked for the best sleeping spot, one where I could see the entrance and as much of the surrounding area as possible. I crawled beneath the trough and tried out different positions, finally lying on my back. I wrapped Hanka's blanket tightly around my body so that I was covered and protected from the concrete floor. One of the watchtowers' searchlights illuminated my hiding place every three or four minutes, and by counting the light I could measure time.

I was surprised that I did not feel the usual nagging pain in my gut that always troubled me when I was in danger. I was calm, serene and indifferent and fell into a half sleep. I dreamed or maybe imagined that I was back home in Katowice, a little boy in my warm bed with my mother crooning my favourite Polish lullaby. The song never ended. After reaching a certain point, she started at the beginning, again and again. I waited for it anxiously, but the ending of the story never came.

She sang the words softly:

The stars in the sky are twinkling,
The sleeping birds no longer sing.
Hush, my angel, close your eyes,
And I will sing you a lullaby.

There once was a king, a princess and a page.
Who lived among the roses, only joy in their days.
Until one day disaster came.
A tragedy, a dreadful shame.
The king was snatched up in a puppy dog's snout.
The page eaten by a cat and the princess by a mouse.
Don't cry, little boy, it's not the end of the story.
The king was made of sugarplums, much to his glory.
The princess, marzipan, and the page, gingerbread.
So don't be sad, my darling, sleep and rest your head.

The room was pitch black when I opened my eyes and I could not work out where I was. The searchlight was off and not even the smallest ray of light pierced the darkness. I stretched my arm above me, touching cold, rough concrete, and started to comprehend my situation. I tried to turn over but could not move. It could have been the middle of the night or early morning. The wind was blowing in my direction and carried voices: loud commands, screaming, sharp orders and finally the sound of marching in the deep mud. I presumed it was the morning shift workers leaving for the plant. Half an hour later the noise faded away, but I did not hear the returning night shift. Something unusual must have happened. I suspected that a grand search for an escaped inmate was in progress. I knew I was in big trouble, afraid to be discovered. I thought of my parents, of Hanka, and my only wish was to be killed instantly when I was caught, unlike Moniek, my very best friend, tortured to death in the most gruesome and dreadful way. I could never forget as long I lived the image of his remains carried to the corpse disposal area. The mass of flesh lying on the stretcher did not resemble any human shape or form – his gouged-out eyes, his ripped-off ears, his skull and torso crushed to a pulp. I recollected that in October 1942, a few days after my arrival in Skarżysko-Kamienna

Werk C, the sadistic German supervisor Zimmermann killed three inmates with a heavy piece of wood, smashing their skulls to an unrecognisable mass because they had not been working fast enough. When I had arrived in Skarżysko for the second time, I considered myself lucky. I had been granted the honour of staying alive to serve their purpose, to their advantage, until I was totally exhausted and obsolete, used up long before my time, a so-called *entlassene Jude*.

I must have dozed for a while and was roused by more marching – the night shift returning, I guessed. I had no idea how long I had slept. It was still dark, but I could not be sure if it was night or early morning. After turning from side to side a few times I eased myself out of the space and began massaging my sore muscles. I ate Hanka's bread and moved carefully towards the door. The only visible light came from the watchtower. I ducked outside, collected a fistful of snow to drink, and found a spot to relieve myself. Back in the room I exercised to keep warm. I now decided to sleep during the day and stay awake at night, which would be easier to endure.

That day seemed terribly long and the sun's brief appearance made it even longer. In January it got dark around 4 pm. I waited and, after identifying various sounds, realised it was close to 7 pm – still two hours to curfew. At last I heard light footsteps. I held my breath and listened carefully. I recognised Hanka's silhouette. I crawled out from beneath the trough and we hugged each other tightly.

She gave me her daily bread allowance.

'I can't take this. You also have to eat.'

'It's half my allowance and half from Stefa.'

'What! You told Stefa that I am in hiding?'

'No, no. I didn't tell her anything. I'll tell her that I lost mine so she will share hers with me. Actually I have difficulty chewing bread now because I had a tooth extracted last night.'

She opened her mouth and showed me.

'But you didn't have a toothache yesterday.'

'No. It's because I'm crying a lot and Stefa wants to know why. I couldn't tell her I'm worrying about you so I told her I had a terrible toothache. She insisted I got rid of the tooth immediately.'

I held her in my arms very tightly, kissing the tears from her cheeks. 'That was a real sacrifice but please don't do anything like that again. Promise?'

'I promise,' Hanka whispered.

'Are they still looking for me? What's happening at the plant?'

'I think so. They've doubled the guards and there's a feeling of doom in the air. Around a thousand inmates were transported to Germany last night – luckily, none from our department. Something strange is going on.'

'Please, be very careful coming here. You might be watched.'

'I will, and I'll be back tomorrow at the same time.'

I kissed her passionately for the very first time. Even though I was weak from hunger, my knees began to tremble with desire. I could hold on to her forever. The rest of the world ceased to exist. I experienced a moment of such bliss. This beautiful budding love was blooming in dark and ugly surroundings, if only for just a few seconds.

I watched her walk away. She had risked her life coming to see me. Sooner or later I would be discovered or I'd give myself up. I had no right to involve her.

I sat away from the windows, counting the intervals between the flashes of the searchlight. I ate some bread and some snow. I was two nights in hiding already. How many more nights could I do this? I didn't know what to do. There would be many empty pallets now – maybe I could sneak into a barrack and shelter there? I heard the camp stirring and, wrapping myself in the blanket, returned to my concrete bed.

*

In the morning my mother woke me instead of my governess. 'No more kindergarten,' she said. 'Today's your first day of school and I'm taking you there, but first Stefan will stop at the photographic studio so we can immortalise this important day.'

As a six-year-old boy I had long, blond curly hair. Under no circumstances did my mother allow anyone to cut or even trim my hair; and Franciska, my nanny, rinsed my hair with chamomile to enhance its colour.

My first day of school! I had a uniform, a school cap, a new schoolbag and a decorated cardboard cone filled to the brim with lollies. But once I was in the classroom a group of children surrounded me. 'Are you a girl or a boy?' 'Why don't you ask your mummy to plait your hair with pink ribbons?' 'Why have you got long hair?' 'You look funny.' I returned home crying, insisting I wouldn't go to school any more to be teased.

'It's only because they envy your beautiful hair,' my mother said.

I pleaded with her to cut my hair like the other children's but she did not listen. Soon after this I asked my father for some money and took myself to a barber. I asked him to cut off my hair with a clipper. Afterwards I hardly recognised myself, but at least I now looked like a boy. I put my cap on and rushed home.

My mother fainted when she saw my bald head, which made me very scared. I ran to my room, crawled into bed and pulled the blankets over my head. Waking up, I expected to see my concerned parents bending over me but all I saw was the bottom of the concrete trough and flurries of snow blowing into the room through the open doorway. Thinking about my dream, which was actually a recollection of events many years earlier, strengthened my will to survive. Now I wanted to fight for the life that I had once had, because the future was so precarious – it was something I couldn't even imagine.

I sensed Hanka's presence and heard her soft footsteps in the snow. She held out her hand to give me her bread and I pulled her towards me. Nestling my face in her neck I was intoxicated by the sweet smell of her hair. The most beautiful and best-groomed girl in the camp. We held each other close for some time. It had been so long since I held another human being that the physical contact engulfed me in a sense of euphoria.

'Today another large transport left for Germany,' Hanka said, breaking the magic spell. 'Inmates were loaded onto the train and only a few hundred people are left. This time some from our department were sent away. Everything in the camp is very tense.'

We chatted a little more before Hanka had to leave. I wondered what was happening to the other inmates in the camp. Something was happening out there and I wanted to live. I was twenty years old and I wanted to live. My mother had promised me that with the help of the thirty-six I would survive. How many nights had I stayed in this place? Three? Four? How many times had Hanka given me her bread? I heard her footsteps in the snow again. *Is she coming back, or was that yesterday she visited?* No. It was her second visit that night. Something *had* happened.

And there she was, standing in front of me, laughing and crying, her arms outstretched. 'They're gone! We are unguarded. We are free!'

I tried to speak but my throat was dry and my words stuck in it. We hugged and cried. We ran from the construction site, bewildered but happy, very happy. I screamed with a fierce joy, as loud as I could: 'Zygmunt Morgen does not exist! He never did. I am Siegmund Siegreich! *Siegreich! Victorious!*'

EPILOGUE

WORLD WAR II, the most destructive war in world history, was the most devastating time of my life. Jews were deceived, brutalised, oppressed and dehumanised. The Germans broke our spirit and the will to defend ourselves. We were orphaned of mothers, fathers and grandparents, bereaved of wives, husbands and children, brothers and sisters, uncles and aunts, cousins, nieces and nephews. We were deprived of the most basic human rights: to live, to breathe, to die with dignity and to rest in a grave. What remained were our hopes, thoughts and dreams. They were private and free. These they could not take away from us.

On the night of 17 January 1945, I was suddenly intoxicated with a sense of freedom. I wanted to forget all I went through and never think of it again.

The morning after liberation, I married Hanka with the blessing of my friend Yumek Kielman's father in front of a group of witnesses. One of them was Adam (Adek) Frydman, who fifty years later witnessed the renewal of our wedding vows in Melbourne, Australia. It took several days before the trains were running and we could leave Częstochowa.

The Red Army took Katowice on 27 January 1945 – five years, five months and a hundred lifetimes after I had first left my home town. On 29 January I travelled back there, via Olkusz, on the same railroad that had carried me away. I was with my wife of eleven days, and her sister. We were skin and bones: Hanka weighed thirty kilograms and I weighed thirty-five. We wore rags, were lice-infested, and had no money, no tickets, no luggage and no belongings, but we were alive and on the road to a new beginning.

Together we moved back into my family home. When Aniela saw the skeleton that I had become, she crossed herself and cried unashamedly, lamenting the fate of her beloved Siegreich family. Later she gave me some precious family photographs. At first I was afraid to look at them should they vanish like the images they captured.

We did not speak about our own personal experiences and tragedies. That subject was taboo – it was suppressed, to be dealt with at some other time. For some the right time never came; the wounds never healed.

I spent nearly fifteen months searching for family survivors through the Red Cross and other agencies, and taped up posters in the surrounding train stations. I knew that my cousin Lunia's daughter, Krysia, had been placed with a gentile family. I searched for Dr Nowak in the hope that he remembered the child's whereabouts and finally found Krysia in Legnica, living with a Polish couple. Tears streamed down my face as I collected the sole survivor of my extended family. Covered in rags and infested with lice, this little girl was desperately neglected and sad. She had her mother's blond hair and blue eyes and looked like a beautiful angel. For some time she lived with us, and Hanka took care of her.

Many of us who had survived were plagued by guilt. Why were we the lucky ones? Why had I survived but not my parents? The guilt was so acute I felt it physically. And when survivors started returning from exile in Russia they were suspicious of how we had managed to survive and were, at times, hostile. Some accused us of collaborating with the Germans.

The fates of those who I knew from the camps are sketchy. My second cousin Mark Faktor survived and became a scientist. Andzia also survived. After the war I learned that her son Ludwig had escaped from Skarżysko-Kamienna and gone south, to the mountains, though that was the last that anyone saw of him. We heard some years later that he had joined the partisans, and had probably been killed fighting with them against the Germans. Iva and Leopold survived and relocated to Canada. Delightful Lillian also survived and lives in Paris. David Nisenbaum moved to Melbourne.

As for the authorities, once Skarżysko-Kamienna had been packed up, all the Jewish functionaries were sent to Buchenwald. At this camp there was a collective of inmates who encouraged newcomers to report on abuse by komendanten. As a result I learned that Mendel Wajntraub, Krzepicki and others were forced to hang themselves as punishment for their cruelty. This form of death, of course, appeared to be suicide.

In April 1946, a woman dressed in rags who looked to be in her fifties knocked on our door. We stared at each other, my gut twisted in shock at this stranger, yet I felt a rush of joy. After a moment I saw a semblance of my beautiful sister Halinka. She was now twenty-five years old. It was the first we had seen of each other since she left Kraków with Don nearly seven years earlier. At last, the two remaining survivors of our family were reunited. Hanka had given birth to our first child, Evelyne, whom we called Ewelinka, just a few months earlier. Halinka and Don had their second child at around this time, and we started a new life together.

A few years later, when Ewelinka was four years old, she returned from her nursery school with a question: 'Daddy, why do the other kids have grandparents picking them up from kinder with treats and I don't?' This beautiful child of mine, this little miracle – the first baby born in Katowice to Holocaust survivors, defying Hitler's promise to annihilate the Jewish people from the face of the earth – touched the deepest wound in my soul. But the time was not yet right to divulge the truth to my little girl. The subject remained taboo for a long time.

In 1951 our second daughter, Aviva, was born. Twenty years later, my wife and I moved to Melbourne, Australia, together with both our daughters, as well as Evelyne's young family, after the persistent urging of my childhood friend Arnold Weisfelner (now known as Adam Weis), who sponsored our migration. We finally set down roots in a truly free and democratic country, where our family has prospered and multiplied.

For the past sixty-odd years, I have had the impossible task of trying to recover my family's stolen assets and seeking compensation for years of forced hard labour and loss of health. My lawyers and I faced arrogance and hostility from bureaucrats, who were simply not interested. Numerous banks, insurance companies and government departments refused access to documents and archives that would enable me to retrieve the substantial wealth rightly belonging to my family.

Years later, when my grandchildren were learning about the Holocaust at school, they asked me to help them with their 'roots project'. I shared some events with them, but I was only touching the surface – I was not able to write of my experiences until now, more than six decades later. The memory of some events may have faded or mellowed with time but everything in this book, no matter how incredible and unbelievable it appears, is all true.

Some readers may think that the world knows enough about the Holocaust, but to understand the enormity of it all would shake humanity to the end of time.

Do I believe in the thirty-six?

I believe in miracles.

INDEX OF NAMES

Flaksbaum, Lilka	Perished in Majdanek, 1943
Franek, 'Szary'	Unknown
Freiberg, Adolf	Perished in Auschwitz, 1943
Freiberg, Cesia	Perished in Auschwitz, 1943
Freiberg, Hela	Perished in Auschwitz, 1943
Freiberg, Lilka	Perished in Auschwitz, 1943
Frenkel, Hipolit	Perished in Auschwitz, 1943
Frenkel, Lusia	Survived
Frenkel, Mania	Perished in Auschwitz, 1943
Frenkel, Tusia	Perished in Auschwitz, 1943
Fromer, Tusia	Survived
Frydman, Adek	Survived
Gąsiorowicz, Bolek	Unknown
Gitl-Leah and her daughter Hela	Perished in Treblinka, 1943
Goldberg	Unknown
Goldfarb, Gilek	Perished in Buchenwald, 1944
Gonzwa, Guta	Perished in Treblinka, 1942
Groshaus, Hanka	Perished in Pionki, 1943
Grünspan, Don	Survived
Grünspan, Eduard Yedidia	Survived
Grünspan, George Joshua	Survived
Grünspan, Halinka (nee Siegreich)	Survived
Herold, Karl	Survived
Hesse, Joachim	Unknown
Horovitz, Borek	Survived
Huzarski, Tusia	Unknown
Idesa (coffeehouse owner)	Perished in Bełżec, 1942
Ipfling, Anton	Survived and imprisoned for life
Jaskółka, Hinda	Unknown
Kalata	Unknown
Kalinowski, Emil	Unknown
Kanencukier, Mrs	Unknown
Kielman, Benjamin 'Yumek'	Survived
Koch	Unknown
Kongrecki, Marian	Perished in Treblinka, 1942
Kotlega, Stanisław	Unknown
Krakowski, Lucia	Unknown

Krzepicki, Ewa	Survived
Krzepicki, Joseph	Killed in Buchenwald, 1944
Kühnemann, Paul	Unknown
Kukielka, Aaron	Survived
Laks, Hanka	Survived
Laks, Mr	Perished in Treblinka, 1942
Laks, Mrs	Perished in Treblinka, 1942
Laks, Rozka	Survived
Laufer, Iva	Unknown
Laufer, Leopold Poldek	Unknown
Leichter, Aaron	Perished in Bełżec, 1942
Leichter, Giza	Perished in Bełżec, 1942
Lichtenstein, Lillian	Survived
Mackiewicz, Danek	Killed in Skarżysko-Kamienna
Majewski (storeman)	Unknown
Mala	Unknown
Mapa, Szymek	Survived
Maria (from Bodzechów)	Unknown
Markowiczowa, Fela	Killed in Skarżysko-Kamienna, 1944
Marysia (from Będzin)	Unknown
Mesing, Henryk	Survived
Mesing, Krysia	Survived
Mesing, Lunia (nee Reichmann)	Perished in Auschwitz, 1943
Najman, David	Survived
Nisenbaum, David	Survived
Nisenbaum, Heniek	Survived
Nojman, Sara	Perished in Bełżec, 1942
Pachter, Wilek	Survived
Patac, Yosel	Unknown
Pawlowski, Dora	Unknown
Pawlowski, Richard	Unknown
Piotrowski, Franciska (governess)	Unknown
Pomeranc, Mrs	Unknown
Proper, Jurek	Perished in Bełżec, 1942
Ptasznik, Mr	Perished in Bełżec, 1942
Ptasznik, Mrs	Perished in Bełżec, 1942
Reichmann, Harry	Unknown

Reichmann, Severin	Unknown
Reichmann, Karl	Perished in Auschwitz, 1943
Reichmann, Regina	Perished in Auschwitz, 1943
Reinicke	Unknown
Rosental, Henryk	Unknown
Safirsztajn (nurse)	Unknown
Saks, Dr	Unknown
Siegreich, Andzia	Survived
Siegreich, Eva	Perished in Treblinka, 1943
Siegreich, Felix	Survived
Siegreich, Isaak Meir	Perished in Auschwitz, 1943
Siegreich, Julius	Perished in Auschwitz, 1943
Siegreich, Karmela	Perished in Auschwitz, 1943
Siegreich, Lilka	Perished in Auschwitz, 1943
Siegreich, Ludwig	Unknown
Siegreich, Rachel	Passed away, 1942
Siegreich, Rose 'Rosa'	Perished in Auschwitz, 1943
Siegreich, Ruth	Survived
Siegreich, Samuel	Killed in Skarżysko-Kamienna, 1943
Siegreich, Samuel David	Perished in Bełżec, 1942
Siegreich, Stefanie	Unknown
Siegreich, Zosia (nee Zachariasz)	Survived
Siegreich, Zosia	Perished in Auschwitz
Silber, Mr (headmaster)	Unknown
Singer, Emanuel	Killed in Staszów, 1942
Singer, Hanka	Perished in Bełżec, 1942
Singer, Efraim	Killed in Staszów, 1942
Sobol, Majlech	Unknown
Sonenberg, Mietek	Unknown
Stanisław (Bodzechów)	Unknown
Stefan (chauffeur)	Unknown
Szafran	Unknown
Szajbe, Eliasz	Unknown
Szlagbaum	Unknown
Tenenbaum, Jurek	Unknown
Teperman, Lejzer	Killed in Buchenwald, 1944
Thaler, Ernst	Perished in Bełżec, 1942

Topioł, Moniek (Busko-Zdrój)	Killed in Busko-Zdrój
Topioł, Moniek (Stopnica)	Killed in Skarżysko-Kamienna
Wacek	Unknown
Wajntraub, Chaim	Killed in Skarżysko-Kamienna, 1944
Wajntraub, Mendel	Kiled in Buchenwald, 1944
Wajsberg	Survived
Wajskop, Janek	Survived
Warman, Salek	Unknown
Wierzbinski, Eva	Perished in Auschwitz, 1943
Wierzbinski, Motek	Perished in Auschwitz, 1943
Wierzbinski, Richard	Perished in Auschwitz, 1943
Yankel	Unknown
Zimmermann, 'Shiviys'	Unknown
Zylberfuden, Haya	Perished in Skarżysko-Kamienna, 1943
Zylberfuden, Wolf	Perished in Skarżysko-Kamienna, 1943

ACKNOWLEDGEMENTS

My appreciation and thanks to the people who have been instrumental in helping me convert my memories into a book. To my beloved wife, Hanka, for her consistent support and encouragement that helped me re-enter and relive the most difficult years of my life. To my treasured daughters, Evelyne and Aviva, and my grandchildren, Eric-David, Natalie-Michelle, Michelle, Tahni and Daniel, for adding such an important dimension to my life, and sharing and taking to heart all my stories throughout their lives.